THE ASSAULT ON MOUNT EVEREST 1922

THE ASSAULT ON MOUNT EVEREST 1922

BY

Brigadier-General Hon. C. G. Bruce, C.B., M.V.O.

AND OTHER MEMBERS OF THE EXPEDITION

WITH MAPS AND ILLUSTRATIONS

GYAN

Published by

GYAN

Gyan Publishing House
5, Ansari Road
Daryaganj, New Delhi-110002
Phone: 011-47034999, 9811692060
E-mail: books@gyanbooks.com

Distribution Network
gyanbooks.com
India, USA, Canada, UK, Australia, France

ISBN : 978-81-212-2355-3 (PB)
First Published, 1923

2nd Impression 2021

Printed at: Gyan Press, Delhi.

The Assault on Mount Everest
1922
Author: Brigadier-General Hon. C. G. Bruce

THE ASSAULT ON MOUNT EVEREST 1922

By

Brigadier-General Hon. C. G. BRUCE, C.B., M.V.O.

AND OTHER MEMBERS OF THE EXPEDITION

WITH MAPS AND ILLUSTRATIONS

NEW YORK

LONGMANS, GREEN & CO.

LONDON: EDWARD ARNOLD & CO.

1923

The Second Climbing Party descending from their second climb

LONDON: EDWARD ARNOLD & Co

PREFACE

The Mount Everest Committee desire to take this opportunity of thanking General Bruce, Mr. Mallory, Captain Finch, Mr. Somervell and Dr. Longstaff for having, in addition to their labours in the field, made the following contributions to the story of an expedition whose chief result has been to strengthen our confidence that the summit of the highest mountain in the world can be attained by man.

CONTENTS

LIST OF ILLUSTRATIONS

MAPS

INTRODUCTION

By

SIR FRANCIS YOUNGHUSBAND,
K.C.S.I., K.C.I.E.

INTRODUCTION

Colonel Howard-Bury and the members of the Expedition of 1921 had effected the object with which they had been despatched. They were not sent out to climb Mount Everest. It would be impossible to reach the summit in a single effort. They were sent to reconnoitre the mountain from every direction and discover what was for certain the easiest way up. For it was quite certain that only by the easiest way possible—and only if there were an easy way—would the summit ever be reached. In the Alps, nowadays, men look about for the most difficult way up a mountain. Hundreds every year ascend even the Matterhorn by the easiest ways up. So men with any turn for adventure have to look about for the difficult ways. With Mount Everest it is very different. The exhaustion produced from the difficulty of breathing in enough oxygen at the great heights is so fearful that only by a way that entails the least possible exertion can the summit be reached. Hence the necessity for spending the first season in thoroughly prospecting the mountain. And this was all the more necessary because no European so far had been within sixty miles of Mount Everest, so that not even the approaches to the mountain were known.

During 1921, under the leadership of Colonel Howard-Bury, this reconnaissance was most thoroughly carried out. Mr. Mallory found what was quite certainly the easiest—indeed the only practicable—way up the mountain, and Major Morshead and Captain Wheeler mapped the mountain itself and the country round. They brought back also much valuable experience of the conditions under which a definite "all-out" attempt to reach the summit might be made. Ample data were therefore now at the disposal of the Mount Everest Committee for organising an expedition to make this attempt.

And first the question of leadership had to be decided. This was a definitely climbing expedition, and a climbing expert would be needed to lead it—and a climbing expert who had experience of Himalayan conditions, which are in so many ways different from Alpine conditions. The one obvious man for this position of leader was Brigadier-General Hon. C. G. Bruce. He could not be expected at his age to take part in the actual climbing. But for the command of the whole Expedition no better could be found. For thirty years he had devoted himself to climbing both in the Himalaya and in the Alps. He was an expert climber, and he knew the Himalayan conditions as no other man. And, what was of scarcely less importance, he knew the Himalayan peoples, and knew how to handle them. Any climbing party would be dependent upon the native porters to carry stores and equipment up the mountain. But climbers from England would know nothing about these men or how to treat them. It was essential, therefore, that there should be with the Expedition some one who could humour and get the best out of them.

This was the more necessary as one of the chief features of these expeditions to Mount Everest was the organisation of a corps of porters specially enlisted from among the hardiest men on that frontier for the particular purpose of carrying camps to high altitudes. This idea originated with General Bruce himself. So far Himalayan climbing expeditions had been dependent upon coolies collected at the highest villages and taken on for a few days while the climb lasted. But this was never very satisfactory, and coolies so collected would be of no use on Mount Everest. General Bruce's plan was very different. It was, months beforehand, to select thirty or forty of the very best men who could be found in the higher mountains, to enlist them for some months, pay them well, feed them well and equip them well, and above all to put into them a real *esprit de corps*, make them take a pride in the task that was before them. But to do all this there was needed a man who knew and understood them and who had this capacity for infusing them with a keen spirit. And for this no one could be better than General Bruce himself. He had served in a Gurkha regiment for thirty years. He loved his Gurkhas, and was beloved by them. He spoke their language; knew all their customs and traditions, and had had them climbing with him in the Alps as well as the Himalaya. And Gurkhas come from Nepal, on the borders of which Mount Everest lies.

For organising this corps of porters, for dealing with the Tibetans, and, lastly, for keeping together the climbers from England, who were mostly quite unknown to each other, but who all knew of General Bruce and his mountaineering achievements in the Himalaya, General Bruce was an ideal chief.

This being settled, the next question was the selection of the climbing party. General Bruce would not be able to go on to the mountain itself, and he would have plenty to do at the main base camp, seeing after supplies and organising transport service from the main base to the high mountain base. As chief at the mountain base, and as second-in-command of the Expedition to take General Bruce's place in case of any misadventure to him, Lieutenant-Colonel E. L. Strutt was selected. He was an Alpine climber of great experience and knowledge of ice and snow conditions. But for the actual effort to reach the summit two men were specially marked out. One, of course, was Mr. George Leigh-Mallory, who had done such valuable service on the reconnaissance of the previous year; and the other was Captain George Finch, who had been selected for the first Expedition, but who had, through temporary indisposition, not been able to go with it. Both of these were first-rate men and well known for their skill in mountaineering. These two had been selected in the previous year. Of new men, Major E. F. Norton was an experienced and very reliable and thorough mountaineer. He is an officer in the Artillery, and well known in India for his skill and interest in pig-sticking. But in between his soldiering and his pig-sticking and a course at the Staff College he seems to have found time for Alpine climbing and for bird observation. A man of high spirit, who could be trusted to keep his head under all circumstances and to help in keeping a party together, he was a valuable addition to the Expedition. Mr. Somervell was perhaps even more versatile in his accomplishments. He was a surgeon in a London hospital, who was also skilled both in music and painting, and yet found time for mountaineering, and, being younger than the others, and possessed of exuberant energy and a fine physique, he could be reckoned on to go with the highest climbers. Another member of the medical profession who was also a mountaineer was Dr. Wakefield. He was a Westmorland man, who had performed wonderful climbing feats in the Lake District in his younger days, and now held a medical practice in Canada. He was bursting with enthusiasm to join the expedition, and gave up his practice for the purpose.

As medical officer and naturalist of the Expedition, Dr. T. G. Longstaff was chosen. He was a veteran Himalayan climber, and if only this Expedition could have been undertaken some years earlier, he, like General Bruce, would have made a magnificent leader of a climbing party. As it was, his great experience would be available for the climbers as far as the high mountain camp. And this time it was intended to send with the Expedition a "whole-time" photographer and cinematographer, both for the purpose of having a photographic record of its progress and also to provide the means by which the expenses of this and a future expedition might be met. For this Captain J. B. Noel was selected. He had made a reconnaissance towards Mount Everest in 1913, and he had since then made a special study of photography and cinematography, so that he was eminently suited for the task.

The above formed the party which would be sent out from England. And subsequently General Bruce, in India, selected four others to join the Expedition: Mr. Crawford, of the Indian Civil Service, a keen mountaineer, who had long wished to join the Expedition; Major Morshead, who had held charge of the survey party in the 1921 Expedition, and now wanted to join the present Expedition as a climber; and two officers from Gurkha regiments, to serve as transport officers, namely, Captain Geoffrey Bruce and Captain Morris.

This completed the British personnel of the Expedition. It had been my hope that a first-rate artist might have accompanied it to paint the greatest peaks of the Himalaya, but the artists whom we chose were unable to pass the medical examination, though the examination was, of course, not so severe as the examination which the actual climbers had to pass.

While these men were being selected, the Equipment Committee, Captain Farrar and Mr. Meade, were working hard. Taking the advice of Colonel Howard-Bury and

Mr. Mallory, and profiting by the experience gained on the previous Expedition, they got together and had suitably packed and despatched to India a splendid outfit comprising every necessity for an Expedition of this nature. The amount of work that Farrar put into this was enormous; for as a mountaineer he knew well how the success of the Expedition depended on each detail of the equipment being looked into, and he spared himself no trouble and overlooked nothing. The stores were of the most varied description, in order to meet the varying tastes of the different members. The tents were improved in accordance with the experience gained. Most particular attention was paid to the boots. Clothing and bedding, light in weight but warm to wear, were specially designed. Ice-axes, crampons, ropes, lanterns, cooking-stoves, and also warm clothing for the porters, were all provided, and much else besides.

But about one point in the equipment of the party there was much diversity of opinion. Should the climbers be provided with oxygen, or should they not? If it were at all feasible to provide climbers with oxygen without adding appreciably to the weight they had to carry, the summit of Mount Everest could be reached to a certainty. For the purely mountaineering difficulties are not great. On the way to the summit there are no physical obstacles which a trained mountaineer could not readily overcome. The one factor which renders the ascent so difficult is the want of oxygen in the air. Provide the oxygen and the ascent could be made at once. But to provide the oxygen heavy apparatus would have to be carried—and carried by the climbers themselves. It became a question whether the disadvantage of having to carry a weight of at least thirty pounds would or would not outweigh the advantages to be gained by the use of the oxygen.

And the Mount Everest Committee were warned of another feature in the case. They were told that if by any misfortune the oxygen were to run out when the climbers were at a considerable height—say 27,000 feet—and they suddenly found themselves without any preparation in this attenuated atmosphere, they might collapse straight away. It was a disagreeable prospect to anticipate. But Captain Finch, who was himself a lecturer on chemistry at the Imperial College of Science, Mr. Somervell, and Captain Farrar, pressed so strongly for the use of oxygen, and Mr. Unna was so convinced he could construct a reasonably portable apparatus, that the Committee decided that the experiment should be made. The value of using oxygen could thus be tested, and we should know what were the prospects of reaching the summit of the mountain either with or without its aid. Captain Farrar, Captain Finch, and Mr. Unna therefore set about constructing an apparatus which would hold the lightest procurable oxygen cylinders, and which could be carried on the back by the climbers.

This final question having been settled, all the stores and equipment having been purchased, packed, and despatched, the members of the Expedition left England in March. But before I leave General Bruce to take up the tale of their adventures, I must say yet one word more about "the good" of climbing Mount Everest. These repeated efforts to reach the summit of the world's highest mountain have already cost human life. They have also cost much physical pain, fatigue, and discomfort to the climbers. They have been very expensive. And there is not the slightest sign of any material gain whatever being obtained—not an ounce of gold, or iron, or coal, or a single precious stone, or any land upon which food or material could be grown. What, then, is the good of it all? Who will benefit in the least even if the climbers do eventually get to the top? These are questions which are still being continually asked me, so I had better still go on trying to make as plain as I can what is the good of climbing Mount Everest.

The most obvious good is an increased knowledge of our own capacities. By trying with all our might and with all our mind to climb the highest point on the earth, we are getting to know better what we really can do. No one can say for certain yet whether we can or cannot reach the summit. We cannot know till we try. But if—as seems much more probable now than it did ten years ago—we can reach the summit, we shall know that we are capable of more than we had supposed. And this knowledge of our capacities will be very valuable. In my own lifetime I have seen men's knowledge of their capacity for climbing mountains greatly increased. Men's standard of climbing has been raised. They now know that they can do what forty years ago they did not deem in the least possible. And if they reach the summit of Mount Everest, the standard of achievement will be still further raised; and men who had, so far, never thought of attempting the lesser peaks of the Himalaya, will be climbing them as freely as they now climb peaks in Switzerland.

And what then? What is the good of that? The good of that is that a whole new enjoyment in life will be opened up. And enjoyment of life is, after all, the end of life. We do not live to eat and make money. We eat and make money to be able to enjoy life. And some of us know from actual experience that by climbing a mountain we can get some of the finest enjoyment there is to be had. We like bracing ourselves against a mountain, pitting our mettle, our nerve, our skill, against the physical difficulties the mountain presents, and feeling that we are forcing the spirit within us to prevail against the material. That is a glorious feeling in itself and a real tonic to the spirit—even when it does not always conquer.

But that is not all. The wrestling with the mountain makes us love the mountain. For the moment we may be utterly exhausted and only too thankful to be able to hurry back to more congenial regions. Yet, all the same, we shall eventually get to love the mountain for the very fact that she has forced the utmost out of us, lifted us just for one precious moment high above our ordinary life, and shown us beauty of an austerity, power, and purity we should have never known if we had not faced the mountain squarely and battled strongly with her.

This, then, is the good to be obtained from climbing Mount Everest. Most men will have to take on trust that there *is* this good. But most of the best things in life we have to take on trust at first till we have proved them for ourselves. So I would beg readers of this book first trustfully to accept it from the Everest climbers that there is good in climbing great mountains (for the risks they have run and the hardships they have endured are ample enough proof of the faith that is in them), and then to go and test it for themselves—in the Himalaya, if possible, or if not, in the Alps, the Rockies, the Andes, wherever high mountains make the call.

THE NARRATIVE OF THE EXPEDITION

By

BRIGADIER-GENERAL HON. C. G. BRUCE,
C.B., M.V.O.

CHAPTER I

TO THE BASE CAMP

The precursor of the present volume, *The Reconnaissance of Mount Everest in 1921*, sets forth fully the successful and strenuous work which was accomplished in that year and which has rendered possible the Expedition of the present year. The whole of our work lying in country which had never previously been explored by Europeans, it was rendered absolutely necessary for a full examination of the whole country to be made before an attempt to climb Mount Everest could possibly be carried out. We have to thank Colonel Howard-Bury and his companions, especially his survey officers, for their important work, which rendered our task in arriving at our base comparatively simple.

The object of the Expedition of 1922, of course, was the actual attack on the mountain in an attempt to climb it; but no great mountain has ever succumbed to the first attempt on it, and therefore it is almost inconceivable that so tremendous a problem as the ascent of Mount Everest should succeed at the very first effort. In fact, I myself am more than satisfied, almost astounded, at the extraordinary success attained by my companions in this endeavour. The problem that lay in front of us, I think, should be first explained.

Mount Everest, as all know, lies on that part of the Himalaya which is narrowest. It is, therefore, exposed very rapidly to the first assaults of the South-west monsoon, and this monsoon advances up the Bay of Bengal at an earlier period in the year than that of its Western branch, the Gulf current. It is this fact which supplies the greatest difficulty to be faced in an attack on any of the great peaks which lie in this region, giving one an unusually short season. However, to a certain extent this is counteracted by the fact that the winter climate in this portion of the Himalaya is far drier than it is in the West. There is less deposit of snow on the mountains in this section of the Himalaya than there would be, for instance, in the Kashmir mountains, and this, to some extent, makes up for the early advance of the monsoon, and consequent bad weather, which renders any exploration of the great heights during the time that the monsoon blows an impossibility.

Towards the end of May the monsoon arrives in Darjeeling, and then, according to the strength of the current, quickly approaches the Southern faces of the Himalaya, and, as the current strengthens, drifts across their summits and through the gorges and over the lower ridges. The problem, therefore, of any party exploring in these mountains resolves itself into the rapidity with which they can establish their base of operations in a suitable locality to explore the mountains and to climb them. During the period of the very great cold, naturally, the upper heights are impossible, and camping on the upper glaciers is in itself also almost impossible. Travelling across Tibet in March, crossing high passes of over 17,000 feet is such that, although it might be perfectly possible to do, it would be a great strain on the stamina of the party, and likely to detract from their condition. We had, therefore, to adapt our advance into Tibet so as to make it at the latest possible moment, in order to avoid the very worst of the weather, and yet at the earliest possible moment, so that we could arrive at the foot of our mountains with sufficient time to attack them before the weather broke up and rendered mountaineering an impossibility at a great height. It resolves itself, then, almost into a race against the monsoon.

This was our problem, and it is my special province in these opening chapters to show how we tackled it.

During the winter of 1921-2, the Mount Everest Committee, owing to the lateness with which the party had returned after the reconnaissance, had to work at very top speed. They had to collect all the necessary stores for the party, and not only that, but also to select a suitable mountaineering team; this was a considerable difficulty. Finally the party was made up as follows: myself as leader, Colonel E. L. Strutt as Second-in-Command, and Dr. Longstaff the official doctor and naturalist of the Expedition. The climbing party pure consisted of Mr. Mallory (of last year's Expedition), Dr. Somervell, Dr. Wakefield, and Major Norton. We had three transport officers, one of whom belonged to the Alpine Club, and was considered an assistant of the climbing party, Mr. C. G. Crawford, of the Indian Civil Service. The official photographer was Captain Noel. Two officers in the Indian Army were attached to the Expedition as transport officers—Captain J. G. Bruce and Captain C. G. Morris. Later, on our arrival in Darjeeling, the party was further reinforced by Major Morshead, who had been one of the survey party of the previous year, and whose general knowledge of Tibet and of Tibetans was of great service to us; and last, but not least, Captain George Finch, who came not only as a most important member of the climbing party, but also as the scientific expert in charge of the entire oxygen outfit.

This large party was collected in Darjeeling by the last week in March, and in a few days we were all ready to make a start. I myself preceded the party by about a month, arriving in Delhi to interview the Indian authorities about the 25th of February. Through the kindness of the Commander-in-Chief, Lord Rawlinson, we were supplied with four young non-commissioned officers of Captain Bruce's regiment, the 2nd Battalion 6th Gurkha Rifles, and an orderly of the 1st Battalion 6th Gurkha Rifles, and right well all these five Gurkhas carried out their duties. As will be seen later, one of them, Lance-naik Tejbir Bura, very highly distinguished himself.

I arrived in Darjeeling with Captain Bruce on March 1, and there I found that our agent in India, Mr. Weatherall, had carried out the instructions which he had received from

England in the most efficient manner. The large quantity of stores which we had ordered previously were all beautifully packed and ready for transportation ; the tents of the previous year all mended and in good order ; the stores of different kinds, such as there were, which had been left also from the previous year, had been put into order ; and last and most important, 150 porters had been collected for our inspection and from whom to make a selection. He had also for us a large number of cooks to choose from, a most excellent individual to look after the tents, Chongay, who proved quite invaluable to us, and a local cobbler who had expressed his willingness to come with the Expedition.

Owing to the tremendous hurry in which all arrangements had to be made in England, the stores were forwarded in different batches. On our arrival in Calcutta, we interviewed Mr. Brown, of the Army and Navy Stores, whose work, both for the Expeditions of 1921 and of 1922, has been quite beyond praise. He told us that only one instalment of stores had yet arrived, but that the ships containing the remainder were expected shortly. Luckily for us, we had at the Army and Navy Stores, and acting in the interests of the Expedition, a most capable agent. As the ships containing the stores arrived, the latter were unloaded, rapidly passed through the Customs, and forwarded on to Kalimpong Road, which is the terminus of the Darjeeling Railway and the Teesta Valley. On arrival there they were met by our representative in no less a person than Captain Morris, handed over to the contractors who were moving our stores, and forwarded on to Tibet in advance of the Expedition. This naturally required a great deal of arranging.

I must mention that, shortly after our arrival in Darjeeling, we were joined by Captain Morris, who immediately left for Kalimpong, two stages on our journey, to which place the whole of the outfit of the Expedition was sent. We could not spare the time to wait for the arrival of the oxygen, and therefore, when the party finally left Darjeeling, Captain Finch, the scientist in whose charge the whole of the oyxgen and scientific apparatus had been put, remained behind with Mr. Crawford to bring it up. Luckily, the ship arrived in Calcutta just as we were leaving, and therefore the delay was less than we had anticipated.

The people of Darjeeling, both the British and the native inhabitants—whether Tibetans or Hillmen—were all immensely interested in our Expedition, and Mr. Laden La, the Deputy Superintendent of Police, was, if anything, the most enthusiastic of them all. Mr. Laden La has himself rendered excellent service to Government, and has travelled greatly in Tibet. He is himself a Tibetan, and, I believe, is an Honorary General in the Tibetan Army. His influence in Darjeeling and the district is great, and his help to the Expedition was invaluable. He arranged in Darjeeling, both as head of the Buddhist Association of Darjeeling, and in conjunction with the Committee of the Hillmen's Association, that the whole of the party should be entertained by these two Associations, and that the chief

Lamas and Brahmins of the district should bless and offer up prayers for the well-being and success of the party. The entertainment went off most excellently, and it was altogether a most interesting function. The Nepalese members of the party were blessed by the Brahmins, but also, in order to confirm this blessing, further received the blessings of the Lamas. I think there is every reason for supposing that this small function assisted in bringing home to all our porters and followers what was expected of them by their own people, and it was very likely a good deal in consequence of this that they behaved on the whole so extremely well. For it must be understood that all these hill people, whether Nepalese or Tibetan, are very light-hearted, very irresponsible, very high-spirited, and up to the present time prohibition as a national measure is not exactly a popular outlook; in fact, none of them on any occasion, unless well looked after, lost any opportunity of looking on the wine when it is red—or any other colour.

Our cooks had to be chosen with a good deal of care. Captain Bruce and myself took the most likely candidates out into the hills and gave them a good trial before we engaged them. One of them, who was a Nepalese, had been an old servant of my own for many months; he was the only Gurkha among them. The other three (for we gave ourselves an ample outfit of four cooks) were Bhotias (Tibetans). They were the greatest success, mostly because they are hard-working and ready to do any amount of work; but they were good cooks too. Captain Noel also engaged an excellent servant (also a cook), and Major Norton's private servant (another Tibetan) was very capable in the same way; so that we were thoroughly well provided with an ample outfit, and wherever we were we could count on having our meals properly prepared. This is one of the important points in Tibetan travel, from the want of which I believe a certain amount of the illness that was experienced in the previous year was due.

We also engaged almost the most important subordinate member of the Expedition—the interpreter, Karma Paul. He was quite young, and had been a schoolmaster in Darjeeling. He had also worked, I believe, for a time in an office in Calcutta. He was quite new to the kind of work that he would have to do. But he was a great acquisition to the Expedition, always good company and always cheerful, full of a quaint little vanity of his own and delighted when he was praised. He served us very well indeed from one end of the Expedition to the other, and it was a great deal owing to his cheerfulness and to his excellent manners and way with the Tibetans that we never had the smallest possible misunderstanding with any officials, even of the lowest grades, to disturb our good relations with the Tibetans of any kind or class. He also was bilingual, for he had been born in Lhasa, and still had relations living there.

On March 26 the whole Expedition started off for Kalimpong by rail, with the exception of Captain Finch and Mr. Crawford, who remained to bring on the oxygen. Owing to the kindness of the Himalayan Railway Company, we were all taken round by rail to Kalimpong Road free, the whole Expedition travelling up the Teesta Valley in the normal manner, with the exception of Captain Noel, who elected to ride on the roof of the carriages in order to take pictures with his cinema camera of the Teesta Valley. The junction at Siliguri, where the Teesta railway branches off from the main line, is only 300 feet above the sea, the terminus at Kalimpong Road about 700 feet above the sea, and therefore as one dives down from the hills one enters into tropical conditions and passes through the most magnificent tropical jungle and the steepest gorges and ravines. It is a wonderful journey. Even the long spell of hot and dry weather and the heat haze at this time of year were unable to spoil the scenery. And though we saw it almost at its worst time, it remained gorgeous.

At Kalimpong the Expedition broke up into two parties, but before we left we had a very pleasant function to attend. I had been charged by Sir Robert Baden-Powell to deliver a message to the scouts of Dr. Graham's Homes for European Children at Kalimpong. Not only that, but incorporated with these scouts was the first small body of Nepalese boy-scouts. It was a very interesting function indeed, and a most enthusiastic one.

From there we pushed on stage by stage over the Jelep La into the Chumbi Valley. Of course, journeys through Sikkim have often been described. Again we were disappointed. On my first arrival in Darjeeling, the cold weather had hardly finished, but now (March 28) we were well into the hot weather of Bengal, and in consequence we were also in the hot-weather haze. During the whole of our journey we never got a single view of the gorgeous Southern faces of the Himalaya, of Kanchenjanga and of its supporters, and especially of the wonderful Siniolchum peak. This was a very great disappointment, as from several points on our road a view of the Southern face can be obtained. Nevertheless, a journey through Sikkim is always a wonderful experience. The steep and deeply cut valleys, the wonderful clear mountain streams, and the inhabitants and their means of cultivation, are all full of interest. The depth of the valleys is always striking, and can never be anything else. When one thinks that from Rongli Chu, situated only at 2,700 feet above the sea, one rises in one continuous pull to close on 13,000 feet on the ridge which looks down on the Gnatong bungalow, and travels through cultivation and forest the whole way, passing through every phase of Eastern Himalayan landscape, one cannot cease to be continually impressed by the scale of the country. We were too early for the rhododendrons on the way to Gnatong, but there were just sufficient in flower to give us a mental vision of what these wonderful rhododendron forests would be like in another three weeks.

On the way to Gnatong, at a height of 11,500 feet, we came to the little village of Lungtung. Here there was a tea-house kept by some Nepalese. It was spotlessly clean, or at least all the cooking arrangements were, and here, as we came up, we all indulged in tea and the local cakes, and found them both excellent. Not only that, but the little lady who kept the shop was full of talk and full of chaff, and we all sat down and enjoyed ourselves for more than an hour, keeping up a continuous flow of conversation. All the men joined us as they came up, and I am afraid we made rather a noise. As a matter of fact, all through Sikkim these little tea-shops are to be found, and the tea is generally quite drinkable. This little lady's shop, though, was particularly well run and attractive. When we left we promised to call and see her again on our return, which promise we were able to fulfil.

The higher portions of the road from Gnatong over the Jelep are a very great contrast. It is almost like a march through the Highlands of Scotland, and hardly represents or brings to one's mind the fact that one is among great mountains. The Jelep, which is 14,300 feet above the sea, is a perfectly easy pass, crossed by a horrid pavé road, very much out of repair, the descent into the Chumbi Valley being, for animals, the last word in discomfort. We employed altogether in our two parties about eighty mules from the Chumbi Valley, and we were all immensely struck by this wonderful transport. There is a considerable trade carried on between Tibet and Chumbi in particular for seven or eight months in the year, as on this road quantities of Tibetan wool are brought down for sale at Kalimpong, very nearly all of it being brought by the Chumbi muleteers, and most efficient they are. They thoroughly understand the loading and care of mules, and the pace they travel at is something to see. It is only understood if one walks for long distances with, or often behind, a train of laden mules. No doubt, owing to the continual changes from cold to warmth and heat, many sore backs are occasioned, and further, owing to the tremendous stress and continuous labour involved, many mules are worked that have no business to be worked. The muleteers themselves, when talked to about it, say that it distresses them, but they are hard put to it to carry out their work, and see no method very often of being able to fulfil their contracts and at the same time lay up their mules.

After crossing the Jelep La, and leaving Sikkim, it is almost like diving into Kashmir, so great is the difference in the general appearance of the country and in its forests. While we were sitting on the top of the Jelep we had the most splendid view of Chomolhari (23,800 feet). It showed itself at its very best; the day was quiet and very warm. Chomolhari stood out clearly, and still with plenty of atmosphere round it. Snow-streamers were blowing out from its summit. It showed its full height, and did full justice to its shape and beauty. It is a great mountain which completely dominates Phari and its plain, and is the striking feature as one enters Tibet from the Chumbi Valley. We all admired it enormously, but the enthusiasm of the party was somewhat damped when I pointed out to them that our high advanced base on Everest, in fact, the camp that we hoped to establish on the North Col, called the Chang La, which had been marked out the year before by Mr.

FROZEN WATERFALL, CHUMBI VALLEY.

Mallory, was, in fact, only about 600 feet lower than the top of Chomolhari itself.

On arrival at Richengong, which is at the foot of the valley which forms the junction between the Jelep Valley and the valley of the Ammu Chu, which is the Chumbi Valley, we were met by Mr. Macdonald, the British Trade Agent, who lives at Chumbi, and his wonderfully dressed chuprassis, and also by a guard of honour of 90 Panjabis, who supplied a small guard both at Yatung, in Chumbi, and also at the British post in Gyantse, on the road to Lhasa. We had a very pleasant ride by the Chumbi Valley to Yatung. I had previously supplied myself in Darjeeling with a treasure of a pony, Gyamda by name, who was locally very well known in Darjeeling. He was only 12½ hands, but had the go and the stamina of a very much bigger animal. He was attended by a sais who was nearly twice as big as himself, and was one of the finest-built Tibetans I saw the whole time. Gyamda himself hailed from the town of Gyamda, which is about 12 miles South of Lhasa. His enormous sais hailed from Lhasa itself, and, unfortunately, could hardly speak a word of anything but Tibetan. However, he improved by degrees, and very soon we got on very well. He adored the pony Gyamda, but had the habit of giving it, unless looked after, at least a dozen eggs mixed with its grain. When we stopped him doing this, he was caught hugging the pony round the neck and saying to it, "Now they have cut your eggs, you will die, and what shall I do?" Gyamda carried me right through the Expedition, and could go over any ground, and came back as well as he left, never sick or sorry, and always pleased with life.

We marched from Chumbi on April 5, accompanied by Mr. Macdonald and his son, who had come to help us make all our transport arrangements when we should arrive in Phari. Mr. Macdonald helped us on all occasions, and we cannot thank him enough for all the trouble he took from now on and during the whole time the Expedition was in Tibet. It was owing very largely to his help that we were able in Phari to get our Expedition on so soon, for he warned the two Dzongpens of Phari Dzong beforehand to obtain adequate transport for us.

Again, the march from Yatung to Phari has been described on many occasions, but it is quite impossible to march through it without mentioning its character. It is, especially at the time of year we went through, one of the darkest and blackest and most impressive forested gorges that I have ever seen, and almost equally impressive is the debouchment on to the Phari Plain at the head of the gorge, dominated as it is by our old friend Chomolhari.

We arrived in Phari on April 6, and made our first real acquaintance with the Tibetan wind. Phari is 14,300 feet, and winter was scarcely over ; the weather also was threatening. Luckily, there is a little British Government rest-house and bungalow and serai at Phari, and there we found comfortable quarters. We were joined on the following day by the rest of the party. This really formed the starting-point of the Expedition, and, further, it was my birthday, and the bottle of old rum, 120 years old, specially brought out for this occasion, was opened and the success of the Expedition was drunk to. If we had known what was in front of us, we should have put off the drinking of this peculiarly comforting fluid until the evening of the day of our first march from Phari. The two Phari Dzongpens, probably owing to the fact that Phari is on the main route between Lhasa and India, were far and away the most grasping and difficult of any officials that we met, but no doubt their difficulties were pretty considerable. Although there is a great quantity of transport to be obtained in Phari, at this time of the year it is in very poor condition. Grazing exists, but one would never know that it existed unless one was told, and also unless one saw herds of yaks on the hillsides apparently eating frozen earth. Everything was frozen hard. We had difficulty, therefore, in obtaining the transport required. We found here collected the whole of our stores, with the exception of the oxygen. Our excellent tindel,[1] Chongay, who had gone on ahead, had got it all marshalled; the tents were also pitched and in good order.

On April 8 we set out from Phari, but had been obliged to reinforce the local transport by re-engaging fifty of the Chumbi mules. We had been obliged to do this because we were unable to get a sufficiency of transport that was capable of carrying loads in Phari itself. But these

[1] Tent-mender.

fifty mules were our salvation; without them, as it turned out, we should have been in a bad way.

There are two roads that lead from Phari to Khamba Dzong, our next objective; the short road passing over the Tang La and the Donka La, and a long road which starts first on the road to Lhasa and turns finally after two marches to the West. On account of the short time at our disposal, and having regard to the fact that we had now in earnest begun our race with the weather, we chose the shorter route. Owing to the condition of the animals, all had agreed that the yaks could not possibly, even by the short road, get to Khamba Dzong under six days. We therefore divided our party again into two. The advance party, with fifty Chumbi mules and a large collection of donkeys and particularly active bullocks, and even some cows, were to march to Khamba Dzong in four days, and were to be followed by 200 yaks in charge of our sardar, Gyaljen, and two of the Gurkha non-commissioned officers, to wit, Naik Hurké Gurung and Lance-naik Lal Sing Gurung, the other two Gurkhas being in charge of the treasure-chest which accompanied the first party; Lance-naik Tejbir Bura and Lance-naik Sarabjit Thapa were to march with the first party.

The sardar Gyaljen had accompanied Colonel Howard-Bury's party on the first Expedition, and had, apparently, from the accounts given of him in last year's volume, not been a very great success. I, however, gave him a second chance. He was a thoroughly capable man, and I had every hope, as he knew that I had heard about him and had also seen the report that had been made of him by Colonel Howard-Bury, that on this occasion he would pull himself together and do well; in this we were not disappointed. Of course, as all sophisticated men in his position are likely to do, he was out to benefit himself; but we were able pretty successfully to cope with this failing, and, generally speaking, his services were of great value, especially on certain occasions. Altogether, I think, he was a success.

Of course, we were rather well qualified from this point of view—both Morris and Geoffrey Bruce had an excellent knowledge of Nepal and of the Nepalese, and Nepalese is the one Eastern language which I may say that I also have a good knowledge of. All Sherpas are tri-lingual—that is to say, they talk their own Sherpa dialect of Tibet, Tibetan as a mother-tongue, and nearly all of them Nepalese as well. Owing to their being subjects of Nepal, the official language (that is, Nepalese) is the one they are obliged to employ in dealing with the authorities. Also nearly every one of the Tibetans we employed and who came with us from Darjeeling spoke Nepali as their second language. In consequence of this, nearly the whole of the work usually done by a sardar of coolies in Darjeeling was carried out by the officers of the Expedition, who dealt directly both with the men and with the people of the country.

On April 8 we started out. There was for a good long time a tremendous scrimmage getting all the different loads packed on to the animals, and dividing the animals, especially as the Tibetans had no idea of being punctual, and in consequence the yaks, ponies for riding, mules and bullocks, all drifted in at different times during the morning. Finally, however, our two large mixed convoys were got off. It was really a great piece of luck being able to keep the fifty Chumbi mules. These were laden in the early morning with what was necessary for our camp and despatched well before the rest of the luggage. The great convoy of 200 yaks was finally marshalled and sent off under the charge of the Gurkhas and the sardar, but the advance party's luggage was spread over miles of country. In consequence of this, Geoffrey, Morris, and myself were delayed until quite late in the morning.

Our first march was about 16 miles, and the day was very threatening. We pushed along on ponies at a good pace and crossed the Tang La, which is a little over 15,000 feet, in rough, but not actually wet, weather. Luckily, the country is very open, over plains of more or less frozen grass. Over the main chain of the Himalaya the clouds had settled, and it was evident that the weather was breaking. A little after noon it broke with a vengeance. The clouds settled down, it began to snow heavily, and the wind increased to half a hurricane. Luckily, however, most of our local men knew the road well, otherwise in this great open and undulating country one could very easily get lost. The track, which was fairly well marked otherwise, was completely and rapidly obliterated in places. It was certainly a rather disheartening start. Morris was delayed for a time to look

NUNS AT TA-TSANG.

after some luggage; Geoffrey and myself pushed on. Going pretty quickly, we were able to pick up different parties, and were lucky enough to pass one small encampment of Tibetans. It was curious to see yaks contentedly chewing the cud, the whole of their weather-side being a mass of frozen snow. They seemed to be quite as happy lying out in a blizzard as though they had been ordinary civilised cows in a barn.

About what is usually known as tea-time we sighted the camp. Our excellent followers had got a few tents up, and I was fortunate enough myself to find that the porter who was carrying my big coat had already arrived. Nearly all Indian camp servants who are accustomed to travelling in the Himalaya are good in a crisis, and, when things get bad, come to the fore; but on this occasion they surpassed themselves. It must be understood that, in Tibet, very, very seldom can anything but dried yak-dung be found to make a fire with. On this occasion the snow had obliterated everything, and in consequence a fire had to be otherwise improvised. Some tents had been pitched, a fire had been got going, and very soon a hot meal and hot tea were forthcoming. The rest of the party gradually collected, but it was not until well after nightfall that the whole of the advance transport had managed to arrive. As a first march it certainly gave the party a very good idea of what they might have to put up with in Tibet; it was a real good entry into Tibetan travel. However, nobody was much the worse, and, the weather having cleared during the night, we had a brilliant sight the following morning.

On April 9, we made what I think was the hardest march undertaken on the Expedition. Our path led us over the ridge in its three bifurcations which runs North from Pawhunri and rapidly rises from our last camp, each of these ridges being just 17,000 feet, slightly more or less, and most of the path being at about 16,000 feet of elevation. At any time early in April great cold would be expected at such a height, but on this day the wind was blowing right over the Himalaya direct from the snows across these passes, and howling down the gorges between them. It was painfully cold, and the wind never abated from morning to night. We left about seven o'clock in the morning, and it was well after nightfall again before our transport was collected at our next camp at Hung-Zung-trak. Longstaff and myself pushed on in search of the camp for most of the day together, arriving before any of the animals at about 4.30 to five o'clock in the evening, and made our camp at the above-named place under some overhanging cliffs with fairly good grazing—such as grazing is in April—and with a stream beneath the camp from which water could be obtained. We were very shortly followed by our magnificent Chumbi transport, which had been pushing along at a tremendous pace the whole day long. I do not know what we should have done without it.

What was very much brought home to us was the absolute necessity of windproof material to keep out the tremendous cold of these winds. Fortunately, I had a very efficient mackintosh which covered everything, but even then I suffered very considerably from the cold. It simply blew through and through wool, and riding without windproof clothing would have been very painful. It was also very fortunate for us that the weather was really fine and the sun shone all day. I think we should have been in a very bad way indeed if the blizzard had occurred on the second day out from Phari, and not on the first.

However, by night we were all comfortably settled down, although the whole of our advance stores did not arrive until after ten o'clock at night again. Unfortunately, three of our porters who had stayed behind with the slowest of the bullocks lost their way after dark. They stayed out the whole night without bedding or covering, and in the morning continued to the nunnery of Tatsang, which was about 4 or 5 miles further down the valley and rather off our direct route. We here heard of them and retrieved them. These men had not yet been issued with their full clothes, and how they managed to sit out the night clothed as they were and without any damage of any kind passes one's comprehension. So low was the temperature that night that the quickly flowing stream outside our camp was frozen solid.

We halted the next day, as the transport was overdone, and the following day (April 11) made another long, but very interesting, march direct to Khamba Dzong, leaving the monastery of Tatsang on our right and crossing high plains on which were grazing large herds of kyang and gazelle. The mounted men had great fun trying to round up and get as close as possible to the herds of kyang; they were trusting up to a point, but never let us go close enough to get a good snap photograph of them. Finally, the road led from the high plateau down to Khamba Dzong, through what to several of us immediately became astonishingly familiar country; for the whole surroundings of the Khamba Dzong Valley reminds one very much of the scenery on the North-west frontier of India. But what a difference in climate!

We camped at Khamba Dzong where last year's Expedition had camped, and were very well received by the same Dzongpen. We were gratified to find Dr. Kellas' grave in good order, and we further added to it a collection of great stones. The inscription on the grave in English and Tibetan was clear and clean. We were delayed in Khamba Dzong for three whole days, partly because of the difficulty in collecting animals; also two days to allow our main convoy of 200 yaks to catch us up, and we had the good luck to be joined by Finch and Crawford, who had pushed on at a great pace with the oxygen apparatus. They showed evident signs of wear and tear, being badly knocked about by the weather. The storm had caught them on the Jelep La, and as this is more South, there had been a very much greater fall of snow, so much so that the Chumbi Valley was inches deep in it. They spoke very highly indeed of all their followers, cooks and Tibetans, and especially of a capital boy, Lhakpa Tsering, who had come along with them as their special attendant. He was quite a young boy, but had made the march in two days with them to Tatsang, where they stayed for the night, without showing any particular signs of fatigue, running along beside their ponies. I make a considerable point of the following: I think great exertions and long marches at these high altitudes before acclimatisation is complete would have tended to exhaust, and not to improve, the training of the party, whereas to have a pony with one and be able to walk or ride when one felt tired or blown, gradually allowed the body to adjust itself. At any rate, I am perfectly certain that if every one had been obliged to walk instead of being able to ride, even on the terribly inadequate ponies that were supplied to them in Tibet, but which, at any rate, gave them the much-needed rest, they would not have arrived at the Rongbuk Glacier fit to do the work which they afterwards successfully tackled.

Our march from Khamba Dzong to Tinki and from Tinki to Shekar was exactly by the route followed by Colonel Howard-Bury in the previous year, and calls for no particular comment on my part, with the exception that two small parties of Finch and Wakefield and Mallory and Somervell made a good attempt at Gyangka-nangpa to climb a 20,000-foot peak, Sangkar Ri, on the way. This they were not quite able to do.

We had no difficulty in crossing the great sand-dunes where the Yaru River joins the Arun, as we were able to cross it in the early morning before the wind had arisen.

But on that morning, when we came to the junction of the valley of the Arun, we had a most wonderful and clear view of Mount Everest to the South. Although it was over 50 miles distant in a straight line, it did not look more than twenty. The whole of the face that was visible to us was smothered in snow. The entire setting of the piece was very strange; the country was almost bare enough to remind one of a crumpled Egyptian desert, and the strangeness and wonder was hugely increased by the South of the valley being filled with this wonderful mountain mass.

At Shekar, where we arrived on April 24, we were again delayed for three days getting transport. We found the Dzong filled with Lamas. There is a great monastery in Shekar itself, and one of less account a little further beyond. The great Lama of Shekar is an extremely cunning old person and a first-class trader. In his quarters at the monastery he had immense collections of Tibetan and Chinese curios, and he knew the price of these as well as any professional dealer. We saw a great deal, in fact, a great deal too much, of the Lamas of Shekar. They were the most inconceivably dirty crowd that we had met in Tibet; the dirt was quite indescribable. Although the people in Lhasa in good positions are reported to be generally cleanish, here in the more out-of-the-way parts of Tibet washing appears to be entirely unknown, except to the Dzongpens, and I believe that the ordinary Dzongpen only has a ceremonial bath on New Year's Eve as a preparatory to the new year, and I should not be at all surprised if Mrs. Dzongpen did too. At any rate, the Dzongpens' families were always infinitely better cared for in this respect than anyone else. These people, however, have the most terribly dirty cooks it is possible for the human imagination to conceive. For this reason I never was very happy as a guest, and although the food provided for one's entertainment was often quite pleasant to eat, it was absolutely necessary not to allow one's imagination to get to work.

The three days' delay at Shekar was greatly due to the movement of officials and troops marching by the same route from Tingri to Shigatse, and as they had commissioned every available animal, they interfered considerably with our movements. Shekar was not comfortable during these days ; the wind was not continuous, but came in tremendous gusts, and dust-devils were continually tearing through the camp and upsetting everything. Shekar, as Colonel-Howard-Bury has described it, is wonderfully situated. The pointed mass of rock rises direct from the plains, and the white monasteries and white town are built on its sides. The illustration will describe it much better than I can. Shekar means " Shining glass." All the towns and houses on the sides of the mountain are brilliantly white and show up very clearly against the dark browns and reds of the hillside. It is no doubt this appearance which gives it its name.

The Dzongpen at Shekar was a most important official. The whole of the country South of Shekar and the Rongbuk Valley where we were going were in his jurisdiction. We hoped that if we could only gain his own goodwill as well as his official goodwill, it would be of very great advantage to us. We entertained each other freely, and he was very pleased with the lengths of kin kob [1] which I gave to himself and his wife, and also with the photographs of the Dalai and Tashi Lamas which I gave to him. By showing him pictures and taking his own picture, we were able to make great friends with him, to our great advantage. He sent with us his agent, Chongay La, who served us well during the whole of our time in the Rongbuk Glacier; in fact, without him we should have had great difficulty in obtaining the large amount of stores, grain, and Tibetan coolies which were necessary for us in order to keep our very large party properly provisioned when we were high up on the mountain-side.

Among our other presents was the inevitable Homburg hat. Wherever we went we presented a Homburg hat. I had provided myself with a large number of these hats from Whiteaway and Laidlaw before leaving Darjeeling. These were a cheap present, but very much valued. Any high man of a village known as a Gembo La would do anything for a Homburg hat; it was ceremoniously placed on his head and was invariably well received. In fact, all recipients visibly preened themselves for some time afterwards.

From Shekar our route differed slightly from Colonel Howard-Bury's. He had taken the direct road to Tingri, but our objective was the Rongbuk. Therefore we crossed

[1] Brocade.

the Arun for the first time, and, crossing by the Pang La, descended into the Dzakar Chu. This was one of the pleasantest marches that we had made. The country was new—even Mallory had only been over part of it. The Pang La (meaning "the Grass Pass") was altogether very interesting, and from its summit, where we all collected and lunched, we had again a fine view of Everest, and on this occasion the mountain was almost clear of snow and gave one a very different impression. We here recognised the fact that Everest, on its North face, is essentially a rock peak. Unfortunately for us, it did not remain clear of snow for long, rough weather again coming up; the next time we saw it we found it again clothed from head to foot in snow.

Four marches from Shekar found us at Rongbuk, the final march from Chodzong to the Rongbuk Monastery being extremely interesting. There is only one word for it: the valleys of Tibet leading up to the Rongbuk Monastery are hideous. The hills are formless humps, dull in colour; of vegetation there is next to none. At our camp at Chodzong, however, on the hillside opposite our camp, there was quite a large grove of thorn-trees. We had visions of a wood fire very quickly damped when we were told that this grove was inhabited by the most active and most malicious of demons, and that he would promptly get to work if we interfered and carried away any sticks from his grove.

The Upper Rongbuk Valley is an extremely sacred

valley; no animals are allowed to be killed in it. In fact, the great Mani at the mouth of the valley opposite the village of Chobu marks the limit beyond which animals are not allowed to be killed. We were told that if we wanted any fresh meat it was all to be killed lower down the valley and carried up to us. The Tibetans themselves live very largely on dried meats, both yak meat and mutton. I have never tried it myself, and its appearance was enough to put off anyone but a hungry dog, but I am told that when cooked it is by no means bad. Most Tibetans, however, eat it raw in its dried state. I bought quantities of both sorts for the porters. They cooked it as they would cook fresh meat, and it seemed to suit them very well. For the sake of their health, however, I gave them, whenever possible, fresh meat, and with the very finest results.

Rongbuk means "the valley of precipices or steep ravines." The Lepchas of Sikkim are occasionally called "Rong Pa," i.e., the people of steep ravines. It is also used for Upper Nepal, or rather for the people on the Southern faces of the Himalayan heights, as they are people of the steep ravines. I have also heard it used to mean Nepal itself. Some five miles up the valley one comes out on to a plateau and is suddenly almost brought up against the walls of the Rongbuk Monastery. Here also, as we came out to the Rongbuk Monastery, we found the whole Southern end of the valley filled with Mount Everest and quite close to us—apparently. In any European climate one would have said that it was a short march to its base, and one would have

Rongbuk Monastery and Mount Everest.

been terribly wrong. The air is astonishingly clear; the scale is enormous. The mountain was 16 miles off.

We pitched our camp just below the monastery with considerable difficulty, as the wind was howling rather more than usual. Then we went up to pay our respects to the Rongbuk Lama. This particular Lama was beyond question a remarkable individual. He was a large, well-made man of about sixty, full of dignity, with a most intelligent and wise face and an extraordinarily attractive smile. He was treated with the utmost respect by the whole of his people. Curiously enough, considering the terrible severity of the climate at Rongbuk, all his surroundings were far cleaner than any monastery we had previously, or indeed subsequently, visited. This Lama has the distinction of being actually the incarnation of a god, the god Chongraysay, who is depicted with nine heads. With his extraordinary mobility of expression, he has also acquired the reputation of being able to change his countenance. We were received with full ceremony, and after compliments had been exchanged in the usual way by the almost grovelling interpreter, Karma Paul (who was very much of a Buddhist here), the Lama began to ask us questions with regard to the objects of the Expedition. He was very anxious also that we should treat his people kindly. His inquiries about the objects of the Expedition were very intelligent, although at the same time they were very difficult to answer. Indeed, this is not strange when one comes to think how many times in England one has been asked—What is the good of an exploration of Everest? What can you get out of it? And, in fact, what is the object generally of wandering in the mountains? As a matter of fact, it was very much easier to answer the Lama than it is to answer inquiries in England. The Tibetan Lama, especially of the better class, is certainly not a materialist. I was fortunately inspired to say that we regarded the whole Expedition, and especially our attempt to reach the summit of Everest, as a pilgrimage. I am afraid, also, I rather enlarged on the importance of the vows taken by all members of the Expedition. At any rate, these gentle "white lies" were very well received, and even my own less excusable one which I uttered to save myself from the dreadful imposition of having to drink Tibetan tea was also sufficiently well received. I told the Lama, through Paul, who, fortunately enough, was able to repress his smiles (an actual record for Paul, which must have strained him to his last ounce of strength), that I had sworn never to touch butter until I had arrived at the summit of Everest. Even this was well received. After that time I drank tea with sugar or milk which was made specially for me.

A word about Tibetan tea: the actual tea from which it is originally made is probably quite sufficiently good, but it is churned up in a great churn with many other ingredients, including salt, nitre, and butter, and the butter is nearly invariably rancid, that is, as commonly made in Tibet. I believe a superior quality is drunk by the upper classes, but at any rate, to the ordinary European taste,

THE EXPEDITION AT BASE CAMP.

Left to Right, Back Row: MAJOR MORSHEAD, CAPTAIN GEOFFREY BRUCE, CAPTAIN NOEL, DR. WAKEFIELD, MR. SOMERVELL, CAPTAIN MORRIS, MAJOR NORTON.
Front Row: MR. MALLORY, CAPTAIN FINCH, DR. LONGSTAFF, GENERAL BRUCE, COLONEL STRUTT, MR. CRAWFORD.

castor-oil is pleasant in comparison. One of the party, however, had managed to acquire a taste for it, but then some people enjoy castor-oil!

The Lama finally blessed us and blessed our men, and gave us his best wishes for success. He was very anxious that no animals of any sort should be interfered with, which we promised, for we had already given our word not to shoot during our Expedition in Tibet. He did not seem to have the least fear that our exploring the mountain would upset the demons who live there, but he told me that it was perfectly true that the Upper Rongbuk and its glaciers held no less than five wild men. There is, at any rate, a local tradition of the existence of such beings, just as there is a tradition of the wild men existing right through the Himalaya.

As a matter of fact, I really think that the Rongbuk Lama had a friendly feeling for me personally, as he told the interpreter, Karma Paul, that he had discovered that in a previous incarnation I had been a Tibetan Lama. I do not know exactly how to take this. According to the life you lead during any particular incarnation, so are you ranked for the next incarnation; that is to say, if your life has been terrible, down you go to the lowest depths, and as you acquire merit in any particular existence, so in the next birth you get one step nearer to Nirvana. I am perfectly certain that he would consider a Tibetan Lama a good bit nearer the right thing than a Britisher could ever be, and so possibly he may have meant that I had not degenerated so very far anyhow. I should have liked to know, however, what the previous incarnations of the rest of the party had been!

I think in my present incarnation the passion that I have for taking Turkish baths may be some slight reaction from my life in the previous and superior conditions as a Tibetan Lama.

The following morning, in cold weather, as usual, we left to try and push our camp as high up as possible. Our march now became very interesting, and we passed on our road, which was fairly rough, six or seven of the hermits' dwellings. These men are fed fairly regularly from the monasteries and nunneries, and do not necessarily take their vows of isolation for ever all at once. They try a year of it and see how they get on before they take the complete vows, but how it is possible for human beings to stand what they stand, even for a year, without either dying or going mad, passes comprehension. Their cells are very small, and they spend the whole of their time in a kind of contemplation of the ōm, the god-head, and apparently of nothing else. They are supposed to be able to live on one handful of grain per diem, but this we were able successfully to prove was not the case; they appear, as far as we could make out, to have a sufficiency of food always brought to them. However, there they are in little cells, without firing or warm drinks, all the year round, and many of them last for a great number of years.

Our march took us right up to the snout of the main Rongbuk Glacier, and on arrival there we vainly endeavoured to get our yak-men to push up the trough between the glacier and the mountain-side. There was promptly a strike among the local transport workers, but the employers of labour were wise enough to give in to their demands. If we had pushed further up, we must have injured a great number of animals, and finally have been obliged to return. So we found a fairly good site, protected to a small extent from the prevailing West wind, and there we collected the whole of our outfit and pitched our camp. I do not think such an enormous cavalcade could possibly have mounted the Rongbuk Glacier before. There were over 300 baggage animals, about twenty ponies, fifty or sixty men in our own employ, and the best part of 100 Tibetans, either looking after us or coming up as representatives of the Shekar Dzongpen. Finally, all were paid off, and the Expedition was left alone in its glory. The date was the 1st of May.

CHAPTER II

THE ASSAULT ON THE MOUNTAIN

Now began in earnest our race against the monsoon. I have often been asked since my return, whether we should not have done better if we had started sooner. I think none of us would have cared to have arrived at our Upper Rongbuk camp a fortnight earlier in the year, nor, having done so, would any good purpose have been served. As it was, the temperature and the coldness of the wind was as much as any of us could keep up with and still keep our good health. This was to be our Base Camp at a height of 16,500 feet. We made suitable dumps of stores, pitched our mess tents, put all our porters in tents at their own particular places, and made ourselves as comfortable as circumstances allowed, strengthening the tents in every way to resist the wind. Noel also pitched his developing tent near the small stream that issues from the Rongbuk Glacier. On our arrival water was hardly available; all the running streams were frozen hard, and we drove the whole of our animals over them. Where the glacier stream flowed fastest in the centre, we got sufficient water for drinking purposes.

The establishment and support of such a large party

VIEW AT BASE CAMP.

(for we were thirteen Europeans and over sixty of what may be termed other ranks) in a country as desolate and as bare as Tibet is a difficulty. There is, of course, no fuel to be found, with the exception of a very little scrubby root which, burnt in large quantities, would heat an oven, but which was not good enough or plentiful enough for ordinary cooking purposes.

Our first work, beyond the establishment of the Base Camp, was immediately to send out a reconnaissance party. Strutt was put in charge of this, and chose as his assistants Norton, Longstaff, and Morshead. The remainder of the party had to work very hard dividing stores and arranging for the movement up to the different camps we wished to make on the way up the East Rongbuk Glacier to the North Col. It was pretty apparent from Major Wheeler's map that our advance up the East Rongbuk to the glacier crossed by Mr. Mallory in 1921, which is below the Chang La, would not be a very difficult road. But it was a very considerable question how many camps should be established, and how full provision should be made for each ? We were naturally very anxious to save our own porters for the much more strenuous work of establishing our camp at the North Col, and perhaps of further camps up the mountain. I had, therefore, on our march up, made every possible endeavour to collect a large number of Tibetan coolies in order that they should be employed in moving all the heavy stuff as far up the glacier as possible; in fact, until we came to ground which would not be suitable to them, or, rather, not suitable to their clothing. They were perfectly willing to work on any ground which was fairly dry, but their form of foot-covering would certainly not allow of continual work in snow. We had a promise of ninety men.

We further had to make full arrangements for a regular supply of yak-dung, the whole of which, as in fact everything to burn in Tibet, is called "shing," which really means wood; all our fuel, therefore, from now on, will be referred to as "shing." All tzampa,[1] meat, and grain for the men had to be procured as far down as Chobu, Tashishong, and even from other villages still further down the Dzakar Chu; that is to say, very often our supplies were brought up from at least 40 miles distant. We required a pretty continuous flow of everything. It is wonderful how much even seventy men can get through.

The preliminary reconnaissance had fixed an excellent camp as our first stage out. Geoffrey Bruce and Morris, with our own porters went up, and, so as to save tents, built a number of stone shelters and roofed them with spare parts of tents. This camp was immediately provisioned and filled with every kind of supply in large amounts in order to form again a little base from which to move up further. Strutt returned with his reconnaissance on May 9, having made a complete plan for our advance and having fixed all our camps up to the flat glacier under the North Col. During this period Finch had also been very active with his oxygen apparatus, not only in getting it all together,

[1] Flour.

but continuing the training of the personnel and in making experiments with the Leonard Hill apparatus as well. He also gave lectures and demonstrations on the use of our Primus stove, with which everybody practised. Primus stoves are excellent when they are carefully treated, but are kittle cattle unless everything goes quite as it should, and are apt to blow up.

Longstaff suffered considerably on the reconnaissance, and was brought down not too fit. We also had a real set-back—our ninety coolies did not eventuate, only forty-five appearing, and these coolies only worked for about two days, when they said that their food was exhausted and they must go down for more. We took the best guarantee we could for their return by keeping back half their pay. They went for more food, but found it in their houses and stopped there; we never saw them again. However, it is not to be wondered at. If ploughing in the upper valleys is to be done at all, it is to be done in May. They were, therefore, very anxious to get back to their homes. Ninety men is a big toll for these valleys to supply, but their behaviour left us rather dispirited. We had to turn every one on to work, and then we had to make every possible exertion to collect further coolies from the different villages. The Chongay La who came with us, and who understood our needs, was frantic, but said he could do nothing. However, we persuaded him to do something, at any rate, and further offered very high prices to all the men who had come. He certainly played up and did his very best. Men came up in driblets, or rather men, women, and children came, as every one in this country can carry loads, and they seem to be quite unaffected by sleeping out under rocks at 16,000 or 17,000 feet.

For the whole time we remained at the Rongbuk Base Camp the equipping and supply of our first and second camps up the East Rongbuk was mostly carried out by local coolies, and the supply of these was very difficult to assure. We never knew whether we should have three or four men working, or thirty; they came up for different periods, so that we would often have a dozen men coming down and four or five going up, and in order to keep their complete confidence, they were received and paid personally by myself or the transport officers. By degrees their confidence was restored, and a very fair stream of porters arrived. Not only that, but many of the men's own relations came over from Sola-Khombu, which is a great Sherpa Settlement at the head of the Dudh Kosi Valley in Nepal. To reach us they had to cross the Ngangba La, sometimes called the Khombu La, which is 19,000 feet in height. Often the men's relations came and were willing to carry a load or two and then go off again. The mothers often brought their children, even of less than a year old, who did not apparently suffer. It is evidently a case of the survival of the fittest.

We had brought also large stores of rice, sugar, tea, and wheat grain, both for the use of the officers of the Expedition and of the porters, for fear we should run short of grain, and

CAMP II. AT SUNSET.

this proved a great stand-by. The very rough tzampa of Tibet is often upsetting even to those most accustomed to it. It was found to be an excellent policy to feed our porters on the good grain when they came down to the Base Camp, and to use the tzampa, which is cooked and ready for eating, at the upper camps. Meat also had to be bought low down, sheep killed low down in the valleys, and brought up for the use of the officers and men, and often fresh yak meat for the porters. The Gurkhas got the fresh mutton. Dried meat was brought up in large quantities for the porters, and proved of the greatest use.

On the return, having received a full report from the reconnaissance party, we tackled in earnest the establishment of the different camps.

Camp III, which was under the North Col, was first established in full. This was to be our advance base of operations; and Mallory and Somervell established themselves there, their business being to make the road to the North Col while the rest of the Expedition was being pushed up to join them. On May 13, Mallory, Somervell, and one coolie, together with a tent, reached the North Col and planted the tent there.

This must be described as the beginning of the great offensive of May, 1922. Owing to the lack of coolies, all our officers and men had been working at the highest possible speed, pushing forward the necessary stores, camp equipage, and fuel to Camps I and II, and from thence moving on to Camp III, Gurkhas being planted at each stage, whose business it was to take the convoys to and fro. Finally, Camps I, II, and III were each provided with an independent cook.

The duties of the cook at Camp III were the duties of an ordinary cook in camp; those of the cooks at Camps I and II were to provide all officers passing through or staying there with meals as they were required, and right well all these three men carried out their duties. The distance from the Base Camp to the advance base at Camp III was fairly evenly divided, Camp I being at about three hours' journey for a laden animal at a height of 17,800 feet; Camp II a further four hours up the glaciers at a height of 19,800 feet, and directly below the lesser peak which terminates the Northern ridge of Everest; Camp III on moraine at the edge of the open glacier below the Chang La, at a height of 21,000 feet, about four hours again beyond Camp II.

As our supply of Tibetan coolies improved, and as the main bulk of the necessary supplies was put into Camp III, and the oxygen and its complete outfit had been deposited in this camp, the hard work of supplying rations and fuel to Camps I and II was entirely in the hands of the local Tibetans. From Camp II to Camp III one encounters real mountaineering conditions, as crevassed glaciers have to be crossed, requiring in places considerable care. The road from the Base Camp to Camp II, rough enough in all conscience, was such as could very easily be negotiated by mountain people.

On May 14, Strutt, Morshead, and Norton left to join

the advance party at Camp III. The weather was even worse than before, the wind blowing a perfect hurricane during the daytime, and the thermometer sinking to zero even in the Base Camp. I asked the Chongay La why it should be that as summer was approaching the weather should be continuously worse. He accounted for this without any difficulty. He said in the middle of the month, each month, in fact, at the Rongbuk Monastery there were special services held. These services invariably irritated the demons on the mountains, and they attempted to put a stop to them by roaring more than usually loud. As soon as the services stopped, these winds would stop too. The services stopped on May 17, and the Chongay La said we could expect better weather on that date.

On May 16 the last of the oxygen, with Finch, left for the upper camps, and it is a curious thing that about that time the weather did slightly improve. On May 20, I received a letter from Strutt telling me of the establishment of the camp on the North Col; he himself also accompanied the party that reached the North Col. Here they made a very considerable encampment, and put in it such light stores and cooking apparatus as would be available for parties stopping there and attacking the mountain from that spot. It is very curious how on this Expedition the standard of what we expected from all our members went up. It was looked upon as a foregone conclusion that any member of the party could walk with comfort to the North Col (23,000 feet). It is quite right, no doubt, that the standard should have been set so high; but it is a little amazing, when one comes to think, that only on one occasion before has a night been spent as high as 23,000 feet, and that on very, very few occasions has this height been even attained. Strutt was quite by way of looking upon himself as a worn-out old gentleman because he felt tired at 23,000 feet. No doubt that is the standard we should set for ourselves; but even 23,000 feet is a tremendous undertaking, and no one at any time or at any age of life need be anything but pleased with himself if he can get there.

The party established at Camp III made little expeditions to the Lhakpa La and Ra-piu-la, and obtained a fine view of Makalu and the Northern face of Everest; but the views so obtained also gave them a sight of the approaching monsoon, and this made every one very nervous about the length of time there was left to us for our actual attack on the mountain. It was this very point, including also the evidence of rough and uncertain weather which had been experienced round the mountain itself, that decided Strutt to allow four members to make an attempt on the mountain without oxygen. Certain defects had been found in the oxygen apparatus, and Finch was employed in rectifying these difficulties, and at the same time he was not quite ready to proceed further. Geoffrey Bruce was also working with him at Camp III, and made great progress in the use of the oxygen. They also roped in as their assistant the Gurkha Tejbir, having for him a special rôle.

It is not for me to describe in detail the great attempt

on the mountain made by the party consisting of Mallory, Somervell, Morshead, and Norton, but I must point out quite clearly that as a *tour de force* alone it stands, in my opinion, by itself. It was the most terrific exertion, carried out during unfavourable weather and in the face of that dreadful West wind. Not only did they reach the prodigious height of 26,985 feet without the assistance of oxygen, but they passed a night at 25,000 feet.

I think it is pretty clear from their accounts that any further expedition must be clothed in windproof suitings, and these of the lightest, when attacking Everest, or probably any other great mountain in this particular part of the world. Morshead, who suffered far more than any of the others from the cold, did not employ his windproof suiting in the early part of the climb, and I believe by this omission he very greatly decreased his vitality, and it was probably this decrease which was the reason of his terrible frost-bites.

It was a tremendous effort, unparalleled in the history of mountain exploration, but it gave immense confidence to all that the mountain was not unconquerable. If on the first occasion such a gigantic height could be reached, we were pretty certain that later, with the experience so gained, and with the weather in the climbers' favour instead of the horrible conditions under which this climb was undertaken, the mountain would in time yield to assault.

The following day, notwithstanding their fatigue, they determined to get down to Camp I. They certainly were a sight on arrival; I have never seen such a crowd of swollen and blistered and weary mountaineers before, but they were all naturally tremendously elated with their performance. Strutt came down with them, and quite rightly too; he had been a very long time living above 21,000 feet, and this in itself is a great strain. I thoroughly endorse his judgment in making this great attempt without oxygen. At first sight it would seem that it was not wise to send so many of the best climbers at once on to the mountain before the oxygen apparatus was ready, but he felt (and I consider he was quite right) that as the weather was so bad and the monsoon was evidently arriving before its time, and as at the moment the oxygen apparatus was in such a doubtful condition, it was far better to make an attempt than possibly to fail in making any attempt at all.

During the time that the great attempt on the mountain without oxygen was being made, Finch was employed in getting the oxygen apparatus into order. It had suffered in a good many ways, and the method of inhaling the oxygen appeared to be deficient, the face-masks, in fact, causing a feeling of suffocation and not allowing a sufficiency of ordinary air to be inhaled. Finch had a very difficult time getting all this apparatus into order in this very high camp. It would have been difficult anywhere, but up here in the great cold and the great height it was infinitely more troublesome. As soon as the apparatus was in working order, they made numerous training walks up on to the passes, looking down into the heart of the Kharta Valley, from where they were able to see the Southern faces of the Himalaya and to

Mount Everest from Camp III.

know the way in which the clouds were pushing up from the South.

They had also instructed, to a certain extent, the Gurkha Tejbir Bura in the use of oxygen, as they intended him to help them in their advance on the mountain.

About the time the other party left for the Base Camp, Finch and Geoffrey Bruce set off for the camp on the Chang La, Camp IV, taking with them twelve laden coolies to carry their outfit. I will not attempt to describe their subsequent mountaineering operations in detail, as these must be left to Finch's narrative in a subsequent chapter, but there are a great many points to which attention might be drawn. First, although Geoffrey Bruce is thoroughly accustomed to work on the hillside, he had never before this big attempt, and before the few practice walks that he had with Finch, attempted a snow mountain in his life; the nearest thing he had been to it was following game in Kashmir. It was, therefore, for him a very great test. The same also applies to the Gurkha; although he is a born mountain man and has hardly been off the hillside the whole of his life, up to the time of the climb he knew nothing about snow and ice as understood by a Swiss mountaineer. However, they had a first-rate leader, and his trust in them proved anything but ill-placed.

Owing to a terrific gale, they had to spend two nights at 25,500 feet. They were all short of food, and no doubt greatly exhausted, and I think they would have been perfectly justified, after two nights spent at this tremendous altitude, if they had given up their attempt and returned, but they had too much grit for that. Here should have come in the use of Tejbir if he had been quite himself. He was given extra oxygen to carry, and their intention was that, after proceeding as far as the ridge, he should be sent back to their camp to wait their descent. However, Tejbir was completely played out when he had reached 26,000 feet.

The party continued until they reached a point which has been found to work out at 27,235 feet. Here Geoffrey had an accident to his oxygen apparatus, and, far from becoming immediately unconscious (as we had been warned would be the case before we left England if climbers were suddenly deprived of their artificial oxygen supply), he was able to attach himself to Finch's instrument while Finch was repairing the damaged apparatus. Slightly higher than this point they were completely exhausted, and had to beat a retreat, the whole party finally descending to the North Col, where food was found ready for them, and by the evening got down to Camp III itself—a great performance, considering the altitude and that the descent was over 6,000 feet. I think it is pretty certain that Tejbir's breakdown was largely due to his not having a windproof suit. This biting West wind goes through wool as if it was paper, and he was exposed to it for a great period of time, and no doubt it very largely sapped his vitality.

One result of this last attempt is that it increases our hopes, almost to the point of certainty, that, with luck and good weather, and when the oxygen apparatus has been further improved, the summit of Everest will be attained.

All the time the porters were working from our Base Camp and up there was great competition between them, and also considerable betting as to who would do the hardest work—the true Tibetan-born porters or the Sherpas from the South. It was rather amusing to see the superior airs which the Sherpas invariably gave themselves in travelling through Tibet. They considered Tibetans undoubtedly jăngli,[1] and treated them very much from the point of view that a clever Londoner does the simplest form of yokel when he appears in London. At any rate, they backed themselves heavily to beat the Tibetans. It was a pretty good race, but finally they came out well on top; in fact, I think all but one who reached 25,000 feet and over were Sherpas. Paul, the interpreter, and Gyaljen, had a great bet also about the officers, Paul favouring Finch and Gyaljen Mallory. As a matter of fact, there was quite a little book made among all the followers with regard to who would go highest among the officers. I did not even belong to the "also rans" between them. Oxygen was looked upon as a matter of no particular importance, and I believe Paul made Gyaljen pay up, as he had won with Finch against Mallory.

On May 27 we welcomed the arrival of John Macdonald with a further supply of money, as, owing to the large calls of our enormous transport, we had been afraid of running short. This was very cheering to us indeed, and also a very

[1] Wild.

great help, for, besides the money, Mr. Macdonald brought with him two or three servants very well accustomed to travel in Tibet and knowing all the people of the country. These we were able to use as special messengers, and we sent off immediately by them an account of the climbs that had occurred. The second of them was unfortunately delayed by illness, and this accounted for the slight delay in letting the world know of our great second " oxygen " climb. The first messenger rode through in ten days from Rongbuk to Phari, and by so doing almost caught up the previous letters which had been despatched through the Dzongpens. Arrangements are, after all, not so bad in Tibet. When one considers that Tibetans themselves have no understanding or care for time, the promptness with which the different communications were sent through was rather wonderful. There were, on occasions, no doubt, hitches, but, generally speaking, the postal arrangements worked very well.

The weather had become more and more threatening, but we could not bring ourselves absolutely to give up for this year the attempts on Everest; at the same time, the casualties were heavy. Our medical members had all got to work and had tested thoroughly each member of the Expedition that had been employed. It was evidently absolutely necessary that Morshead should return as quickly as possible into hospital in India, and there were also several other members who were suffering from their hard work. Longstaff had " shot his bolt " as far as this year's work was concerned, and it was also most important that Morshead should have a doctor with him. Strutt, too, was very much overdone, and it was time for him to return. Norton was strained and tired, and Geoffrey's toes, though not so bad as Morshead's, required that he should quickly go down to a warmer climate. We therefore made up two convoys, which were to start together from the Base Camp. Longstaff, Strutt, and Morshead to go with the sardar Gyaljen direct to Darjeeling, travelling viâ Khamba Dzong, and from Khamba Dzong directly South to Lachen and Gangtok and Darjeeling by the shorter and quicker route. This would bring them quite a week sooner to Darjeeling than the route by which we entered Tibet. It was most important that Morshead should be got back as quickly as possible; in fact, we were all very nervous about his condition, and we were afraid that it might be necessary for some operation to be carried out actually on the march.

It had always been our idea that as soon as we had finished with our summer attack on Everest, the whole Expedition should go into the Kharta Valley, where Colonel Howard-Bury in 1921 made his camps, and there recover from our labours. The Kharta Valley is far lower than any other district in this part of Tibet, lying between 11,000 and 12,000 feet above sea-level; there are also many comforts which do not exist in other parts. There is good cultivation, trees and grass to a certain extent, and even some vegetables are obtainable. It is altogether a charming spot—very charming compared with any other country we were likely to see. The road was very high for sick men, as it led over the Doya La, which is only 3 feet under 17,000 feet, but having once got there, they would be in comfort compared with the Rongbuk Glacier.

Having decided on sending off this large convoy of invalids and semi-invalids, we then began to organise our third attempt on Everest, but so doubtful was the weather that the party was organised for two complete purposes. It was fully provided with porters, far more than would in the ordinary way be necessary for an attempt on the mountain itself, considering that the camps were all fully provisioned. We had brought every single man off the glacier after the last attempt in order to give them all a complete rest. Every one had now had a long rest, with the exception of Finch, who had only had five days. He, however, was very keen to join the party.

The second rôle of this party was to evacuate as many camps as possible, according to the condition of the weather, and it was carefully explained to them that if in their opinion the weather was such as to preclude an attempt on the mountain, they were to use the greatest possible care and run no undue risks. It was organised as follows: The climbing party to consist of Finch, Mallory, and Somervell; the backing-up party, Crawford and Wakefield, to remain at Camp III; and Morris, in whose charge the whole of the transport arrangements were, was to take charge of the evacuation of camps either after the attempt had been made, or if no attempt was made, immediately. Such was the condition of the weather that I had no very great hope that even the Chang La camp could be evacuated, but it was most necessary to recover all stores left at the great depôt at Camp III. This was of the utmost importance, as not only was the oxygen apparatus there, but also a great number of surplus stores—stores which we should be in need of. We had, of course, rationed these camps with a view to staying there probably a fortnight longer, but this year the monsoon had evidently advanced at least ten days earlier than usual. That, however, we could not foresee, nor could we foresee the very great severity of the 1922 monsoon of the Eastern Himalaya. This we only heard about on our return to India later on. It was a curious thing that the Rongbuk Lama had sent up to congratulate the porters, and ourselves also, on having come back safely from the earlier attempts, but he warned the porters to leave the mountain alone, as he had had a vision of an accident.

On June 3 the great convoy set off and spent the night at Camp I. On June 4 we were rather overwhelmed to see Finch staggering into camp. He was very much over-done, and had by no means recovered from his terrific exertions on the mountain. It was quite evident that he was finished for this year, and he was lucky to be just in time to join the detachment returning to India direct. It was a very great loss to the party. Not only would he have been of special assistance as the oxygen expert, but his experience and knowledge of snow and ice under the conditions then prevailing would have been of the greatest advantage to the party.

The weather now had completely broken. It was snowing hard; even at our Base Camp we had 2 inches of snow; the whole of the mountains were a complete smother of snow. Notwithstanding this, and, under the conditions, quite rightly, the convoy pushed on to Camp III. On arrival at Camp III the weather cleared. The wind temporarily went round to the West, and one perfect day of rest and sunshine was enjoyed.

Morris all this time was on the line of communication. He had the whole of the service of evacuation to arrange, and was laying out his convoys of Tibetan coolies and others with that point of view in his mind. It was lucky he did so. The great foe, generally speaking, on Everest during the dry period is the horrible West wind, but now the monsoon had to all intents and purposes arrived. The West wind now was our one and only friend. If it would again blow for a short period, the mountain would probably return temporarily to a fairly safe condition. The South wind is a warm and wet, though fairly strong, current, but the result of even a short visit from it absolutely ruins the mountain-side. However, at Camp III they enjoyed one full day of sunshine, followed by a very low temperature (12° below zero) the following night, and it was considered, owing both to the strength of the sun and to the fact that the West wind had temporarily got the better of the South wind, that the mountain would in all probability be safely solidified so as to render an attempt justifiable. Therefore on the morning of June 7 a start was made to reach the North Col, with the object of spending a night there and making an assault on the mountain the following day. It was also proposed to carry up as much oxygen as possible to the greatest height they could get the porters to go, and from that point only to use the remaining oxygen to make a push over the summit. I think this was a thoroughly sound proposition. They were all acclimatised, and it seems to me that it is probably better, especially if there is any chance of a shortage of oxygen, to use one's acclimatisation to go as high as one can without undue fatigue, and from thence on to use the oxygen. No doubt it would be possible and of advantage, if the oxygen apparatus should ever be improved, to use it for the whole of an ascent, say, from 20,000 feet or so, but against that comes the chance that, in case of any cessation of the oxygen supply, the danger would be very much greater.

The caravan consisted of Mallory, Somervell, and Crawford, who was going with them as far as the North Col to assist them and to relieve them of the hard labour of re-making the path up to that point. Mallory will relate further on how at about one o'clock, when about half the journey had been completed, the snow suddenly cracked across and gave way, and the whole caravan was swept down the hillside, and seven porters killed.

On return to Camp III, a porter was despatched to take the news down to the Base Camp, and arrived that same night at about nine o'clock, having travelled at full speed—really a wonderful performance. There was nothing to be done—that was quite evident—and all I could do was to await the return of the party for a full account, sending news at the same time to Morris to evacuate the camps at the greatest possible speed. Mallory arrived by himself, very tired, and naturally very upset, on Thursday, the 8th. Again was shown what a terrible enemy the great Himalaya is. Risks and conditions which would appear justifiable in the Alps can never be taken in the Himalaya. So great is the scale that far greater time must be allowed for the restoration of safe conditions. When once the condition of a mountain is spoiled, the greater size requires more time for its readjustment. The odds against one are much greater in the Himalaya than in the smaller ranges. Its sun is hotter; its storms are worse; the distances are greater; everything is on an exaggerated scale.

Mallory was followed next morning by Wakefield, Crawford, and Somervell, who brought down with them a certain amount of the lighter equipment. Morris was all this time working to salvage as much as he possibly could from the different camps. We had a large number of Tibetans pushed up as far as Camp II, and as many of our own porters as were available (not very many, I am sorry to say, by now) working with Morris in the evacuation of Camp III. In this work the cooks and orderlies also joined.

It was perfectly evident by now that the monsoon had set in in full force. On his return, Morris gave me a very vivid description of how, even during the one day that he stayed up after the others had left at Camp III, although the weather was fairly fine, the whole face of the mountain sides began to change; how under the influence of the soft South wind the mountains seemed to melt and disintegrate. Not only that, but even the great teeth formed by the pressure of the collateral glaciers, probably great séracs that spring out like the teeth of a huge saw on the glacier, and which seemed solid enough to last for all time, were visibly crumbling up, and some of them were even toppling over. The great trough of black ice up the centre of the glacier which Strutt has described had turned into a rushing torrent—and all this in an incredibly short period of time. Snow also fell at intervals, and it was quite apparent that when the monsoon settled down the whole of Camp III would be under a great blanket of fresh snow. Under these conditions a good deal of stuff, especially the supplies of grain, tzampa, and so on, for our porters, had to be abandoned. As for Camps IV, V, and VI, there was naturally no chance of rescuing anything from them. Thus was occasioned a fairly large loss of outfit; nor was there any possibility that any of it could have stood under any conditions more than a month's exposure to the weather. There was a considerable loss in the oxygen apparatus, but Morris managed to bring down three full outfits in more or less dilapidated condition.

On Morris's return to the Base Camp, the party was completed. One of the difficulties in having so large an outfit as ours was the difficulty of obtaining transport when necessary. Therefore, as soon as we saw signs of the monsoon, it was necessary to make arrangements for our return, as at least fifteen days were required to collect the still large number of animals required for our moving. These animals have to be searched for all down the Dzakar Chu, collected, and brought up; nor when once collected could they be kept waiting for very long, as the supply of fodder in the upper valley was absolutely nil—fodder did not exist. When we sent off the previous party they travelled as lightly as possible, but even then the small number of animals which was required for their transport had not been obtained with any great ease. Fortunately, John Macdonald was with us and was free, and it was owing to his help (for he speaks Tibetan as well as Nepali, and is thoroughly accustomed to deal with the people) that the two parties of Strutt and Norton were able to proceed with such little delay. It had required a full fifteen days to collect enough animals to move the main body. I had arranged for a latitude of one or two days, which meant that they should have spare food up to that extent, but beyond that it would be quite impossible, naturally, to make provision. Of course, as one of our secondary objects we had hoped, if our party had not been exhausted, to have explored the West Rongbuk and the great glens on the Western faces of Everest. And besides this most interesting piece of exploration, of which really not very much more than glimpses were obtained during 1921, there is the prodigious and fascinating group of Cho Uyo and Gyachang Kang to be explored.

Watching the Dancers, Rongbuk Monastery.

As I before pointed out, of course, not only was our major work and the whole object of the Expedition the tackling of the great mountain, but also it was a race against the weather, so we could let nothing interfere with our main object. It was quite clear now, as we were situated, that an exploration of the West Rongbuk was entirely beyond consideration. Not only was the whole party fairly played out, but to get up enthusiasm in a new direction after what we had gone through was pretty nearly out of the question. Somervell, the absolutely untireable, had very strong yearnings in that direction, but it would have been nothing more than a scramble in the dark if he had gone. The weather was broken and was getting worse and worse every day. Snow fell occasionally even at our camp. Further up everything was getting smothered. Everest, when we had glimpses of it, was a smother of snow from head to foot, and no one who saw it in these days could ever imagine that it was a rock peak.

I am afraid also that most of us had only one real idea at the time, and that was to get out of the Rongbuk Valley. However, during our wait for the transport the annual fête of the Rongbuk Monastery occurred. There was a great pilgrimage to the monastery to receive the blessing of the Lama and to witness the annual dances. Most of our party went down to see dances, and Noel especially to cinematograph the whole ceremony, dances as well as religious ceremonies. I have not done justice up to this point to Noel's work. He was quite indefatigable from the start, and had lost no opportunity during our march up, not only of taking many pictures of the country and Expedition, both with his ordinary camera and with his cinema camera, but of studying Tibetan life as well. He had in the Rongbuk Valley pitched his developing tents near the only available clear water at the moment, and had there been untiring in developing his cinema photographs. He had made two expeditions to the head of the East Rongbuk Glacier, and had even taken his cameras and his cinema outfit on to the North Col itself where he remained for no less than four days—a most remarkable *tour de force.* On the last occasion he had accompanied the evacuation party, and had been actually taking pictures of the start of the last attempt to get to the North Col and to climb Everest. Of course, his performances with the camera are entirely unprecedented. The amount of work he carried out was prodigious, and the enthusiasm he displayed under the most trying conditions of wind and weather was quite wonderful. We now feel that we can produce a real representation of our life and of life in Tibet in a manner in which it has never hitherto been brought before people's eyes, and this gives a reality to the whole Expedition which I hope will make all those who are interested in mountain exploration understand the wonderful performances and the great difficulties under which the climbing members of this Expedition and the transport officers laboured.

After the news of the accident had been received, we immediately got in touch with the great Lama of Rongbuk, who was intensely sympathetic and kind over the whole matter. It is very strange to have to deal with these curious people; they are an extraordinary mixture of superstition and nice feelings. Buddhist services were held in the monasteries for the men who had been lost and for the families; and all the porters, and especially the relations of the men who were killed, were received and specially blessed by the Rongbuk Lama himself. All the Nepalese tribes who live high up in the mountains, and also the Sherpa Bhotias, have a belief that when a man slips on the mountains and is killed, or when he slips on a cliff above a river and falls into it and is drowned, that this is a sacrifice to God, and especially to the god of the actual mountain or river. They further believe that anyone whosoever who happens to be on the same cliff or on the same mountain at the same place, exactly at the same time of year, on the same date and at the same hour, will also immediately slip and be killed.

I also received during our return a very kind letter from the Maharajah of Nepal condoling with us on the loss of our porters. He writes as follows:—

"Personally, and as a member of the Royal Geographical Society, I share with you the grief that must have resulted from the frustration of the keen hope entertained by you and the party. My heartiest sympathies go to you and to the families of the seven men who lost their lives in the attempt. This puts in my mind the curious belief that persistently prevails with the people here, and which I came to learn so long ago in the time of our mutual friend, Colonel Manners Smith, when the question of giving permission for the project of climbing the King of Heights through Nepal was brought by you and discussed in a council of Bharadars. It is to the effect that the height is the abode of the god and goddess Shiva and Parvati, and any attempt to invade the privacy of it would be a sacrilege fraught with disastrous consequences to this Hindu country and its people, and this belief or superstition, as one may choose to call it, is so firm and strong that people attribute the present tragic occurrence to the divine wrath which on no occasion they would draw on their heads by their actions."

This, I must point out, is, of course, the Southern and Hindu people's tradition, and did not in the same way affect all the porters whom we employed, as they were Buddhists by faith. The whole of our people, however, took the view common to both and dismissed their troubles very rapidly and very lightly, holding simply that the men's time had come, and so there was no more to be said about it. If their time had not come, they would not have died. It had come, and they had died and that was all. What need to say any more? As a matter of fact, this philosophic way of looking on everything also allowed them to say that they were perfectly ready to come back for the next attempt, because if it was written that they should die on Everest, they should die on Everest; if it was written that they would not die on Everest, they would not, and that was all there was to be said in the matter.

CHAPTER III

THE RETURN BY KHARTA

On June 14 we were cheered with the news that our transport was approaching, and I think a good many sighs of relief were uttered. We had quite made up our minds to cross over into the Kharta Valley, and, having had a sufficiency of rest, to explore the Kama Chu more completely than had been done in 1921, and, if possible, to examine the whole gorge of the Arun where it breaks through the great Himalayan range; but our first idea was to get down to a decent elevation where some rest could be obtained, where we could get adequate bathing and washing for our clothes and get everybody into a fairly respectable condition again. Living continuously for many weeks at elevations never below, and generally far above, 16,500 feet, does not tend to general cleanliness, and it also, after a time, I think, tends to general degeneration. At the same time, we were by no means convinced that at medium elevations there is any particular loss of physical powers or that acclimatisation takes long to complete. I found, personally, that I was getting better and better when exerting myself at the medium heights to which I went. I found, during the march that was in front of us, that I could walk at elevations of over 16,000 feet very much more easily than when I first arrived at the Rongbuk Glacier, and this certainly does not show that one had been degenerating physically. I think, really, that the strain was more a mental one; and this remark probably also applies to every member of our party. At the same time, it was most exhilarating to think that one was descending to a low altitude.

We made our first march back to the Rongbuk Glacier, and that evening we were left in peace—by the Lamas, that is to say, but not by the wind, which howled consistently, bringing with it thin driving sleet.

On the following morning we arranged that we should all meet the Rongbuk Lama; and so, having got our kit packed, we left it to be loaded by the Tibetans, and the whole party, including all our followers, porters, all the Gurkhas who were with us (with the exception of Tejbir, who had gone on in advance with Geoffrey Bruce and Norton), went up to the monastery. There we waited in the courtyard until the Lama himself descended from his inner sanctuary in state. Tea was first served in the usual way, ordinary tea being provided, I am glad to say, for the others and myself by special arrangement of the interpreter. I think Noel, however, a man of infinite pluck, took down a bowl or two of true Tibetan tea. The Lama made special inquiries after the Expedition, and then began the blessing. He offered us his very best

The Chief Lama, Rongbuk Monastery.

wishes, and presented me, through Paul, with a special mark of his goodwill, a little image of one of the Taras, or queens, of Tibetan mythology. My special one was the Green Tara, who takes precedence among all ladies. This was a mark of very great favour. Paul was also presented with another little mark and many little packets of medicine, which were to preserve him from all and every description of the illnesses which afflict and worry humanity. The Buddhistic side of Paul came up on this occasion, and he received his blessings and the medicines in the most humble and reverent spirit. The Gurkhas all went up too, and were suitably blessed, being even more humble in their aspect than the very much overcome and reverent porters themselves; they could hardly be induced to approach his Holiness. However, we all parted on the most friendly terms, and left our own good wishes, for what they were worth, with the old gentleman.

By three o'clock in the afternoon we arrived at Chodzong. But what a difference there was in our march! The few days of the monsoon and the small amount of rain which had fallen, even this little way back from the mountains, had changed the whole aspect of the valley. Flowers had begun to show, and in places there was even a little green grass. At Chodzong there was quite a considerable amount of grass, and we enjoyed here what was more pleasant than anything we had experienced for a long time—a shower of rain. We had almost forgotten the existence of rain, and the relief from the very trying dryness of the Tibetan atmosphere, which parches one's skin as if one was in the Sahara, was immense. Still, at Chodzong it was cold at night and the temperature below freezing-point. Here we found all our ponies and their saises returned from taking Norton and Geoffrey Bruce over to the Kharta Valley. Also the gigantic D(r)ubla and his small Gyamda very fit and well.

This camp at Chodzong was a place particularly impressed on our minds on our way up, as we had there the very coldest breakfast that we anywhere indulged in. The wind was blowing half a hurricane, and the temperature nearly at zero, while our breakfast was actually being brought to us in the morning, and the misery and discomfort of that particular temperature was in great contrast to the delightful weather we were now experiencing. From this place we diverted a large convoy of our spare baggage to Shekar, to await our return after we had finished our further wanderings in Kharta. The following day took us up the Rebu Valley. It was a fairly long and very windy march, but the climate was so greatly improved that, generally speaking, it was very enjoyable, and again we camped in a very pleasant spot in grassy fields—such a change from our late life. Not only that, but in the evening, as the people up here had no prejudices, we caught a sufficient number of snow-trout, really a barbel, to make a dish. My own servant, Kehar Sing, the cook, always had a reputation for being, and always was, a first-rate poacher. At any form of netting or tickling trout he was a great hand. However, he was completely eclipsed later on by one of Macdonald's servants, to whom I am quite certain no fish-poacher that ever was could have given a wrinkle. He was also quite a good hand at catching fish with rod-and-line. The Gurkhas, as usual, took a hand; they are immensely fond of fish, and their methods are primitive. Tejbir, who came along with us, was nearly recovered from his exertions with Finch and Geoffrey; he had lost a good deal of skin from seven or eight fingers and a large patch off his foot, but though his frost-bites were many, they were slight. He was really suffering from being rather overdone, and took at least a fortnight to recover.

The next day's was an interesting march, though very long, and tiring for the animals. Our way led over the high ridge which divides the Dzakar Chu country from the Kharta district. Although the rise was not very great from our camp at approximately 13,500 feet, still the pass itself was just 17,000 feet, or rather, to be absolutely accurate, just 3 feet under. The way led for several miles, hardly rising at all, up a grassy valley, and then over the strangest and wildest and most completely barren of hillsides. From here, no doubt, we should have a fine view of the great supporters of Everest, but clouds completely obliterated the mountains. We had the ordinary balmy Tibetan breezes through the snows, but modified to what they would have been quite a short time before.

The descent from the Doya La was very fine indeed; the colour wonderful, and very soon giving promise of a greener land. The first 300 feet on the Kharta side is down a very steep rocky track, and I was told afterwards by Geoffrey Bruce that he never dismounted, and that the wonderful Gyamda had carried him down without making a mistake. On that day we all of us well overtopped 17,000 feet. There was a little joke about Crawford, who was not very tall, but who certainly did not deserve his nickname of the "Two-and-a-half-footer" given him by the porters. It was a joke among them afterwards, when told the height of the pass, that he had just missed the 17,000 feet by 6 inches.

It was a very long descent, but into a valley rapidly changing from bare hillsides to grassy banks. Never was there a more welcome change, and here we came into a real profusion of Alpine flowers. It was a full 20-mile march to our halting-place at Trateza, and as we got down where the valley narrowed we passed the very picturesquely situated village of Teng. Everybody was delighted with the change. Our camp was pitched near the village on quite thick and beautiful green grass, and the hillsides were green and covered with bushes. We were absolutely happy and intensely relieved, and pleased with our surroundings. The ponies and animals simply pounced on the green grass, and were even more happy than their masters.

The following morning we all started off in wonderful

spirits, shared in by the yaks, several of whom took it into their heads to run amuck, and we had a first-class scene of confusion in the rather tight camp before we could get matters straightened out. One yak especially was peculiarly gay here, and took to the hillside after throwing his load on three or four occasions. We had, in fact, a real hunt after him; everybody joined in the fun, and I am afraid on one or two occasions some of the more light-hearted of the porters kept him going on purpose. This march, however, was even pleasanter than the one before. The part we were travelling down grew richer and richer; the hillsides were thickly clothed in cedar trees and in shrubs of many kinds; the valley itself, wherever possible, was cultivated. We passed on our way two or three small villages extremely well situated, and finally debouched into an open valley full of fields and cultivation, where we joined the main Arun Valley and the district of Kharta proper. Kharta is a fairly large district, and not a village. The largest settlement is called Kharta Shika, and it is there that the Dzongpen has his abode. The whole of this district, also, is under the Dzongpen of Shekar Dzong, and the Dzongpen of Shika apparently has not as full powers by any means as the Dzongpen at Shekar Dzong. However, for all that, he appears to be quite a little autocrat.

It was quite delightful riding out into the main valley, and there also we were cheered by meeting Geoffrey Bruce and John Macdonald, who had come out some miles from where our camp had been established at the small village of Teng. We passed, also, the old gentleman, known, I think, in the last year's Expedition as "the Havildar," but whom Geoffrey and Norton had promptly christened Father William. He was a rather officious, but at the same time most helpful, old man, and on our way back he asked us to come in for a meal into his very attractive garden; but as it was only a mile or so from Teng, where our camp was pitched, we did not think it was worth while then, knowing we should see a good deal more of the old gentleman. He brought us plenty of what we were yearning for—fresh green vegetables, the very greatest boon.

We found our invalids very nearly recovered; Norton's feet, however, were tender, and Geoffrey's toes still in a distinctly unpleasant condition. It was wonderful, nevertheless, how well both were able to get about with the help of plenty of socks. Our camp was pitched in fields at a height of about 10,800 feet, and below us, at about the distance of 3 miles, we could see the entrance to the great Arun Gorge where it cuts through the Himalaya. On the opposite side of the Arun the two mountains, old friends of ours that we had noticed on our way up, looked down on the camp. On the whole of my way down I was struck with the resemblance between these valleys and parts of Lahoul and Kailang. They were less rich, however, and the forests of pencil cedar not so fine, but still the whole character of the country and of the hill-sides was very much the same.

Tibetan Dancing Man.

Tibetan Dancing Woman.

Above the camp at Teng was a very well situated monastery, which Noel afterwards photographed. Soon after our arrival during the afternoon, the Dzongpen from Kharta Shika arrived to meet us. He was reported at first to be very suspicious of the party, and such, indeed, appeared to be the case. However, after a long conversation, and having presented him with pictures of the Dalai Lama and of the Tashilumpo Lama, as well as with the ubiquitous Homburg hat, he became much more confidential, and we finished up very good friends. He also told us that on the following day he would bring down some Tibetan dancers and acrobats to give us a performance.

The rapidity with which the whole party seemed to recover at Kharta was perfectly wonderful. Everybody was in first-class health and spirits, especially all our porters, and that night their high spirits were not only due to the atmospheric conditions, but were taken into them in a manner they thoroughly approved of and of which they had been deprived for some time. However, after all their very hard work and the wonderful way in which they had played up, it is not altogether to be wondered at if they did occasionally "go on the spree" on their way back.

So attractive was the whole country, and so strong was the call of the Kama Valley, that we were all very soon anxious to get a move on again. Tejbir was still not quite recovered, and would be all the better for further rest, so he was detailed with one of the other Gurkhas, Sarabjit, to stay behind and take charge of our camp and spare equipment. The rest of us all set to work and planned an advance into the Kama Valley, and, we hoped also, an exploration of it, both towards the snows up and to the Popti La, which is the main road into the valley of the Arun, and, if possible, up the great Arun Gorge itself. But this year's monsoon never gave us a chance of carrying out more than a small portion of that programme. We were now living in an entirely different climate. We had many showers of rain, which were hailed with delight by the people of the country, as their crops were now fairly well advanced. The crops at Kharta consist chiefly of peas and barley, as usual, but there is a certain amount of other grain and vegetables to be obtained from the gardens.

Having arranged the transport, we started our caravan off to Kharta Shika. Norton had issued a large-hearted invitation for us to lunch with him at the mouth of the Arun Gorge. Previously Norton and Geoffrey had explored, while they were waiting, the country round as far as they could go on horseback, and Norton had discovered at the mouth of a gorge an alp like those on the Kashmir Mountains, surrounded with a forest which he described as equal to a Southern Himalayan forest, and we positively must go and see it, and climb up the hillsides and look down into the gorge itself.

We all accepted his invitation with the greatest alacrity. On the afternoon of the day before starting, the Dzongpen, as he had promised, produced us his acrobats and dancers, and we had a very hilarious afternoon. They were not particularly good either as actors or as acrobats, but they danced with prodigious vigour, and it was altogether great fun. Before all the dances and the little plays they covered their faces with masks of an extremely primitive kind. They failed at most of their tricks once or twice before accomplishment, and these failures were invariably greeted both by the spectators and by the actors with shrieks of laughter.

On the following day (June 19) we all set off, the luggage proceeding direct to Kharta Shika under the charge of the interpreter and the Gurkhas, while we switched off to Norton's alp. It really was delightful, and though the forest was rather a dwarfed forest, it contained several kinds of fir trees, birch, and rhododendron scrub, and, after Tibet, was in every way quite charming. We climbed up the hillsides and suddenly came round the corner on to great cliffs diving straight down into the Arun Valley, and we could see further down how enormously the scale of the mountains increased. It was a most attractive gorge, but on our side it appeared to be almost impossible to have got along, so steep were the hillsides. On the far bank, that is, the true left bank, the East bank, there was a well-marked track, and it appears that lower down it crosses to the right bank and then continues on the right bank to the junction with the Kama Chu. Later on Noel and Morris were able to explore and photograph the greater part of the gorge. We all sat on the top of the cliffs and indulged in the very pleasant amusement of rolling great rocks into the river a thousand feet below us—always a fascinating pursuit, especially when one is quite certain that there is no one in the neighbourhood. The lunch did not turn up for some time, when an exploring party discovered that our porters, who had been detailed to carry it, had dropped in at a village and visited the Barley Mow, and could hardly get along at all in consequence; finally, however, the lunch was rescued and an extremely pleasant time passed. It was absolutely epicurean: Gruyère cheese, sardines, truffled yaks, and, finally, almost our last three bottles of champagne. It was intended to be an epicurean feast—and it was so.

By the evening we arrived in Shika, and found our camp pitched in beautiful grassy fields high above the village of Shika. The Dzongpen was very anxious to entertain the whole party, but we were rather lazy and did not want to go down to his village, which was some way off, but promised him that we would pay him a visit on our return from Kama. The Dzongpen, however, imported his cooks and full outfit and gave us a dinner in our own tent, himself sitting down with us and joining in. He was a plump and very well dressed little man, and by now had completely recovered his confidence in us. He was, however, very anxious that we should do no shooting, and this anxiety of his was no doubt very largely occasioned by the fact that he had only arrived from Lhasa about a fortnight before our arrival. We were to reach in two marches Sakiathang, in the Kama Valley, where Colonel Howard-Bury and his party had encamped the year before. Our first march led us over the Samchang La to a camp called Chokarbō. It was a steep and rough walk over the pass, but knowing the wonderful capacity of the Tibetan pony, several of the party took ponies with them. It was necessary both for Geoffrey and for Norton to rest their feet as much as possible until completely cured, and so on arrival at Chokarbō they took their ponies on over our next pass, the Chog La, which is no less than 16,280 feet, and down into the Kama Chu. This is a very rough road indeed.

We had here reached the most perfect land of flowers, and in the low land which lies between the Samchang La and our camp at Chokarbō we found every description of Alpine flora, reinforced by rhododendrons—the very last of the rhododendrons. We also found several kinds of iris.

The road leading up to the Samchang La was extremely steep and rough, but the path was well marked, and it was evident there was a considerable amount of traffic leading into the Kama Chu. The local people stoutly denied that yaks could cross, but later on we actually found yaks carrying loads over this road. I can quite understand their reason for not wishing to send their yaks, as the road from one end to the other is very bad for animals. At Chokarbō all the riding ponies were dispensed with, with the exception of Geoffrey's and Norton's; these two ponies they particularly wished to look after, as they had bought them, knowing that they must assure mounts, probably to the end of the journey. They had certainly picked up the most useful little couple. All the same, they had to walk most of the way, as it was quite out of the question for anyone to have ridden at all, except over short pieces of open ground, and it was perfectly wonderful the way in which these two ponies got over the most shocking collection of rocks, big and little, and how they negotiated the extremely slippery and rocky path which led down from the Chog La. The ascent to the Chog La was easy, and the latter half of it still under winter snow, as also was the first thousand feet of the descent. The mountains were interesting on each side, so much so that Somervell and Crawford went off for a little climb on the way. The descent was delightful, although the road was, as I have said, very stony indeed. One passes through every description of Eastern Himalayan forest and wonderful banks of rhododendrons of many kinds. We were, unfortunately, much too late for their full bloom, but a month earlier this descent must be perfectly gorgeous, the whole hillsides being covered with flowering rhododendrons.

The descent to Sakiathang is at least 5,000 feet, and may be a little more. Thang means "a flat bench," and

Old Tibetan Woman and Child.

such was Sakiathang, set in gorgeous forest, and deep in grass and flowers. But the weather was breaking fast, and by evening the clouds had descended and wiped out the whole of the valley. Before it was quite obliterated we got glimpses of what it must be like in fine weather.

In the early morning of the following day (Thursday, June 22), when I woke up and looked out of my tent, the mouth of which looked straight up the valley between the big mountains, the clouds had lifted somewhat, and the whole end of the valley was filled with the gorgeous Chomolönzo peak, and for an hour or so I was able to watch it with the clouds drifting round its flanks, and then, just as the sun lit up the valley for a moment, the great monsoon clouds coming up from the valley of the Arun, driven by the wind up the Kama Chu, completely wiped it out again. It was a glorious glimpse, and the only one we obtained during our stay of more than a week in Sakiathang.

We found encamped in the neighbouring woods Nepalese shepherds, with their flocks of sheep, and saw for the first time the very fine type of sheep which these men own—a far bigger and better breed of sheep than exists in Tibet, and also carrying a very much finer coat of wool. They were rather strange to look at at first, as the whole fore-part of their body was black and the hind-part white. We also found that the Nepalese shepherds thoroughly understood the value of their own sheep. They keep them all to make butter from their milk, which they collect and sell in the bazaars in Nepal. All these shepherds were Gurkhas belonging either to the Gurung tribe or Kirantis, and, curiously enough, one of them was related to my servant Kehar Sing, he having gone through the "mit" ceremony with his relations, and that is quite sufficient for him to be also a "mit." This "mit" ceremony is rather difficult to explain. It is not exactly blood-brotherhood, it is more of the nature of religious brotherhood; but it is quite binding, as much so as an ordinary relationship. This eased the situation for us pretty considerably in the matter of obtaining milk and butter. As I have before mentioned, I do not myself eat butter in an uncooked state, but the remainder of the party reported that this sheep's butter was of very fine quality, and it was certainly very clean. These shepherd establishments are known as gôts. Naturally forgetting that certain terms are unfamiliar, I told Wakefield that I had bought two sheep from the gôts. He seemed more confused than usual by the strangeness of the country.

As we were rather short of provisions, we despatched Noel's servant and our excellent Chongay Tindel to obtain supplies for us; the first down to the junction with the Arun, and the second over the Popti into Damtang, a large Nepalese settlement.

The remainder of the party stayed behind, hoping for better weather in order to explore the upper valley of the snows, and up to the Popti to get a view of the country into Nepal, if possible. It was no use attempting to move unless the weather cleared to a certain extent. Meanwhile we were living in a smother of cloud, mist, and rain. But how delightful it was to have an ample supply of firewood and to be able to build, for the first time since we had entered Tibet, a reckless camp-fire round which we could all sit! It is a real hardship in Tibet never to have a good roaring fire, and it is a little damping to one's spirits having always to go to bed in order to get warm. Whenever it cleared, we went for short walks through the neighbouring forests and into the neighbouring valleys, and saw quite enough to fill us with a desire for much more exploration. The forest of the Kama is unbelievably rich; the undergrowth, especially the hill bamboo, of a very vivid green, and the cedar and fir appear very dark, almost black, against it. But the forest also contains every other kind of tree and shrub proper to the Eastern Himalaya, and the river-banks were, in places, overhung with the most glorious Himalayan larch, identical with the European larch in appearance, but with possibly a greater spread of branch.

The weather got worse and worse, and our food supplies lower and lower. There were no signs of the return either of Noel's servant or of the Chongay from Nepal, and so, with the greatest reluctance, we gave up further exploration as a body. We were reduced to only half a day's grain-food for our following, and not only that, but the Tibetan porters whom we were expecting to help us back, and who had been ordered, showed no signs of arriving.

Having searched the country round, we managed to rope in a few local people, mostly Tibetans, who had come over from Kharta for wood. There is considerable traffic from the Tibetan side, as in this well-wooded country they cut most of the timber required for their houses and carry it over on their own backs, or else on the backs of unfortunate yaks, when they can bring themselves to risk their yaks' legs over this awful road. We carried as much luggage as we possibly could with us, not knowing how many men we should be able to obtain to send for the remainder. We had not enough men with us to carry the whole camp, and so two Gurkhas were left here in charge of what remained. They were also to meet Chongay and bring him back with them, and it was considered an absolute certainty that he would be in time to save them from a shortage of rations; also, they would be able to get enough to keep themselves alive from the Gurkha gôts, although these gôts themselves are on a very short ration of grain, living largely on sheep's milk.

Our own porters and a few local people, with the help of a little chaff to excite them, vied with each other in the size of the loads they could carry, and they certainly gave us a first-class exhibition of load-carrying. One girl, about eighteen years of age, actually carried a 160-lb. tent by herself from Sakiathang to Chokarbō, over the top of the Chog La. Moreover, this tent had been wet for the last ten days, and although we did our best to dry all our camp as much as possible before starting, it must have been at least 20 to 30 lb. heavier than it ought to have been. I am quite certain that not a single man or woman carried less than 100 lb. that day over the pass, and this they did apparently without undue fatigue, arriving quite cheerful at Chokarbō. We started in fairly fine weather—a break, we thought; but before we had gone half-way up the hill the clouds descended on us, and it was raining hard when we got to our camp. The day before we left we came to the conclusion that it would be quite possible for a very small party to get down to the junction of the Kama Chu over the Arun, and Noel himself was intensely anxious to photograph the Kama Chu and the gorges of the Arun itself. He had also a plan, if possible, to get up the gorge and to cross up over the high cliffs and hillsides, which would bring him down almost to the alp where we had our picnic with Norton. This was a magnificent conception, but, considering the weather, we thought that he would have a very rough time of it. He chose Morris as his assistant; he took off his own particular porters, reinforced by some Tibetans, and left on the 27th, we leaving on the 28th.

While we had been over there, Geoffrey's feet had completely recovered, and he was able to walk now as of old. Norton could walk uphill, but his feet pained him when descending; his ear had by this time completely recovered.

On the 29th, Geoffrey and I, leaving the remainder of the party, went down to see the Dzongpen of Kharta, with a view to making arrangements for our final return.

I had, previous to this, written to the Maharajah of Nepal with a scheme by which Mallory should be allowed to cross the upper end of the Wallung and Yallung valleys and to cross into British territory by the Khang La, returning to Darjeeling by the ordinary route along the Singalela Ridge. The Maharajah gave his consent to this expedition, but unfortunately it had to be modified, owing to difficulties of transport and to the very bad weather; but as Mallory was rather pressed for time, it was arranged that he, Somervell, and Crawford, should return direct to Tinki, crossing the Arun by the rope bridge which was utilised in 1921 for the return of the party, and from thence descending into Sikkim and travelling viâ Lachen and Gangtok back to Darjeeling. The remainder of the party, with the heavy luggage, would have to return viâ Shekar and the way we came in order to square up our various accounts with the different Dzongpens and with the authorities, postal and other, in Phari Dzong and the Chumbi Valley. All this required a certain amount of arrangements. Before going into Kama, we had given the Dzongpen an outline of our requirements, but everything in Tibet, as elsewhere, requires a considerable supervision, and so Geoffrey and I went down before the rest of the party to complete our arrangements. On our way down we met a large contingent of Tibetan porters coming over to move our camp. This eased matters off very considerably. They were sent off into the Kama to bring the remainder of the camp, and on their return to move the full camp down to Teng. Meanwhile we descended and had a long and very interesting interview with the Dzongpen, who by this time had quite lost all suspicion of us. He entertained us splendidly, and presented us each with a jade cup before leaving.

On July 1 we were all assembled in Teng, and packing up and dividing our luggage preparatory to the return of the party by the different routes. On July 3 Mallory's party set off, and we did not see him nor the rest of the party again until our arrival in Darjeeling, more than a month later. We were now joined by Noel and Morris, back from their adventurous journey up the Arun. They gave me a report of their travels. I think it would be worth while once more to point out what the course of the Arun is. The Arun is one of the principal tributaries of the Kosi River (that is evident from the map), and has a very long journey through Tibet, where it is known as the Bhong Chu.

It rises near and drains the plains of Tingri and Khamba, and then turning due South, forces its way through the main chain of the Himalaya directly between the mountain passes of the Everest group on the one side, and of the Kanchengjanga group on the other. Between our camp at Kharta and the village of Kyamathang, which is on the actual Nepal frontier, a distance of some 20 miles, the river drops a vertical height of 4,000 feet; and therefore we were particularly interested in the exploration of this wonderful gorge, and we wished to find out, if we could, whether this tremendous vertical drop consisted of a series of great rapids and waterfalls or a steady fall in the bed of the river. It was also clear, from first glimpses that we had had of the Arun Gorge, that lower down they must be of the greatest possible grandeur and interest. I have before described how we looked down from our picnic into the Arun and hoped we should be able to explore it.

When we despatched Noel and Morris it was in terribly bad weather, the whole of the Lower Kama being a smother of mist and the jungle dripping with moisture. We had most of us been down as far as a place called Chotromo, where the river is crossed by the road which leads up to the Popti La, and this is the common road down into Nepal. From there the road is far less well known, and is not so well marked.

I will now give Noel's description of his journey.

"On the evening of the 27th June, at the end of our first day's march, we pitched our camp on a little pleasant grassy shelf situated in a small clearing in the forest near empty shepherd huts, which comprise the camp at Chotromo. The hot, damp atmosphere of the Ka(r)ma here at 9,000 feet harbours a world of insect life. No sooner had the sun set that evening than swarms of tiny midges emerged. They annoyed us for most of the night, except when, in moments of exasperation, we got out of bed and drove them away by lighting a small fire of juniper-wood at the mouth of our tent. From Chotromo a little

Fording the Bhong Chu.

shepherd track leads down the left bank of the river to Kyamathang. In actual distance Kyamathang is not far, but the road is scarcely level for more than a few yards. It zigzags precipitously a thousand feet up and down in order to avoid the ravines through which the river rushes, thus trebling the marching distance. The forest here becomes more tropical; bamboos and ferns are thick in the undergrowth, the trees increase enormously in size, and leeches make their appearance. The path where it descends to the river passes through bog and marsh, where the Nepalese shepherds, who mostly use this road, in order to reach the upper grazing grounds, have cut and laid tree-trunks along the path. The forest here darkens owing to the height of the trees, junipers being particularly noticeable; most of the trees being festooned with thick grey lichen. Here and there on level spots beside the river-bank one marches from the forest into delightful glades carpeted with moss and thick with banks of purple irises in full bloom.

"Ascending and descending precipitously the hillsides, and covering all the time horizontal distance at a despairing rate, we came at last, tired out, to the bridge which leads across the Kyamathang, and there found that another climb of some 1,500 feet remained before reaching the village, which is perched on a small plateau overlooking the junction of the rivers. Kyamathang, though, strictly speaking, in Tibet, is a typical Nepalese village. The neat little chalets are each surrounded by well-kept fields of

Indian corn, wheat, and barley. The fields are bounded by stone walls, and each contains a small machan (a small raised platform), from where a look-out is kept for bears at night. Kyamathang and the surrounding villages are so inaccessible that the people do not appear to come under the influence of Tibet or Nepal, leading an independent life. The village boasts of five Gembus (headmen), all of whom, so excited at seeing Europeans for the first time, did all they could to help us, and insisted on accompanying us on our first march up the gorge.

"The road from Kyamathang, after passing the fields of Lungdo, plunges once more into the forest. The path mounts up over cliffs, hiding the view of the river in the gorge below, but revealing across the valley the magnificent waterfalls of Tsanga, some thousand feet in height.

"At our first halting-place we met a fine old Gurkha shepherd, Rai or Karanti by tribe, a man of some seventy years of age, who many years ago had been employed by the Survey of India. He was able to tell us much about our route ahead. This stretch of country, although inhabited by Tibetans, is yearly visited by Nepalese shepherds, who use the rough track in order to reach the grazing grounds on the mountain-tops above the gorge. He told us we should find a track of sorts along the right bank of the river, which would eventually bring us out at Kharta again.

"The Arun has no great waterfalls, but passes through three deep gorges, one at Kyamathang and one near

Kharta, where it enters the main chain. There is another also between these two. For the rest it is a raging torrent running through a narrow forested defile.

"In order to pass these gorges, the path ascends and descends many thousands of feet. Looking down from the ledges of the precipices, one gets occasional glimpses of the torrent below; the cliffs above frequently rising as much as 10,000 feet above the river-bed, and ending in snow-capped peaks. Here and there the promontories of the cliffs afford a grandiose panorama, which rewards the exertions of the terrific ascents, but as these alternate ascents and descents are not single occurrences, but the normal nature of the track, ever climbing up by crazy ladder-paths and plunging amongst tangled undergrowth, one ceases to revel in the scenery, and would forego those bird's-eye views from the cloud-level for the sake of a few yards of marching on the flat.

"At the end of our second march, where the track appeared to come to an end, while pitching our camp in a small clearing, swarms of bees descended upon us, scattering our porters in all directions; they did no harm, however. Our third march was a struggle through pathless jungle, and, mounting over the great central gorge, on the far side of which we dropped down to the river-bed, we found a narrow strip of sand, just room enough to pitch our camp. This was one of the most beautiful spots seen in the valley. Wild flowers grew here in great profusion, the most conspicuous amongst them being some great white lilies fully 6 feet in height. That evening the rain, which had been falling most of the day, cleared, and the rising clouds revealed the luxuriant walls of the valleys, which seemed to rise almost vertically above us, with black caverns beneath, where the trees trailed and projected over the water's edge.

"During the fourth march we again struck the track which is apparently used by Tibetans who come down from the Kharta end of the valley to get wood. This led us up the side valley, descending from the mountains round about Chog La. We camped towards the top of the valley, and next day crossed by a new pass, which we judged to be about 16,000 feet in height, and then crossed the Sakia Chu, which descends from the Samchang Pass across the Yulok La, and descended on Kharta."

Well, I think that is a very fine description of an intensely interesting journey. One thing the party was quite certain of, and that was that they never would have got through had they numbered any more. It was very difficult to get supplies even for themselves, as the roads were so very, very bad, and camping grounds so very, very small. They said all their men had worked like horses, but it was so warm that they took nearly all their clothes off and worked almost entirely naked. It is an extraordinary thing how, when one gets far back into the Himalaya at altitudes at 7,000, 8,000, and 9,000 feet, one is often extremely warm. This is generally due to the fact that most of these places are usually between mountains and in confined conditions; such altitudes on the lower spurs of the Himalaya are by no means so warm. We all envied Noel and Morris their trip and the gorgeous country which they had seen, and, further than that, I in particular envied them the occasional glimpses which they could get right down the Arun Valley into Nepal, glimpses of country which I believe no European has yet looked on.

As a matter of fact, I had also written to the Maharajah to find out whether it would not be possible for me to return to Darjeeling viâ this same Arun Valley. It was a mere *ballon d'essai*; I had no real hope that the rules and regulations of the Nepal Durbar would be overridden in my favour, but it is probably not more than 50 miles from Kyamathang down the Arun Valley to Dhankuta, which is a large Nepalese town, and only some five or six days' travel from Darjeeling itself. What a wonderful experience it would have been! The Maharajah was extremely kind about it, but quite firm.

At the same time as Noel and Morris arrived, our Chongay also came from the Popti route, and he brought with him quite a number of chickens and vegetables and excellent potatoes. He had been delayed at Damtang by the weather. There was quite a change in Chongay on his arrival. We were filled with admiration. He wore a Seaforth Highlander's bonnet and a Seaforth Highlander's tunic, both of which he had obtained from some demobilised Gurkha who had sold his effects in the Upper Arun Valley.

We joined hands and danced round him with cheers; Chongay bridled from head to foot.

Soon after Mallory's party left, a note arrived from Crawford to say that his pony and his pony-man had run away during the night, and asking us to find out about it, as he had been paid for the full journey. This was reported immediately to the Dzongpen. He knew exactly what to do. Without a moment's hesitation he seized the man's elder brother, down with his clothes, and gave him a first-class flogging, and nearly flogged old Father William himself, so angry was he, as this man was one of Father William's underlings. Father William was humbler than ever after this, and produced more and more green vegetables.

On July 4 the main body set off, even now very considerable. We were to march direct by a road up to the present date untravelled, our first march being to Lumeh, which was also on the road used by Mallory and by last year's Expedition. From there we marched up the Dzakar Chu instead of turning to our right and crossing the Arun. We had been largely in summer in Kharta, but on our way to Lumeh we came in, for a time, to some of the very strongest winds we had met since leaving the Rongbuk Glacier. Crossing a little gully, I was nearly blown off my pony. Our camp at Lumeh has been described by Colonel Howard-Bury, and is a very charming spot.

The following march to Dzakar Chu was quite new ground, not travelled by any European, and was very interesting indeed, but extremely rough. It led for part of the way through a steep and deep gorge, extraordinarily like the gorges in the Hindu Kush in Gilgit and Chambal. The gorge, owing to its elevation, is of less depth, but the whole colour and form of the mountains, their bareness and barrenness, and the smell from the wormwood scrub, brought back to me the Hindu Kush in very vivid recollection. Those gorges, however, as so often in the West, are terribly and oppressively hot, but here, at 12,500 to 13,000 feet above the sea, we were in a fresh and exhilarating air. We camped at a village called Dra, at the foot of the pass we were to cross, which is called the Chey La. Our camp was pitched in a very pleasant grove, and here we had, for the last time until we arrived at the Chumbi Valley, a gorgeous and glorious camp-fire. Curiously enough, the wood was willingly given to us by the inhabitants.

The following morning there was a long march and a continual pull to the top of the Chey La, about 17,000 feet, the last thousand feet being a very rapid ascent, but from the top we were almost in sight of Shekar and the Arun Valley. The camp at which we stopped was a very short morning's walk from our old camp at Pangli, and separated from it by a low ridge.

The next morning, after crossing the Arun at the Arun Bridge, we reached Shekar, where we had a great reception. The Dzongpen played up, and he had no less than 160 mules all collected and ready for us the following morning; and not only that, but every one turned out the evening, and we had a little race meeting of our own and a great tea with exchange of cakes and compliments with the Dzongpen himself. Altogether we were evidently in very good favour both with the Dzongpen and with the great Lama of Shekar. Noel and others paid a very interesting visit to the great Lama, and were shown by him his collections of curios of all kinds. They thought at first that the old gentleman prized and guarded these as Gömpa property, but they were rather surprised to discover that he was perfectly ready to sell at a price—and that his own. He was by far the shrewdest trader that we had come across in Tibet. Most of the things that he was ready to part with, however, were beyond the pockets of our party.

John Macdonald, who has a very good eye for a pony, took out a likely mount in the horse-races and himself won no less than three races that day. He bargained for it, as he was looking forward to the Darjeeling pony-races in the autumn, and before we left Macdonald, to his great joy, had concluded a very respectable bargain.

The following morning we got off not quite as well as we should. We had difficulty in loading and some difficulties on the march. Shekar had proved altogether too much for the porters and the following morning they were not of much use; in fact, it was with the greatest difficulty that many of them were produced at the next camp. The place was called Kyishong. It had not been a very

Panorama at Shekar Dzong.

promising little camp, so we thought of stopping down by the river on a very pleasant plot of grass, but on arrival there we found a dead Tibetan in a basket moored to the bank in the water about a hundred yards above our camp, so that was no place for us. Instead of marching back exactly the same way we had come, viâ our camp at Gyangka-Nangpa, we determined to follow up a smaller branch of the Arun which would bring us finally down on to Tinki itself. By so doing we avoided wading the Yaru in two places, and also the rather high and steep Tinki Pass. On our way across the plains of Teng, before one arrives at the great sand dunes of Shiling, we passed a Sokpo, a true Mongolian, whose home was in Northern Mongolia, near Urga, a religious devotee. He was travelling from Lhasa to Nepal, that is, to Khatmandu, on a pilgrimage, by the time-honoured method of measuring his length on the ground for every advance. He was a young man and apparently well fed, trusting to the kindness of the villages through which he passed for his food. He told us that he had been continually travelling and that it had taken him one year to reach the place where we found him from Lhasa, and that he hoped to get to Khatmandu in another year, if he was lucky and able to cross the mountains. We encouraged him the best way we could and left him to his work.

Our halt that night was in a very pleasant camp surrounded by low cliffs at a place called Jykhiop. Our march up this valley was a great contrast to our march into Tibet. A warm sun and a pleasant cool breeze blowing; the clouds drifted across us and we had some rain, which only added to our comfort. We camped one night at a place called Chiu, where we all bathed, and bathed the ponies into the bargain.

Our last march before reaching Tinki was over an interesting pass, which suffers under the terrible name of the Pharmogoddra La, down to a pleasant little camping ground with a very dirty village near it. Here we caught an enormous number of fish, the inhabitants proving quite ready to help us do so. Every one fed freely on fresh fish that night.

An easy pleasant pass the following morning led us down in 2½ hours to Tinki. Here we met the Dzongpen of Tinki for the first time. He was an extremely pleasant individual, and the most friendly and intelligent official we met in Tibet. He helped us in every way, and had previously helped Strutt's party on their journey through. We heard excellent reports also of him afterwards from the advance parties. When we had gone through in the spring this Dzongpen had been away collecting his dues for the Tibetan Government. Tinki was a very different place, very green, and altogether very lovely. Before travelling in Tibet we had heard so much of the wonderful colour of Tibetan scenery. It was only on our return journey when there was a considerable amount of moisture in the air, when clouds rolled up from the South, that one obtained a real notion of what Tibet could be like when at its best, and Tinki, which had been an absolute sandy waste when we marched up, was now covered with beautiful green grass and flowers. Nor was the air of that horrible and rather irritating dryness, but was almost balmy, considering the height of the country.

Two days later we reached Khamba Dzong. The Dzongpen was absent, but his two head men helped us in his place. We had pouring rain the whole of the following night. There must have been from 1½ to 2 inches of rain, a most surprising experience in Tibet and one for which we were hardly prepared. The men had been breaking out a little again, and one sportsman had broken out considerably more than anybody else. For purposes of letting the porters down easily we never considered a man was inebriated as long as he could lie on the ground without holding on, but this man for three days in succession had been hopeless, giving no reaction whatever to the smartest smacks with our sticks, and finally having to be brought into camp and giving a great deal of trouble. So we determined on an exemplary punishment. The other men who had broken out badly had all been given loads to carry for a march, but the next day this man was condemned to carry an enormous load from Khamba Dzong to Phari. Considering what his condition had been we were absolutely astounded when the following day he carried the whole of well over 100 lb. for a 20-mile march to Tătsăng, over a pass of 17,000 feet, grinning and smiling the whole way as if it was the finest joke he had heard of. Everybody "pulled his leg" on the way, but nothing could possibly interfere with his good temper. He was condemned to carry this load right into Phari Dzong, crossing the three high ridges of the Donka La, and never for a moment did he lose his temper or bear any ill-will. This is characteristic of the people: as long as your treatment of them is understood by them to be just they bear no ill-will whatever, nor does it interfere in any way with one's friendly relations; but still, for all that, it seems to me that they are unkillable. After his behaviour and the condition he was in for so long, to do such terrific hard labour as we condemned him to do without the smallest sign of fatigue was pretty remarkable. But, after all, my own particular Angturke had only complained of being a little dazed after falling 60 feet on to his head at the time of the accident.

We camped at Tătsăng, and here we parted with Noel, who carried off his own people and left us for Gyantse; he was very much afraid of bringing his cinema films down into the warmth and damp of Sikkim until they were properly developed, but not only this: it was now the season of the great meetings and dances of Gyantse, and he hoped to get first-rate studies of Tibetan life generally. The climate and accommodation also at Gyantse would just suit him, and he would be able there to put in a full month's work completing his films and adding immensely to his collection of pictures of Tibetan life. He accompanied us for 5 miles, almost up to the camp we had

IN KAMPA DZONG.

occupied on our arrival in the spring, and we left him with great regret.

We had a long march that day from Tătsăng, and again crossing the ridges of the Donka La a very cold wind and sleet and rain overtook us. It was the last shot at us the typical Tibetan weather had, and considering the time of year it did its very best for us, but we camped that night under the Donka La at a great height, not far from 17,000 feet. While we were waiting for our luggage we took refuge in a Tibetan encampment. The Tibetans were out with their herds of yaks, grazing them over the hillsides. We were rather amused to find that they had guns in their encampment, which they evidently used for sporting purposes, and we thought regretfully of the limitations which had been put on our expedition.

Next morning we had a delightful march crossing the last and highest ridge of the Donka La and camped half-way to Phari, finally reaching Phari Dzong after a very pleasant morning's ride over delightful green turf and passing immense flocks of sheep grazing on the hillsides.

Here, on July 20, we found a welcome post and spent the day in great comfort in the Phari Dzong bungalow. Two days later we reached Chumbi and met the Macdonalds again, and were, as usual, sumptuously entertained by them. Here our transport had to be reorganized to take our still rather large convoy down to India. Geoffrey and I climbed the neighbouring hills and really revelled in the whole journey down, which had been very reminiscent of the Western Himalaya in summer. Chumbi is wonderful; even in the rains the climate is delightful. It cannot have more than one-third of the rainfall which falls only 20 miles away on the other side of the Jelep: in fact, when two days later we crossed the Jelep, we were immediately involved again in the mists and rains and sleets, and were again in a completely and absolutely different type of country.

We arrived at Gnatong on July 27 in pouring rain, but next morning it had cleared, and on the way down as we started the clouds showed signs of really lifting. On arrival at the ridge over which the road crosses before beginning the long descent to Rongli Chu, about 400 feet above Gnatong, we were lucky enough to come in for one of those sudden breaks which occasionally occur during the monsoon, and if one is at the moment in a position to profit by them one obtains one of the most glorious sights to be found in this world. Such was our luck this morning. Standing on the ridge we were able to see the plains of India stretched out beneath us to the South, the plains of Kuch Behar with the Mahanadi River running through them quite clear, while on our right Kanchengjanga rose through the clouds—a perfectly marvellous vision of ice and snow, looking immeasurably high. The clouds were drifting and continually changing across the hillsides and the deep valleys. The extremely deep and, in places, sombre colour, the astonishingly brilliant colour where the sun lit up the mountains, and the prodigious heights, made a mountain vision which must be entirely unsurpassed in any other portion of the globe. It was a moment to live for; but the moment was all too short. In half an hour the vision of the plains and the mountains was completely blotted out.

At Lungtung we visited the little tea-shop where we had all collected, as we had promised the patroness on our way up. There she was again, full of smiles, with her family round her, and we all stayed there and drank hot tea, which we thoroughly enjoyed after the cold and driving mist, and the flow of chaff I think even surpassed that of our first visit. So exhilarated were we that Geoffrey and I ran at top speed down to Sedongchen, which is only 6,000 feet, tearing down the hillsides, and by so doing, although we occasionally took short cuts over grassy banks and through forest where it was not too thick, we arrived at Sedongchen, having entirely baffled the leeches which swarm in this part of the forest. Not so, however, Wakefield; he also had been exhilarated and had taken a short cut down, but he had been too trusting, and he arrived with his legs simply crawling with leeches.

The rest of our journey through Sikkim requires no particular comment, except that the weather behaved itself in a wonderful way, and we escaped any real heavy duckings. The heat, although considerable in the lower valleys and moist, was not at all oppressive. So much so that we were able to travel at a great pace down to Rongli bridge, which is only 700 feet above the sea.

We arrived in Darjeeling on August 2, every one by now in thoroughly good health. Here we were to await the arrival of Crawford and Somervell, who were making tremendous attempts, considering that it was the height of the monsoon, to see something of the South face of Kanchen, and even, if possible, to do a little climbing—a rather ambitious programme under the circumstances. Five or six days later they arrived, quite pleased with themselves and having had a very strenuous time, but naturally having seen a minimum of the country they travelled over. At Darjeeling the party rapidly broke up, although the Staff of the Expedition had about a fortnight's work clearing up business matters, which included the proper provision for the families of the unfortunate porters who had been lost in the avalanche.

Thus ended the first attempt to climb Mount Everest. I think on the whole we may be quite satisfied with the results. It would have been almost unthinkable if a great mountain like Everest—the highest in the world, almost the greatest in scale as well—had yielded to the very first assault. After all, it took a very long time, many years in fact, to climb the easier of the great mountains of the Alps. It took many years to find the way, even, up the North face of the Matterhorn, a problem which would now only be considered one of the second class. How, then, could we expect on the very first occasion to solve all the different problems which are in-

LINGGA AND THE LHONAK MOUNTAINS.

cluded in an assault on Everest? It is not merely a case of mountaineering, or of mountaineering skill, nor even of having a most highly-trained party; there are many other problems which we also have to consider. Our methods had almost to be those of an Arctic expedition; at the same time our clothing and outfit in many ways had to be suitable for mountain climbing. Our climbing season was extraordinarily short, far shorter than it would have been in any mountains in the West.

Not only that, but all the warnings of the scientists tended to show that no very great height could probably be reached without oxygen, and that even with an oxygen apparatus there were a great many dangers to be faced. Among other things we were told that having once put on the oxygen apparatus, and having once for any continuous period worked on an artificial supply of oxygen, the sudden cessation of that supply would certainly cause unconsciousness, and probably would cause death. Luckily for us this was proved not to be in accordance with actual practical experience, as the height reached by our climbing party which had not used oxygen was more than 2,000 feet higher than any point yet reached. For the Duke of Abruzzi, in his great attempt on the Bride Peak on the Baltoro Glacier in Baltistan, did not quite reach 24,600 feet. While Mallory, Somervell, and Norton reached 26,985 feet.

In the whole range of the mountains of the world there are only four peaks that top this great height, namely,

Mount Everest itself, K² in the Karakorum in Baltistan; Broad Peak on the Baltoro Glacier, and Makalu in the Everest group. Therefore this climb stands actually as the fifth of the great altitudes of the world. It is a perfectly prodigious performance, and taken simply as a *tour de force* stands in the front rank in no matter what department of sport or human endeavour. The men who took part in this climb have every reason to be proud of themselves.

As I have pointed out, Finch and Geoffrey Bruce, using oxygen, took a route traversing the face of the mountain to the West, and before they were completely played out and conditions were such that they had to return, reached a height of 27,235 feet. If they had directly mounted up the ridge they would undoubtedly have reached the point on the main Everest crest which is marked at 27,390 and have progressed along it to a greater altitude. There is no doubt in my mind whatever of this: not only would their route have been far more direct, but the actual ground over which they would have to climb would have been easier. It is quite certain that with the same exertions on the same day they could have reached a higher point than they did. That does not, however, in the least detract from their performance. Their experiences, as has been pointed out by Finch, ease the oxygen question immensely. It was shown that it was quite possible to remove the oxygen apparatus altogether, having used it fully and having reached a height of 25,500 feet, nor was the accident to Geoffrey's apparatus attended with any of the terrible consequences which we were led to expect. These conclusions are all very satisfactory from the point of view of our final success in climbing Everest. There is no doubt that the height will be attained provided the very best men, the best apparatus, and an outfit of porters equally as good as our own, attempt it. And there are plenty of men to draw from for porters. We could probably obtain without difficulty a team as good, or better. Of that I am quite certain.

It was pretty evident that one of the secrets of living with immunity high up is that the actual clothes on the men's backs should be as light as possible and as windproof as possible. Proper protection should be taken against the wind for the head also, and the greatest care must be taken and the necessity for care be understood by everybody in the protection of their hands and feet. It is quite possible that with a little more care we might have escaped this year without any serious consequences from that point of view.

These remarks apply equally to the outfit for the porters. Men who worked with so little experience, and took camps for us to a height of 25,500 feet, would, if correctly outfitted, take the camp 500 to 1,000 feet higher: of that I am quite convinced. An improved and lighter oxygen apparatus is under construction; when this has been completed I have every reason to believe that an oxygen depôt could be well established at 26,000 feet, thus allowing a full time for the attempt on the greater heights. This year there was always at the back of the oxygen-carriers' minds a slight doubt that their oxygen might give out and that the consequences to them would be most unpleasant.

Another problem that must always be borne in mind when one's object is the assault of a great mountain in the Himalaya, is to bring one's whole party there in first-class health and training. This sounds an unnecessary remark to have to make, but as a matter of fact the task is not as easy as it appears. The great danger lies in fatiguing and exhausting one's party before the real test comes. This year there was great danger of our working the porters out, and this question gave me a good deal of anxiety. But they were all absolute gluttons for work, and I never would have believed that men could have carried out such tremendous hard labour in establishing our high camps and apparently continuing fit and well, showing no signs of staleness and quite ready to continue up the mountain.

Before we left Darjeeling I forwarded to the Dalai Lama, on behalf of the Mount Everest Committee, a letter of thanks for all the assistance which he had given to our Expedition, and sent with it, for him and for the Tashilumpo Lama also, a silk banner on which was printed a coloured picture of the Potālā, the great palace of the Dalai Lamas in Lhasa.

THE FIRST ATTEMPT

By

GEORGE LEIGH-MALLORY

CHAPTER IV

THE PROBLEM

I

It is very natural that mountaineers, particularly if they are members of the Alpine Club, should wish success to the Everest Expedition; for in a sense it is their own adventure. And yet their sympathies must often wobble. It is not always an undiluted pleasure to hear of new ascents in the Alps, or even in Great Britain; for half the charm of climbing mountains is born in visions preceding this experience—visions of what is mysterious, remote, inaccessible.

By experience we learn that we may pass to another world and come back; we rediscover the accessibility of summits appearing impregnable; and so long as we cannot without a tremor imagine ourselves upon a mountain's side, that mountain holds its mystery for us. But when we often hear about mountaineering expeditions on one or another of the most famous peaks in the world, are told of conquests among the most remote and difficult ranges or others continually repeated in well-known centres, we come to know too well how accessible mountains are to skilful and even to unskilful climbers. The imagination falters, and it may happen that we find ourselves one day thinking of the most surprising mountain of all with no more reverence than the practised golfer has for an artificial bunker. It was so, I was once informed by a friend, that he caught himself thinking of the Matterhorn, and he wondered whether he shouldn't give up climbing mountains until he had recovered his reverence for them. A shorter way, I thought, was to wait until the weather broke and then climb the Matterhorn every day till it should be calm and fine again, and when he pondered this suggestion he had no need to test its power, for he very soon began to think again of the Matterhorn as he ought to think. But from the anguish of discovering his heresy he cherished a lesson and afterwards would never consent to read or hear accounts of mountaineering, nor even to speak of his own exploits. This was a commendable attitude in him; and I can feel no doubt, thinking of his case, that however valuable a function it may have been of the Alpine Club in its infancy to propagate not only the gospel, but the knowledge of mountains, the time has come when it should be the principal aim of any such body not only to suppress the propagation of a gospel already too popular, but also to shelter its members against that superabundance of knowledge which must needs result from accumulating records. Hereafter, of contemporary exploits the less we know the better; our heritage of discovery among mountains is rich enough; too little remains to be discovered. The story of a new ascent should now be regarded as a corrupting communication calculated to promote the glory of Man, or perhaps only of individual men, at the expense of the mountains themselves.

It may well be asked how, holding such opinions, I can set myself to the task of describing an attempt to reach the highest summit of all. Surely Chomolungmo should remain inviolate; or if attempted, the deed should not be named. With this point of view I have every sympathy, and lest it should be thought that in order to justify myself I must bring in a different order of reasons from some other plane, and involve myself in a digression even longer than the present, I will say nothing about justification for this story beyond remarking that it glorifies Mount Everest, since this mountain has not yet been climbed. And when I say that sympathy in a mountaineer may wobble, the mountaineer I more particularly mean is the present writer. It is true that I did what I could to reach the summit, but now as I look back and see all those wonderful preparations, the great array of boxes collected at Phari Dzong and filling up the courtyard of the bungalow, the train of animals and coolies carrying our baggage across Tibet, the thirteen selected Europeans so snugly wrapt in their woollen waistcoats and Jaeger pants, their armour of wind-proof materials, their splendid overcoats, the furred finneskoes or felt-sided boots or fleece-lined moccasins devised to keep warm their feet, and the sixty strong porters with them delighting in underwear from England and leathern jerkins and puttees from Kashmir; and then, unforgettable scene, the scatter of our stores at the Base Camp, the innumerable neatly-made wooden boxes concealing the rows and rows of tins—of Harris's sausages, Hunter's hams, Heinz's spaghetti, herrings soi-disant fresh, sardines, sliced bacon, peas, beans, and a whole forgotten host besides, sauce-bottles for the Mess tables, and the rare bottles more precious than these, the gay tins of sweet biscuits, Ginger Nuts and Rich Mixed, and all the carefully chosen delicacies; and besides all these for our sustenance or pleasure, the fuel supply, uncovered in the centre of the camp, green and blue two-gallon-cans of paraffin and petrol, and an impressive heap of yak-dung; and the climbing equipment—the gay little tents with crimson flies or yellow, pitched here only to be seen and admired, the bundles of soft sleeping-bags, soft as eiderdown quilt can be, the ferocious crampons and other devices, steel-pointed and terrible, for boots' armament, the business-like coils of rope, the little army of steel cylinders containing oxygen under high pressure, and, not least, the warlike sets of apparatus for using the life-giving gas; and lastly, when I call to mind the whole begoggled crowd moving with slow determination over the snow and up the mountain slopes and with such remarkable persistence bearing up the formidable loads, when after the lapse of months I envisage the whole prodigious evidences of this vast intention, how can I help rejoicing in the yet undimmed splendour, the undiminished glory, the unconquered supremacy of Mount Everest?

Base Camp and Mount Everest in Evening Light.

It is conceivable that this gréta mountain, though still unsubdued, may nevertheless have suffered some loss of reputation. It is the business of a mountain to be ferocious first, charming and smiling afterwards if it will. But it has been said already of this mountain that the way to the summit is not very terrible, it will present no technical difficulties of climbing. Has it not then, after all, a character unsuitably mild? Is it not a great cow among mountains? It cannot be denied that the projected route to the summit presents no slopes of terrible steepness. But we may easily underrate the difficulties even here. Though some of us have gazed earnestly at the final ridge and discussed at length the possibility of turning or of climbing direct certain prominent obstacles, no one has certainly determined that he may proceed there without being obliged to climb difficult places; and the snow slope which guards the very citadel will prove, one cannot doubt, as steep as one would wish to find the final slope of any great mountain. Again, the way to the North Col, that snow-saddle by which alone we may gain access to the North Ridge, has not always been simple; we know little enough still about its changing conditions, but evidently on too many days the snow will be dangerous there, and perhaps on many others the presence of bare ice may involve more labour than was required of us this year. But granted this one breach in the defence of Mount Everest, shall we only for that think of it as a mild mountain? How many mountains can be named in the Alps of which so small a part presents the hope of finding a way to the summit? Nowhere on the whole immense face of ice and rocks from the North-east ridge to Lhotse and the South-east ridge is the smallest chance for the mountaineer, and, leaving out all count of size, Mont Blanc even above the Brenva Glacier has no face so formidable as this; of the Southern side, which we know only from a few photographs and sketches, one thing is certain—that whoever reaches it will find there a terrific precipice of bare rock probably unequalled for steepness by any great mountain face in the Alps and immeasurably greater; the single glimpse obtained last year of the Western glacier and the slopes above it revealed one of the most awful and utterly forbidding scenes ever observed by men; how much more encouraging, and yet how utterly hopeless, is the familiar view from the Rongbuk Valley! Mount Everest, therefore, apart from its pre-eminence in bulk and height, is great and beautiful, marvellously built' majestic, terrible, a mountain made for reverence; and beneath its shining sides one must stand in awe and wonder·

II

When we think of a party of climbers struggling along the final ridge of Mount Everest, we are perhaps inclined to reject an obvious comparison of their endeavour with that of athletes in a long distance race. The climbers are not of course competing to reach the goal one before another; the aim is for all to reach it. But the climbers' performance, like the runners', will depend on two factors, endurance and pace; and the two have to be considered together. A climber must not only keep on moving upwards if he is to succeed, he must move at a certain minimum pace: a pace that will allow him, having started from a given point, to reach the top and come down in a given time. Further, at a great height it is true for the climber even more than for the runner on a track in England that to acquire pace is the chief difficulty, and still more true that it is the pace which kills. Consequently it is pace more than anything else which becomes the test of fitness on Mount Everest.

Every man has his own standard, determined as a result of his experience. He knows perhaps that in the Alps with favourable conditions he is capable of ascending 1,500 feet an hour without unduly exerting himself and without fatigue; if he were to bring into action the whole of his reserves he might be able to double this figure. He will assuredly find when he comes up into Tibet and lives at a mean height of 15,000 feet that he is capable of very much less. And then he begins to call in question his power, to measure himself against his European standard. Every member of both Everest Expeditions was more or less of a valetudinarian. He had his eye on his physical fitness. He wondered each day, Am I getting fitter? Am I as fit as I should expect to be in the Alps? And the ultimate test was pace uphill.

The simpler phenomena of acclimatisation have frequently been referred to in connection with Mount Everest. But still it may be asked why improvement should be expected during a sojourn at 15,000 feet. It is expected because as a matter of experience it happens: though why the red corpuscles in the blood whose function is to absorb and give up oxygen should multiply in the ratio of 8 : 5, I leave it to physiologists to explain. Whatever explanation they may give I shall not cease to regard this amazing change as the best of miracles. And this change in the hæmoglobin content of the blood evidently proceeds a long way above 15,000 feet. Nevertheless the advantage thereby obtained by no means altogether compensates at very high altitudes the effects of reduced atmospheric pressure. It enables a man to live in very thin air (11½ inches barometric pressure, at 27,000 feet), but not to exert himself with anything like his normal power at sea-level. His pace suffers. If at 23,000 feet he were able to exercise no less power than at 10,000 feet after a few well-spent days in the Alps, he would probably be able to ascend the remaining 6,000 feet to the summit in a single day. But if you cut off the supply of fuel you cannot expect your engine to maintain its pace of working; the power exercised by the climber in the more rarefied atmosphere at these high altitudes must be less; a rise of 6,000 feet in a day will be beyond his capacity. Therefore he must have camps higher on the mountain, and ultimately he must have one so high that in nine or ten hours even his snail's pace will bring him to the summit.

We must remember too that not only will his pace have suffered, his mind will be in a deplorable state. The experiments conducted in pressure chambers have a bearing on this point. I treasure the story of Prof. Haldane who, while in such a chamber, wanted to observe the colour of his lips and for some minutes gazed into his mirror before discovering that he held the back towards his face. Mountaineers have often observed a lack of clarity in their mental state at high altitudes ; it is difficult for the stupid mind to observe how stupid it is, but it is by no means improbable that the climbers of Mount Everest will try to drink their food or proceed crabwise, or do some quite ridiculous thing. And not only is it difficult to think straight in thin air, it is difficult to retain the desire to do anything at all. Perhaps of all that tells against him the mere weakness of a man's will when he is starved of oxygen is beyond everything likely to prevent his success.

Since the problem of climbing Mount Everest presented itself physiologically, it was only natural in us on the Expedition continually to be watching acclimatisation. We watched it in connection with the whole idea of being trained for the event. Probably each of us had a different notion as to how he should be trained, and some thought more about training than others. On this point I must confess a weakness when I foresee an event in which my physical strength and condition are to count for so much ; I am one of those who think more about training. I consider how I may add a cubit to my stature and all the time I am half aware that I might spare myself the trouble of such futile meditations. Experience seems only to show that, provided I habitually eat well and sleep well and take a moderate amount of exercise, I can do nothing to improve my endurance on a mountain. Probably some men may do more to this end. The week we spent in Darjeeling sufficed for all of us to brace ourselves after the enervating effects of our journey from England. Norton, who had come out rather earlier and prepared himself in the most strenuous fashion for the immense exertions of the Khadir Cup, was already finely trained—too well, I thought, for so lean a man. He and Geoffrey Bruce, my companion in the first party, together with General Bruce, Longstaff, and Noel, elected to walk a great deal in Sikkim, and so I believe did Somervell, Wakefield, and Morshead in the second party. The General, very frankly expressing the probable advantage to his figure of profuse perspiration in those warm valleys, also walked a great deal. For an exactly contrary reason—I hate the inconvenience that must arise on the march from wet clothes—I walked less than any of these; probably Longstaff and I rode more than the rest up to Phari Dzong. But when I heard how wonderfully fit were the two most energetic walkers of our party, and learned from Geoffrey Bruce of Norton's amazing pace uphill, I could not refrain from testing my own condition on the first occasion that we approached a comparatively high altitude: coming up to Gnatong, where the bungalow is situated above 12,000 feet, I walked for all I was worth, and was well satisfied. Next day I felt far from well with indigestion and headache. General Bruce and Longstaff were also unwell, and it was a cheerless afternoon and evening in the two little rooms at Kupup, with hailstorms outside and too little light within. Norton and Bruce elected to sleep on the verandah, and these two, with me, if I were fit enough, intended starting early next morning so as to climb a small mountain, diverging thus from our path over the Jelep La (14,500 feet) for the sake of the view. We set off not much later than we had intended; but it was now Norton's turn to be unwell, and he was properly mountain-sick 1,000 feet below the pass. However, we were not inclined to pay much attention to these little troubles; with a day's rest at a lower elevation (9,000 feet), and the pleasures of feasting with the Macdonalds in Yatung, we were quickly restored.

The continuous process of acclimatisation was due to begin at Phari Dzong. There we should stay three days above 14,000 feet, and after that our marches would keep us between that level and 17,000 feet, so that a man would surely find out how he was affected by living at high altitudes. At Phari the whole party seemed remarkably fit, and any amount of energy was available for sorting out and checking our vast mass of stores. But the conditions of travel on these high plains became evident so soon as we were on the march again. Those who gaily started to walk, not troubling to provide themselves with a pony, found after a time that they were glad enough to ride; but then it became so bitterly cold that riding was more disagreeable than walking, and most of us, as we pushed along in the teeth of a blizzard, preferred to walk, and were surprisingly fatigued. Two of the party were ill when we reached camp, but more perhaps from chill than mountain-sickness. On the following day a system of sharing ponies to allow alternate walking and riding was more carefully organised. Even so, most of us must have walked two-thirds of that long rough march (about 25 miles), and while crossing the "Concertina pass," as we called it, a name which explains itself, we had ample opportunities of testing our powers of walking uphill between 16,000 and 17,000 feet; it was evident that we were already becoming acclimatised and able to enjoy those mild competitions in which a man will test his powers against another as they breast a hill together. This was encouraging enough; but how far we were from "going" as we would go at 10,000 feet lower could easily be observed from our puffing and blowing and the very moderate pace achieved by great efforts.

It was a week later before we had another opportunity of testing our acclimatisation as we came up to the Tinki La, a rise of nearly 3,000 feet up to 17,000 feet. I suppose there may have been some slight improvement in this week; for my part, I was fairly fit, and after riding over the comparatively flat approach, walked up about 2,000 feet without a halt and experienced no sort of fatigue. But the party as a whole was disappointing, and several members were distinctly affected by the height. Perhaps this pass was one of those places where some local circumstance emphasises the altitude, for the ponies stopped and puffed in a way we had never seen before; but I fancy the reason of their condition was to be found in the steepness of the ascent.

The day after crossing the Tinki La, we had a short march to Gyangkar Nangpa, and, coming across the flat basin, had full in view before us Sangkar Ri, a prominent rock peak, the most northerly of a remarkable range above the left bank of the Arun River. The desire to vary the routine of the daily march by climbing a mountain had already stirred a number of suggestions among us, and now the opportunity seemed to offer itself; we were further incited by the prospect of a splendid view of Mount Everest if we could reach this summit, which lay not so very far out of our way. No doubt unconscious motives, too, promoted our attempt on Sangkar Ri. The pleasures of mountaineering must always be restricted for those who grapple with the highest mountains, if not denied *in toto*; but the ascent of a little rock peak of 20,000 feet might help to keep alive in us some appreciation of mountaineering as an enjoyable pursuit. And then we wanted confidence in ourselves. At present we could only feel how unequal we were to the prodigious task in front of us; so were we urged to try conclusions with Sangkar Ri, to put ourselves to the test.

The project demanded a high camp, at 17,000 feet, nearly 4,000 feet above Gyangkar Nangpa. Seeing that it would clearly be undesirable to employ more than a very small number of porters to carry up tents and sleeping-bags for the night, Somervell and I at first made a plan for ourselves alone; but when it was found that two others wanted to come with us, this plan was amplified to include them, and it was arranged that the four of us should sleep at close quarters in a Whymper tent. The porters who carried for us in the evening would take down their burdens in the early morning, in time to get them loaded on to the animals at Gyangkar without delaying the main body. The establishment of our camp did not proceed without some little difficulty; one of the porters gave out and had to be relieved of his load, and it was not until we had contoured a hillside for an hour in the dark that we found a suitable place. So soon as we had lain down in our tent, a bitter wind sprang up and blew in at the door; the night was one of the coldest I remember.

We had ascended not more than 1,000 feet next morning when one of the party decided that he was too ill to go on; he exhibited the usual symptoms of mountain-sickness. While the other two suffered the disappointment of turning back, Somervell and I pushed on towards a snow col on the North ridge of the mountain. As it was desirable to reach this point without delay in order to see the view while it was yet unclouded, and to take photographs, I continued at my own pace, and eventually found myself looking down on Somervell some distance below me as he struggled up with frequent halts. I very soon made up my mind that we should get no higher than this. But after a brief halt and some refreshment when he had rejoined me, Somervell announced that he was prepared to go on. We began to make our way along a rock ridge, which became ever steeper as we mounted. Our progress was slow indeed, and I kept thinking, as I found myself more and more fatigued, "Surely we must give up now; a man in his state can't go on climbing such rocks as these." But whenever I asked how he was feeling, he would answer that he was getting along well enough; and as we gradually won our way up, and I kept my eye on my watch, I began to see that we had really a chance of reaching the summit. The rocks were by no means easy, and it is commonly said that the effort of climbing difficult rocks is just what will prove most exhausting, if it can be undertaken at all, to men affected by altitude. The struggle to overcome a steep obstacle must always interfere with regular breathing. Nevertheless, I am inclined to think that the advantage in sheer exhilaration of climbing difficult rocks compensates the greater trouble in breathing, and that so long as I am still in a state to climb them, I prefer even difficult rocks to snow. The actual exertion put forth in mounting even the steepest cliff is often overrated. If there are moments of intense struggle, these are rare, and though the demand on nervous concentration is great, the climber proceeds for the most part with balanced movements, requiring, indeed, the sureness of trained muscles, but no tremendous output of strength. With such balanced movement the two of us were able to go slowly upwards, without a rapidly increasing exhaustion, to the foot of a formidable gendarme. We had hopes in the first instance that he might be compelled to yield to a frontal attack. But, 30 feet up, we found our way barred by a slab, which was at once so smooth and so exposed that, though we felt it might conceivably be climbed, we decided it was not for us to climb it at the present moment; our allowance of rope was insufficient for operations which might require an "abseil"[1] on the descent. We therefore turned to the West side of our ridge. Here, of course, we were out of the sun, and the rocks were so cold that they felt sticky to the skin and blistered our finger-tips. However, we managed to execute a sensational traverse, and afterwards climbed a steep wall, which brought us out above the slab from which we had turned back. It was here that we experienced both the difficulty and the danger of rock-climbing at high altitudes. It was necessary, in a terribly exposed position, to pull oneself over an edge of rock on to a little platform. A big effort was required: but the reserve of strength had been exhausted. Having committed myself to this taxing struggling, the grim thought arose in my mind that at the critical moment I might be found wanting and my body refuse to respond when the greatest effort was required of it. A great effort was required before I arrived panting on the airy stance.

After these exciting moments, we reached the top of the gendarme without much trouble. But he had cost us too much time. We had to start from Gyangkar this same day in pursuit of General Bruce, and ought to cross the quick-sands of the Shiling Plain before dark. We had already overstepped the time allowed for the ascent according to

[1] A method of coming down on a double rope.

our intention. The summit now appeared perhaps 500 feet above us, and the intervening rocks were evidently going to provide some stiff passages. It was necessary, therefore, to turn back here and waste no time on the descent. The descent proved longer than we had expected; we chose a long traverse over steep snow to avoid the gendarme, and neither of us was in a condition to cut steps quickly. We observed, in fact, what I had observed last year with Bullock, that one may go down a considerable distance at a high altitude, and instead of recovering very quickly, as may happen in the Alps, one only becomes progressively more fatigued. It was 4.30 p.m. when we reached Gyankar and found ourselves happily recovered from our exertions. Sangkar Ri was still unclimbed. But we looked back on our expedition with some satisfaction. We had been little short of 20,000 feet when we turned back, and I had been greatly impressed by Somervell's endurance. For though very much fatigued before reaching the col at the foot of our ridge, and further enervated by an attack of dysentery which had begun on the previous day, his condition seemed rather to improve than to deteriorate above that point. For my part, I had come near enough to exhaustion, considering the difficulties of the climb, and had suffered from a severe headache, but certainly felt no worse than I expected at this stage of our training.

I entered upon this tale with the object of illustrating the course of acclimatisation among us; but the return to Gyangkar was not for us the end of the story. It was now clear that we could not hope to cross the quicksands before night. However, we might hope to reach the ford by which we must cross the river Yaru with still enough light to recognise the spot, and thereafter we could rest in a sheltered place I knew of until the late rising moon should show us the tracks of the main body. We set off accordingly in high haste on the ponies we found waiting for us. Our instruction had been that these animals should be specially selected for their fleetness of foot—for Tibetan ponies can, some of them, travel at a fair speed, while others no amount of flogging will urge beyond 3 miles an hour. The beast I rode very quickly showed that he was one of these last. I had entrusted my ice-axe to a porter who accompanied us, and now told him to ride behind me and use it if necessary. For 5 miles he used it with a dexterity and energy beyond praise. Then I abandoned the pony, and, walking ahead of the party, easily outstripped the rest encumbered with this beast. Night fell when we were still 2 miles short of the ford. But as Somervell and I approached the spot and wondered exactly where it might be, we perceived lights a little way ahead on the further bank of the river, presumably those of a Tibetan camp, and soon a figure appeared on that side. We were hailed in Tibetan; our sirdar, coming up, spoke Tibetan in reply; the figure waded across to us; and it was explained to me that this good Samaritan was prepared to carry me over on his back. I readily agreed to so generous a proposition. He was not an easy steed, but I was able to hang on to him for a hundred yards or so until he deposited me on the other bank, a light enough burden, apparently, to be picked up and set down like a child. And 400 yards further we reached the lights. It was no stranger camp; the tents were ours, and the General and the rest were sitting in the Mess while dinner was keeping hot in the kitchen against our return.

Ten days later we reached our Base Camp at the foot of the Rongbuk Glacier (16,800 feet) and contemplated the prospect of rising another 12,000 feet and more to the summit of Mount Everest. At all events the whole party had reached this point remarkably fit, and no one now showed signs of distress from staying at this elevation. Remembering how Bullock and I had felt after our first exertions up here last year, I hoped to spend a few days at the Base Camp before doing very much, and as General Bruce's plans worked out nothing was required of me at present. But much was asked of the reconnaissance party which started out on May 4.

It has been recorded in earlier chapters how in three days from the Base Camp they reached a height of 21,500 feet on the East Rongbuk Glacier. The cold was great and their hardships were unrelieved by the greater comfort of established camps enjoyed by those who followed the pioneers. From their accounts they were evidently affected a good deal by altitude before turning back with their work accomplished, and in spite of the cold they experienced the familiar phenomenon of lassitude so painfully and particularly noticeable on the glaciers when the sun makes itself felt. But on the whole they had been less affected by the want of air than was to be expected. They had this advantage—that they proceeded gradually; the distance to travel was long, but the ascent was never steep, and they found the upper glacier very lightly covered with snow; and it is heavy going and a steep ascent that most readily induce the more distressing symptoms of mountain-sickness. However, from the point of view of acclimatisation it was highly satisfactory that this party should have proceeded with so little delay to reach 21,000 feet.

Meanwhile Somervell and I, chafing somewhat at our inactivity and with the idea that a long day on the mountains would do us good at this stage, on May 6 climbed a small peak above the left bank of the Rongbuk Glacier. It was a day of small misfortunes for me. As we were walking on the stony slopes in the early morning my triconni nails of hard steel slipped on a granite slab and I contrived to leave there an incredible amount of skin from the back of my right hand. And higher, as we worked along a broken ridge, a large boulder poised in unstable equilibrium slipped as I brushed it with my knee and fell on the big-toe joint so as to pinion my right foot. It was an awkward moment, for the place was steep; I just had strength to heave it over and down the mountain-side, and luckily no bones were broken. But walking was very painful afterwards, and perhaps this accident had something to do with the fatigue I felt as we neared the summit. On the lower slopes I had been going well enough and seemed fitter than

SERAC, EAST RONGBUK GLACIER.

Somervell; at 21,000 feet he was apparently no more fatigued than at 18,000 or 19,000 feet, while I could scarcely drag one leg after the other. And when we came back to camp I was surprisingly glad to take a little whisky in my tea.

III

I have said too much already about the early stage of acclimatisation: my excuse must be that much will depend upon this factor. The issue will depend no less on organisation and transport; and though this subject is General Bruce's province, at all events so far as Camp III, I have a few words to add to what he has written.

In the calculation of what will be required at various stages in order to reach the summit of Mount Everest it is necessary to begin at the highest; and the climber imagines in the first place where he would like to have his camps. He may imagine that on the final day he might rise 2,000 feet to the summit; if he is to give himself the best chance of success he will not wish to start much lower than 27,000 feet, and in any case he cannot camp much higher, for he is very unlikely to find a place on the ridge above the North-east shoulder (27,400 feet) or on the steep rocks within 200 feet of it. We may therefore fix 27,000 feet approximately as the desirable height for the last camp. And we have another camping-ground fixed for us by circumstances, approximately at 23,000 feet, the broad shelf lying in the shelter of the ice-cliffs on the North Col—there is no convenient place for a comparatively large camp for a considerable distance either above or below it. But to carry up a camp 4,000 feet at these altitudes would be to ask altogether too much of the porters. We must therefore establish an intermediary camp between these two, say at 25,000 feet if a place can be found.

Now what will be required at these three camps? We must ask first with what number of climbers the assault is to be made. A party of two appears insufficient, for if one man should become exhausted the other will probably want help in bringing him down. This difficulty is met by having three climbers. But since an exhausted man cannot be left alone, certainly not without the shelter of a tent, nor should one man go on alone, a party of three must turn back so soon as one man is unable to go further. Four men would give a better chance of success in this case, for then two might go on and still leave one to look after the sick man. Granted, then, that the best hope is for four men to start from a camp at 27,000 feet, we have firstly to provide them with tents. Two tents are better than one, for it may be difficult to find a place for four men to lie side by side, and the greater weight of two smaller tents above one larger is inconsiderable; and they must have sleeping-bags, provisions for two days, fuel, and cooking-pots. All these necessities have been previously carried up to the camp below at 25,000 feet; but other things besides are required there. We may assume that this camp is to be used as a stage on the way up only and not on the way down. Even so, six porters at least will have to sleep there before carrying up the highest camp, and their requirements will be the same as we have laid down for the four climbers; we must add another day's provisions and fuel for the climbers themselves.

It will be understood from this method of calculation how we arrive at the number of loads which must be carried up to any given camp; it is observable that at each stage downwards the number increases in a proportion considerably greater than 2 : 1. Fortunately we are not obliged to proceed strictly on these lines; to the lower camps we need not carry up the whole of our stores on one day, and consequently we need not increase in this alarming ratio the number of our porters. But in any case when we get down to the North Col we must clearly have a large bulk of stores; and the fewer porters we employ between one stage and another, economizing on tents and sleeping-bags, the more time we shall require.

It was clear from the start that time was likely to be a formidable enemy. General Bruce's problem was not only to move our vast quantity of stores across an almost barren country, but to move them in a given time. It was fortunate for this reason that the number of porters who came with us was not increased, for every man must add something to our burdens. No one who knows that arid country could fail to be surprised that we reached our Base Camp below the Rongbuk Glacier so early as the 1st of May. But now the number of Nepalese porters—only forty were available for carrying—was too small for all our needs. If they alone were to shoulder all our loads when should we reach the North Col? Some sort of depot must be established below it at 21,000 feet for the supply of all higher camps on the mountain before we could proceed; and the reconnaissance party determined that two staging camps would be required between the Base Camp and this depot. The existence and the solution of so large a problem of transport have so important a bearing on our later plans that I must refer to it again in this place. General Bruce has told how he impressed Tibetans into his service, and by using them up to Camp II was able to liberate our own porters much earlier than might have been expected for work further on. But the system of employing Tibetans did not work without a hitch. It was because the first labour battalion absconded that General Bruce gave orders for only two of us to go forward and use the first opportunities for pushing on from Camp III. With the prospect of an early monsoon and a shortage of transport it was desirable that, so soon as any porters were available for work above Camp III, this work should be pushed on without delay, and if necessary an assault should be made with the minimum of stores required by a party of two climbers. Without a further supply of transport there was no question of using the oxygen, for we should have more than enough to carry up without it.

On May 10 Somervell and I started from the Base Camp for Camp I. The way already customary among the porters led us at first over the flat waste of stones, intersected occasionally by dry stream-beds, which lies below the black, humpy snout of the Rongbuk Glacier; we then followed the deep trough below the glacier's right (west) bank, an obvious line, but rough with great boulders. It is not before reaching the head of this trough, where one must turn up towards the East Rongbuk Glacier, that a problem arises as to how best to proceed; here we found that an adequate path had already been stamped on the loose moraine, and after ascending steeply we contoured the hillside at an easy gradient—a little forethought and energy had devised so good a way that we could walk comfortably from one camp to the other in two hours and a half. Moreover we were highly pleased by Camp I. The draught perpetually blowing down the main glacier was scarcely noticed in this side-valley; the afternoon sun was shining to cheer the stony scene, and away to the West some noble peaks were well placed for our delight. But beyond æsthetic satisfaction we were soon aware of a civilized habitation. We had been in camp only a few minutes when a cook brought us tea and sweet biscuits and demanded to know what we would like for dinner; we ordered a good dinner and proceeded to examine our apartments. Geoffrey Bruce, we knew, had been busy here with certain constructional works to obviate the difficulty of carrying up heavy tents which were required in any case at the Base Camp. We found a little house reserved for Europeans, one of four solidly built with stones and roofed, with the outer flies of Whymper tents. I never measured up this chamber; I suppose the floor must have been 8 feet × 10 feet and the roof 4 feet high. It is true the tent-poles bridging across from side to side in support of the roof were in dangerously unstable equilibrium, and there were windy moments when valetudinously minded persons might have pronounced it a draughty room. But we were far from hypercritical on this first night, particularly as no wind blew, and a wonderful and pleasant change it was, after living in tents, to sit, eat, and sleep in a house once more.

The greater part of our alpine stores, with which I was especially concerned, had already reached Camp I, and there I found the various bundles of tents, ropes, sleeping-bags, crampons, paraffin, petrol, primus stoves, cooking-sets, etc., which I had carefully labelled for their respective destinations. The great majority were labelled for III—no higher destination had yet been assigned, and I speculated, not altogether optimistically, as to the probable rates of their arrival. As the general order of transport was interrupted for the present, we had to decide what we should take on with us both of food and alpine stores. Somervell, who by now was an expert in the numbers and contents of food-boxes, vigorously selected all that we preferred, and we went to bed with very good hopes for the future, at least in one respect. In consequence of these puzzling problems it took us some little time in the morning to make up our loads; it was past ten o'clock when we started on our way to Camp II.

I was surprised, after we had proceeded some distance

View from Ice Cavern.

along the stones on the left bank of the East Rongbuk Glacier, to observe a conspicuous cairn, evidently intended to mark our way over the glacier itself. But the glacier in this lower end is so completely covered with stones that in choosing the easiest way one is only concerned to find the flattest surfaces, and as we mildly followed where the route had been laid out by Colonel Strutt and his party we found the glacier far less broken than was to be expected. Ultimately we walked along a conspicuous medial moraine, avoiding by that means some complicated ice, and descended it abruptly, to find ourselves on the flat space where Camp II was situated.

By this time we had seen a good deal of the East Rongbuk Glacier. As we came up the moraine near its left bank we looked northwards on a remarkable scene. From the stony surface of the glacier fantastic pinnacles arose, a strange, gigantic company, gleaming white as they stood in some sort of order, divided by the definite lines of the moraines. Beyond and above them was a vast mountain of reddish rock known to us only by the triangulated height of its sharp summit, marked in Wheeler's map as 23,180. The pinnacles became more thickly crowded together as we mounted, until, as we followed the bend southwards, individuals were lost in the crowd and finally the crowd was merged in the great tumbled sea of the glacier, now no longer dark with stones, but exhibiting everywhere the bright surfaces of its steep and angry waves. At Camp II we were surrounded on three sides by this amazing world of ice. We lay in the shelter of a vertical cliff not less than 60 feet high, sombrely cold in the evening shadow, dazzlingly white in the morning sun, and perfectly set off by the frozen pool at its foot. Nothing, of course, was to be seen of Mount Everest; the whole bulk of the North Peak stood in front of it. But by mounting a few steps up some stony slopes above us we could see to the south-east, over the surface of the ice, the slopes coming down from the Lhapka La, from which high pass we had looked down the East Rongbuk Glacier in September, 1921, and observed the special whiteness of the broken stream, at our own level now, and puzzled over its curious course. We had yet another sight to cheer us as we lay in our tents. On the range between us and the main Rongbuk Glacier stood, in the one direction of uninterrupted vision, a peak of slender beauty, and as the moon rose its crests were silver cords.

Next morning, May 12, according to Colonel Strutt's directions, we worked our way along the true left edge of the glacier and the stones of its left bank. The problem here is to avoid that tumbled sea of ice where no moraine can be continuously followed. Probably it would be possible to get through this ice almost anywhere, for it is not an ice-fall, the gradient is not steep, the pinnacles are not seracs, and there are few crevasses: but much time and labour would be wasted in attempting such a course. Further up the surface becomes more even, and the reconnaissance party had reached this better surface by only a short and simple crossing of the rougher ice. We easily found the place, marked by a conspicuous cairn, where they had turned away from the bank. Their tracks on the glacier, though snow was lying in the hollows, were not easy to follow, and we quickly lost them; but presently we found another cairn built upon a single large stone, and here proceeded with confidence to cross a deep and wide trough of which we had been warned; and once this obstacle was overcome we knew no difficulty could impede our progress to Camp III. The laden porters, however, did not get along very easily. Their nails, for the most part, were worn smooth, and they found the ice too slippery. As I had never seen in the Alps a glacier-surface like this one I was greatly surprised by the nature of the bare ice. In a sense it was often extremely rough, with holes and minute watercourses having vertical side 6 inches to 13 inches high; but the upper surfaces of the little knobs and plateaus intervening were extraordinarily hard and smooth and the colour was very much bluer than the usual granular surface of a dry glacier. It was also surprising to find at most a thin coating of fine snow as high as 20,500 feet; for in 1921 we had found, even before the first heavy snowfall, plenty of snow on the glaciers above 19,000 feet. For my part, with new nails in my boots, I was not troubled by the slippery surfaces. But we decided to supply the porters with crampons, which they subsequently found very useful on this stage of the journey.

CHAPTER V

THE HIGHEST CAMP

IV

The situation of Camp III when we reached it early in the afternoon was not calculated to encourage me, though I suppose it might be found congenial by hardier men. We had turned the corner of the North Peak so that the steep slopes of its Eastern arm rose above us to North and West. Our tents were to be pitched on the stones that have rolled down these slopes on to the glacier, and just out of range of a stone fall from the rocks immediately above us. A shallow trough divided us from the main plateau of the glacier, and up this trough the wind was blowing; since the higher current was hurrying the clouds from the normal direction, North-west, we might presume that this local variation was habitual. But wind we could hardly expect to escape from one direction or another. A more important consideration, perhaps, for a mountain camp is the duration of sunshine. Here we should have the sun early, for to the East we looked across a wide snowy basin to the comparatively low mountains round about the Lhakpa La; but we should lose it early too, and we observed with dismay on this first afternoon that our camp was in shadow at 3.15 p.m. The

Seracs, East Rongbuk Glacier, above Camp II.

water supply was conveniently near, running in a trough, and we might expect it to be unfrozen for several hours each day.

Whatever we might think of this place it was undoubtedly the best available. Very little energy remained among the party, most of whom had now reached 21,000 feet for the first time in their lives. However, a number soon set to work levelling the ground which we chose for two tents. It was necessary to do this work thoroughly, for, unlike the smooth, flat stones at Camp I, these, like those at Camp II, of which we had obtained sufficient experience during the previous night, were extremely sharp and uncomfortable to lie on. After it was done we sent down the main body of the porters, keeping only one man for cook and each the man specially attached to him as servant by Geoffrey Bruce's command long ago in Darjeeling. With these we proceeded to order our camp. The tents were pitched, some sort of a cookhouse was constructed from the wealth of building material, and we also began to put up walls behind which we could lie in shelter to eat our meals. Perhaps the most important matter was the instruction of Pou, our cook, in the correct use of the Primus stove; with the purpose of giving him confidence a fine fountain of blazing paraffin was arranged and at once extinguished by opening the safety valve; for the conservation of our fuel supply we carefully showed him how the absolute alcohol must be used to warm the burner while paraffin and petrol were to be mixed for combustion. Fortunately his intelligence rose above those disagreeable agitations which attend the roaring or the failure to roar of Primus stoves, so that after these first explanations we had never again to begrime our hands with paraffin and soot.

In our tent this evening of May 12, Somervell and I discussed what we should do. There was something to be said for taking a day's rest at this altitude before attempting to rise another 2,000 feet. Neither of us felt at his best. After our first activities in camp I had made myself comfortable with my legs in a sleeping-bag, Somervell with his accustomed energy had been exploring at some distance—he had walked as far as the broad pass on the far side of our snowy basin, the Rápiu La, at the foot of Everest's North-east ridge, and had already begun a sketch of the wonderful view obtained from that point of Makalu. When he returned to camp about 5.30 p.m. he was suffering from a headache and made a poor supper. Moreover, we were full of doubts about the way up to the North Col. After finding so much ice on the glacier we must expect to find ice on those East-facing slopes below the Col. It was not unlikely that we should be compelled to cut steps the whole way up, and several days would be required for so arduous a task. We decided therefore to lose no time in establishing a track to the North Col.

It was our intention on the following morning, May 13, to take with us two available porters, leaving only our cook in camp, and so make a small beginning towards the supply of our next camp. But Somervell's man was sick and could not come with us. We set out in good time with only my porter, Dasno, and carried with us, besides one small tent, a large coil of spare rope and some wooden pegs about 18 inches long. As we made our way up the gently sloping snow it was easy to distinguish the line followed to the North Col after the monsoon last year—a long slope at a fairly easy angle bearing away to the right, or North, a traverse to the left, and a steep slope leading up to the shelf under the ice-cliff on the skyline. With the sun behind us we saw the first long slope, nearly 1,000 feet, glittering in a way that snow will never glitter; there we should find only blue ice, bare and hard. Further to the North was no better, and as we looked at the steep final slope it became plain enough that there and nowhere else was the necessary key to the whole ascent; for to the South of an imaginary vertical line drawn below it was a hopeless series of impassable cliffs. The more we thought about it the more convinced we became that an alternative way must be found up to this final slope. We had not merely to reach the North Col once: whatever way we chose must be used for all the comings and goings to and from a camp up there. Unless the connection between Camps III and IV were free from serious obstacles, the whole problem of transport would increase enormously in difficulty; every party of porters must be escorted by climbers both up and down, and even so the dangers on a big ice slope after a fall of snow would hardly be avoided.

Endeavouring to trace out a satisfactory route from the

shelf of the North Col downwards, we soon determined that we should make use of a sloping corridor lying some distance to the left of the icy line used last year and apparently well covered with snow. For 300 or 400 feet above the flat snowfield it appeared to be cut off by very steep ice-slopes; nevertheless the best hope was to attempt an approach more or less direct to the foot of this corridor; and first we must reconnoitre the steepest of these obstacles, which promised the most convenient access to the desired point could we climb it. Here fortune favoured our enterprise. We found the surface slightly cleft by a fissure slanting at first to the right and then directly upwards. In the disintegrated substance of its edges it was hardly necessary to cut steps, and we mounted 250 feet of what threatened to be formidable ice with no great expenditure of time and energy. Two lengths of rope were now fixed for the security of future parties, the one hanging directly downwards from a single wooden peg driven in almost to the head, and another on a series of pegs for the passage of a leftward traverse which brought us to the edge of a large crevasse. We were now able to let ourselves down into the snow which choked this crevasse a little distance below its edges, and by means of some large steps hewn in the walls and another length of rope a satisfactory crossing was established. Above this crevasse we mounted easy snow to the corridor.

So far as the shelf which was our objective we now met no serious difficulty. The gentle angle steepened for a short space where we were obliged to cut a score of steps in hard ice; we fixed another length of rope, and again the final slope was steep, but not so as to trouble us. However, the condition of the snow was not perfect; we were surprised, on a face where so much ice appeared, to find any snow that was not perfectly hard; and yet we were usually breaking a heavy crust and stamping down the steps in snow deep enough to cover our ankles. It was a question rather of strength than of skill. An East-facing slope in the heat and glare of the morning sun favours the enemy mountain-sickness, and though no one of us three was sick our lassitude increased continually as we mounted and it required as much energy as we could muster to keep on stamping slowly upwards.

We lay down at length on the shelf, not yet shaded by the ice-cliff above it, in a state of considerable exhaustion. Here presumably was the end of a day's work satisfactory in the most important respect, for we felt that the way we had found was good enough, and with the fixed ropes was suitable for use under almost any conditions. It occurred to us after a little interval and some light refreshment that one thing yet remained to be done. The lowest point of the North Col, from which the North ridge of Everest springs a little way to the South of our shelf, is perhaps ten minutes' walk. We ought to go just so far as that in order to make quite sure of the way onward.

In the direction of the North-east shoulder, now slightly East of South from us, the shelf slopes gradually upwards, a ramp as it were alongside the battlements almost attaining the level of the crest itself. In the whirl of snow and wind on that bitter day of September 1921, Bullock, Wheeler, and I had found it necessary, in order actually to gain this level, to take a few steps to the right round the head of a large crevasse slanting across our line to the North Col. Somervell and I soon found ourselves confronted by this same crevasse, and prepared to evade it by the same manœuvre. But during those intervening months the crack had extended itself some distance to the right and prevented the possibility of getting round at that end. It was also much too wide to be leapt. The best chance was in the other direction. Here we were able to work our way down, before the steep slopes plunge over towards the head of the East Rongbuk Glacier, to a snow bridge within the crevasse giving access to a fissure in its opposite wall. We carefully examined the prospects of an ascent at this point. Our idea was to go up in the acute angle between two vertical walls of ice. A ladder of footsteps and finger-holds would have to be constructed in the ice, and even so the issue would be doubtful. When we set against the severe labour our present state of weakness and considered the consequences of a step into the gulf of the crevasse while steps were being cut—how poor a chance only one man could have of pulling out his companion—it was clear that a performance of this kind must wait for a stronger party. In any case, we reckoned, this was not a way which could safely be used by laden porters. If it must be used we

PARTY ASCENDING THE CHANG LA.

should apply to General Bruce for a 15-foot ladder, more permanent than any we could make in the ice, and no doubt the mechanical ingenuity so much in evidence at the Base Camp would devise a ladder both portable and strong. Even this thought failed to inspire us with perfect confidence, and it seemed rather a long way to have come from England to Mount Everest, to be stopped by an obstacle like this.

But was there no possible alternative? On this side of the crest we had nothing more to hope; but on the far side, could we reach it, there might exist some other shelf crowning the West-facing slopes of the Col, and connecting with the lowest point. We retraced our steps, going now in the opposite direction with the battlement on our left. Beyond there was a snow slope ascending towards the formidable ridge of the North Peak. The crevasse guarding it was filled with snow and presented no difficulty, and though the slope was steep we were able to make a staircase up the edge of it and presently found ourselves on the broken ground of the Northern end of the crest. As we turned back toward Everest a huge crevasse was in our way. A narrow bridge of ice took us across it and we found we were just able to leap another crevasse a few yards further.

We had now an uninterrupted view of all that lies to the West. Below us was the head of the main Rongbuk Glacier. On the skyline to the left was the prodigious North-west ridge of Everest, flanked with snow, hiding the crest of the West Peak. Past the foot of the North-west ridge we looked down the immense glacier flowing South-westwards into Nepal and saw without distinguishing them the distant ranges beyond. Near at hand a sharp edge of rocks, the buttress of Changtse falling abruptly to the Rongbuk Glacier, blocked out vision of the two greatest mountains North-west of Everest, Gyachung Kang (25,990) and Cho Uyo (26,367). But we could feel no regret for this loss, so enchanted were we by the spectacle of Pumori; though its summit (23,190) was little higher than our own level, it was, as it always is, a singularly impressive sight. The snow-cap of Pumori is supported by splendid architecture; the pyramidal bulk of the mountain, the steep fall of the ridges and faces to South and West, and the precipices of rock and ice towards East and North, are set off by a whole chain of mountains extending West-north-west along a frail, fantastic ridge unrivalled anywhere in this district for the elegant beauty of its cornices and towers. No more striking change of scenery could be imagined than this from all we saw to the East—the gentle snowy basin; the unemphatic lines of the slopes below and on either side of the Lhakpa La, dominated as they are by the dullest of mountains, Khartaphu; the even fall of rocks and snow from the East ridge of Changtse and from the North-east ridge of Everest. Pumori itself stood only as a symbol of this new wonderful world before our eyes as we stayed to look westwards, a world exciting, strange, unearthly, fantastic as the sky-scrapers in New York City, and at the same time possessing the dignity of what is enduring and immense, for no end was visible or even conceivable to this kingdom of adventure.

However, even Somervell's passion for using coloured chalks did not encourage him to stay long inactive in a place designed to be a funnel for the West wind of Tibet at an elevation of about 23,000 feet. We sped again over snow-covered monticules thrust up from the chaos of riven ice, and at last looked down from one more prominent little summit to the very nape of the Chang La. We saw our conjectured shelf in real existence and a fair way before us. In a moment all our doubts were eased. We knew that the foot of the North Ridge, by which alone we could approach the summit of Mount Everest, was not beyond our reach.

Dasno meanwhile was stretched in the snow on the sheltered shelf, which clearly must serve us sooner or later for Camp IV. As we looked down upon him from the battlements, we noticed that their shadow already covered the greater part of the shelf. It was four o'clock. We must delay no longer. The tent which Dasno had carried up was left to be the symbol of our future intentions, and we hastened down. Since 7 a.m. Somervell and I had been spending our strength with only one considerable halt, and latterly at a rapid rate. For some hours now we had felt the dull height-headache which results from exertion with too little oxygen, a symptom, I am told, not unlike the effect of poisoning by carbon monoxide. The unpleasing symptom became so increasingly disagreeable as we came down that I was very glad to reach our tent again. As it was only fair that Somervell should share all my sufferings, it now seemed inconsiderate of him to explain that he had a good appetite. For my part, I took a little soup and could face no food; defeated for the first and last time in either expedition before the sight of supper. I humbly swallowed a dose of aspirin, lay my head on the pillow and went to sleep.

V

For three days now we made no expedition of any consequence. The question arises, then, what did we? I have been searching the meagre entries in my journal for an answer, with no satisfactory result. The doctrine that men should be held accountable for their days, or even their hours, is one to which the very young often subscribe as a matter of course, seeing in front of them such a long way to go and so little time: the futility of exact accounts in this sort is apparent among mountains; the span of human life appears so short as hardly to be capable of the usual subdivisions, and a much longer period than a day may be neglected as easily as a halfpenny in current expenditure; and while some hours and days are spent in doing, others pass in simply being or being evolved, a process in the mind not to be measured in terms of time. Nevertheless, it is often interesting to draft a balance-sheet covering a period of twenty-four hours or seven days if only to see how much must truthfully be set down as "unaccounted."

In the present instance my first inclination is to write off in this bold fashion a full half of the time we spent in Camp III. But I will try to serve my accounts better cooked. The largest item in a balance of hours, even the least frank, will always be sleep. Here I prefer to make the entry under the heading Bed. This will enable me to write off at once a minimum of fourteen or a maximum of sixteen hours, leaving me only eight to ten hours to account for. It is also a simplification, because I am able by this means to avoid a doubtful and perhaps an ugly heading, Dozing. No one will ask me to describe exactly what goes on in bed. At Camp III it will be understood that supper is always included, but not breakfast, for as the breakfasting hour is the most agreeable in the day, it must be spent out-of-doors in the warm sun. Supper, unlike most activities, takes less time than in civilised life. Wasted minutes allow the food to cool and the grease to congeal. The porter serving us would not want to be standing about longer than necessary, and the whole performance was expeditious. Perhaps the fashion of eating among mountaineers is also more wolfish than among civilised men. The remaining 13½ or 14½ hours were not all spent in sleep. Probably on the night of May 13–14 I slept at least ten hours after the exertions of our ascent to the North Col. But though one sleeps well and is refreshed by sleep in a tent at an altitude to which one is sufficiently acclimatised, the outside world is not so very far away. However well accustomed to such scenes, one does not easily lose a certain excitement from the mere presence beyond the open tent-door of the silent power of frost suspending even the life of the mountains, and of the black ridges cutting the space of stars. The slow-spinning web of unconscious thought is nearer consciousness. One wakes in the early morning with the mind more definitely gathered about a subject, looks out to find the stars still bright, or dim in the first flush of dawn, and because the subject, whatever it be, and however nearly connected with the one absorbing problem, commands less concentrated attention—for the unwilled effort of the mind is more dispersed—one may often fall asleep once more and stay in a light intermittent slumber until the bright sun is up and the tent begins to be warm again. No sleeper, so far as I know on this second expedition, could compete either for quantity or quality with the sleep of Guy Bullock on the first; but all, perhaps with different habits from either his or mine, but at all events all who spent several nights at this camp or higher, slept well and were refreshed by sleep, and I hope they were no less grateful than I for those blessed nights.

I often remarked during the Expedition how large a part of a day had been spent by some of us in conversation. Down at the Base Camp we would often sit on, those of us who were not expert photographers, or painters, or naturalists, sit indefinitely not only after dinner, but after each succeeding meal, talking the hours away. When a man has learned to deal firmly with an imperious conscience, he will be neither surprised nor ashamed in such circum-

PEAK, 23,180 FEET (KELLAS' DARK ROCK PEAK) FROM THE RONGBUK GLACIER ABOVE CAMP II.

stances to enter in his diary, "so many hours talking and listening." It is true that conscience has the right to demand, in the case of such an entry, that the subjects talked of should also be named. But our company was able to draw upon so wide a range of experience that a fair proportion of our subjects were worth talking of. Perhaps in the higher camps there was a tendency to talk, though from less active brains, for the sake of obliterating the sense of discomfort. However, I believe that most men, once they have faced the change from armchairs and spring mattresses, and solid walls and hot baths, and drawers for their clothes and shelves for their books, do not experience discomfort in camp life except in the matter of feeding. However good your food and however well cooked, sooner or later in this sort of life meals appear messy. The most unsatisfactory circumstance of our meals at the Base Camp was the tables. In a country where wood is so difficult to obtain you cannot construct solid tables, still less can you afford to carry them. Our ingenious "X" tables had thin iron legs and canvas tops. On the rough ground they were altogether too light, too easily disturbed, and for this reason too many of our victuals erred on to these tables; their surfaces appeared under our eyes with constantly accumulating stains, but half rubbed out by a greasy rag. Efforts truly were made to control the nightly flow, proceeding from X and Y in their cups—had they been cups of beer or whisky, we might have minded little enough, but the sticky soiling mess was soup or cocoa; offenders were freely cursed; tables were scrubbed; table-cloths were produced. In the long run, no efforts availed. If the curry were tasty and the plate clean, who would complain of a dirty table-cloth at the impurification of which he had himself assisted? But I have little doubt that this circumstance, more than any gradual drift of the mountaineer back towards the Stone Age, was to be held accountable for the visible deterioration of our table manners. With no implication of insult to General Bruce and Dr. Longstaff, I record my belief that our manners at Camp III were better than those at the Base Camp. It may suggest a lower degree of civilisation that men should be seated on the ground at boxes for eating rather than on boxes at a table. On the contrary, the nice adjustment of a full plate upon one's lap, or the finer art of conveying and forking in the mouthfuls which start so much further from the face, requires a delicacy, if it is to be accomplished at all, which continually restrains the grosser impulses. And, though it might be supposed that as we went higher up the mountain we should come to feeding entirely *sans façon*, it was my experience that the greater difficulties at the higher altitudes in satisfying the appetite continually promoted more civilised habits of feeding. To outward appearance, perhaps, the sight of four men each with a spoon eating out of a common saucepan of spaghetti would not be altogether reassuring. But one must not leave out of the reckoning the gourmet's peculiar enjoyment in the steamy aroma from things cooked and eaten before any wanton hand has served them on a dish, still less the finer politeness required by several persons sharing the same pots in this manner.

On the whole, therefore, we suffered, either morally, æsthetically, or physically, little enough in the matter of meals; still less from any other cause. The bitter wind, it is true, was constantly disagreeable. But such wind deadens even the senses that dislike it, and the wind of Tibet was admirable both as an excuse for and necessary contrast with luxurious practices. Just as one most enjoys a fire when half aware of unpleasant things outside, or is most disgusted by a stuffy room after breathing the soft air of a South-west wind, so in Tibet one may delight merely in being warm anywhere. Neatly to avoid the disagreeable is in itself a keen pleasure and heightens the desire for active life. It was only rarely, very rarely, that one suffered of necessity, and generally, if a man were cold, he was himself to blame; either he had failed to put on clothes enough for the occasion, or had failed, having put them on, to stimulate circulation. In a sleeping-bag such as we had this year, with soft flannel lining the quilted eiderdown, one need not be chilled even by the coldest night; and to lie in a tent no bigger than will just hold two persons, with 20° of frost inside and 40° without, snugly defying cold and wind, to experience at once in this situation the keen bite of the air and the warm glow in one's extremities, gives a delicious sensation of well-being and true comfort never to be so acutely provoked even in the armchair at an English fireside.

But to return to the subject from which I have naughtily digressed, time passed swiftly enough for Somervell and me at Camp III. We did not keep the ball rolling so rapidly and continuously to and fro as it was wont to roll in the united Mess; but we found plenty to say to one another, more particularly after supper, in the tent. We entered upon a serious discussion of our future prospects on Mount Everest, and were both feeling so brave and hardy after a day's rest that we decided, if necessary, to meet the transport difficulty half-way and do without a tent in any camp we should establish above the North Col, and so reduce the burden to be carried up to Camp IV to three rather light or two rather heavy loads. Our conversation was further stimulated by two little volumes which I had brought up with me, the one Robert Bridges' anthology, *The Spirit of Man*, and the other one-seventh of the complete works of William Shakespeare, including *Hamlet* and *King Lear*. It was interesting to test the choice made in answer to the old question, "What book would you take to a desert island?" though in this case it was a desert glacier, and the situation demanded rather lighter literature than prolonged edification might require on the island. The trouble about lighter literature is that it weighs heavier because more has to be provided. Neither of my books would be to every one's taste in a camp at 21,000 feet; but *The Spirit of Man* read aloud now by one of us and now by the other, suggested matters undreamt of in the philosophy of Mount Everest, and enabled us to spend one evening very agreeably. On another occasion I had the good fortune to open my Shakespeare at the very place where Hamlet addresses the ghost. "Angels and

Ministers of Grace defend us," I began, and the theme was so congenial that we stumbled on enthusiastically reading the parts in turn through half the play.

Besides reading and talking, we found a number of things to do. The ordering of even so small a camp as this may occupy a good deal of attention. Stores will have to be checked and arranged in some way so as to be easily found when wanted. One article or another is sure to be missing, too often to be retrieved when it lies on the stones only after prolonged search, and even to find a strayed stocking groped for on hands and knees in the congested tent may take a considerable time. Again, the difficult and important problem of meals will have to be considered in connection with the use of available food supplies. We have one ox tongue. Shall we open it to-day, or ought we to keep it to take up with us ? And so on. But with a number of details to be arranged, I was impressed not so much by the amount of energy and attention which they demanded as by the time taken to do any little thing—and most of all to write. Undoubtedly one is slower in every activity, and in none so remarkably slower as in writing. The greater part of a morning might easily be consumed in writing one letter of perhaps half a dozen pages.

In referring to my own slowness, particularly mental slowness, I must hasten to exclude my companion. His most important activity when we were not on the mountain was sketching. His vast supply of energy, the number of sketches he produced, and oil-paintings besides, was only less remarkable than the rapidity with which he worked. On May 14 he again walked over the uncrevassed snowfield by himself to the Rapiu La. Later on I joined him, and, so far as I could judge, his talent and energy were no less at 21,000 feet than on the wind-swept plains of Tibet.

VI

On May 16 Somervell and I spent the morning in camp with some hopes of welcoming sooner or later the arrival of stores, and sure enough about midday the first detachment of a large convoy reached our camp. With the porters, somewhat to our surprise, were Strutt, Morshead, and Norton. The whole party seemed rather tired, though not more than was to be expected, and when a little later Crawford, the responsible transport officer, came in, he told us he had been mountain-sick. We were delighted to learn that General Bruce was now much happier about transport —hence these reinforcements; twenty-two Tibetan coolies were now working up to Camp I, more were expected, and the prospects were definitely brighter. A start had even been made, in spite of Finch's continued sickness, with moving up the oxygen cylinders. We at once proceeded to discuss with Crawford how many porters could remain with us at Camp III. Taking into consideration the oxygen loads, he suggested a number below the hopes I had begun to entertain. It was agreed that eight could be spared without interfering with the work lower down. We had two before, so we should now have ten in all.

It was clear that all must carry up loads to Camp IV with the least delay in reason. But in view of the tremendous efforts that would be required of these men at a later stage, it was a necessary act of precautionary wisdom to grant the porters a day's rest on the 16th; and in any case an extra day was advisable for the acclimatisation of us all before sleeping at 23,000 feet. Meanwhile we should be able to formulate exact plans for climbing the mountain. It had hitherto been assumed that the first attempt should be made only by Somervell and me, and General Bruce had not cancelled our orders; but he had now delegated his authority to Strutt, as second-in-command, to decide on the spot what had best be done. The first point, therefore, to be settled was the number of climbers composing the party of attack. Strutt himself took the modest rôle of assuming that he would not be equal to a considerable advance above Camp IV, but saw no reason why the other four of us (Crawford returned on the 15th to a lower camp) should be too many for one party provided our organisation sufficed. Norton and Morshead were evidently most anxious to come on, and for my part I had always held, and still held, the view that four climbers were a sounder party than two for this sort of mountaineering, and would have a better chance of success. It remained to determine what could be done for a party of four by the available porters. To carry the whole of what we should need up to Camp IV in one journey was clearly impossible. But we reckoned that twenty loads should be enough to provide for ourselves and for nine porters, who would have to sleep there and carry up another camp. The delay in making two journeys to the North Col was not too great; the one sacrifice involved by this plan was a second camp above the North Col. In my judgment, the chances of establishing such a camp, even for two climbers, with so small a number as ten porters, without reckoning further loss of time, would be small in any case. We were necessarily doubtful as to how much might be expected of our porters before the North Ridge had been explored, and before we had any evidence to show that these men were capable of much more than other porters had accomplished before. It was right, therefore, for the advantages of the stronger party, to sacrifice so uncertain a prospect. Nevertheless, we realised the terrible handicap in this limitation.

I shall perhaps appear as affirming or repeating what is merely commonplace if I venture to make some observations about the weather, but I must here insist upon its importance to mountaineers; and though I cannot remember that the subject was much discussed among us at Camp III, it remained but a little way below the surface of consciousness. In settled weather among mountains one has not a great deal to observe. The changing colours at sunrise and sunset follow an expected sequence, the white flocks of fleecy clouds form and drift upwards, or the midday haze gathers about the peaks, leaving the climber unperturbed. He has sniffed the keen air before dawn when he came out under the bright stars, and his optimism is assured for the day.

On Mount Everest it had been supposed that the season preceding the monsoon would be mainly fair; but we knew that the warm moist wind should be approaching up the Arun Valley, pushing up towards us during the month of May, and we must expect to feel something of its influence. Moreover, we did not know very well how to read the signs in this country. We anxiously watched and studied them; each of us, I suppose, while he might be engaged upon one thing or another, or talking of matters infinitely and delightfully remote from Mount Everest, like a pilot had his weather-eye open. And what he saw would not all be encouraging. The drift of the upper clouds, it is true, was fairly consistent; the white wisps of smoke, as it seemed, were driven in our direction over the North Col, and occasionally the clear edge of the North Ridge would be dulled with powdery snow puffed out on the Eastern side. But looking across the snowfield from near our camp to where the head of Makalu showed over the Rapiu La, we saw strange things happening. On May 16, our day of rest, a number of us paid a visit to this pass, and as we stood above the head of the Kama Valley, the clouds boiling up from that vast and terrible cauldron were not gleaming white, but sadly grey. A glimpse down the valley showed under them the sombre blue light that forebodes mischief, and Makalu, seen through a rift, looked cold and grim. The evidence of trouble in store for us was not confined to the Kama Valley, for some clouds away to the North also excited our suspicion, and yet, as we looked up the edges of the North-east arête to its curving sickle and the great towers of the North-east shoulder, here was the dividing-line between the clear air and fair weather to the right, and the white mists to the left streaming up above the ridge and all the evil omens. The bitterest even of Tibetan winds poured violently over the pass at our backs. We wondered as we turned to meet it how long a respite was to be allowed us.

Preparation for what we intended to attempt was not to be made without some thought, or at all events I do not find such preparation a perfectly simple matter. It requires exact calculation. The first thing is to make a list—in this case a list of all we should require at Camp IV, with the approximate weights of each article. But not every article would be available to be carried up on the first of the two journeys to the North Col; for instance, we must keep our sleeping-bags for use at Camp III until we moved up ourselves. It was necessary, therefore, to mark off certain things to be left for the second journey, and to ascertain that not more than half of the whole was so reserved. It might be supposed that the problem could now be solved by adding up the weights, dividing the total by ten (the number of our porters), and giving so many pounds, according to this arithmetical answer, to each man for the first journey. In practice this cannot be done, and we have to allow for the fallibility of human lists. However carefully you have gone over in your mind and provided for every contingency, you may be quite sure you have omitted something, probably some property of the porters regarded by them as necessary to salvation, and at the last moment it will turn up. The danger is that one or two men will be seriously overloaded, and perhaps without your knowing it. To circumvent it, allowance must be made in your calculations. On this occasion we took good care to carry up more than half of what was shown on our list on the first journey. Another difficulty in the mathematical solution is the nature of the loads. They cannot be all exactly equal, because they are composed of indivisible objects. A tent cannot be treated like a vulgar fraction. The best plan, therefore, is to fix a maximum. We intended our loads to be from 25 to 30 lb. They were all weighed with a spring balance, and the upper limit was only exceeded by a pound or two in two cases, to the best of my remembrance.

On May 17 the fifteen of us, Strutt, Morshead, Norton, Somervell, and I, with ten porters, set off for Camp IV. The snow was in good condition, we had our old tracks to tread in, and the only mishap to be feared was the possible exhaustion of one or more porters. It was necessary that all the loads should reach their destination to-day; but the five climbers were comparatively unladen, and constituted a reserve of power. My recollections of going up to the North Col are all of a performance rather wearisome and dazed, of a mind incapable of acute perceptions faintly stirring the drowsy senses to take notice within a circle of limited radius. The heat and glare of the morning sun as it blazed on the windless long slopes emphasised the monotony. I was dimly aware of this puzzling question of light-rays and the harm they might do. I was glad I wore two felt hats, and that Strutt and Somervell had their solar topis. Morshead and Norton had no special protection, and the porters none at all. What did it matter ? Seemingly nothing. We plodded on and slowly upwards ; each of us was content to go as slowly as anyone else might wish to go. The porters were more silent than usual. They were strung up to the effort required of them. No one was going to give in. The end was certain. At length our success was duly epitomised. As he struggled up the final slope, Strutt broke into gasping speech : "I wish that—cinema were here. If I look anything like what I feel, I ought to be immortalised for the British public." We looked at his grease-smeared, yellow-ashen face, and the reply was: "Well, what in Heaven's name *do* we look like ? And what do we do it for, anyway ? "

At all events, we had some reason to feel hopeful on our subsequent day's rest, May 18. Somervell more particularly pronounced that his second journey to Camp IV had been much less fatiguing than the first. I was able to say the same, though I felt that a sufficient reason was to be found in the fact that far less labour had been required of me. It was more remarkable, perhaps, that those who went for the first time to 23,000 feet, and especially the laden men, should have shown so much endurance.

On May 19 we carried up the remainder of our loads. And again we seemed better acclimatised. The ascent to the North Col was generally felt to be easier on this day ; we had strength to spare when we reached the shelf. With all our loads now gathered about us at Camp IV, the first stage up from the base of the mountain was accomplished. To-morrow, we hoped, would complete the second. The five light tents were gradually pitched, two of them destined for the climbers a few yards apart towards the North Peak, the remaining three to accommodate each three porters in the same alignment ; in all, a neat little row showing green against the white. The even surface of the snow was further disturbed by the muddled tracks, soon to be a trampled space about the tent-doors. For the safety of sleep-walkers, or any other who might feel disposed to take a walk in the night, these tent-doors faced inwards, toward the back of the shelf. There the gigantic blocks of ice were darker than the snow on which their deep shadow was thrown. Their cleft surfaces suggested cold colours, and were green and blue as the ocean is on some winter's day of swelling seas—a strange impressive rampart impregnable against direct assault, and equally well placed to be the final defence of the North Col on this section, and at the same time to protect us amazingly, entirely, against the unfriendly wind from the West.

Other activities besides demanded our attention. It had been resolved that one more rope should be fixed on the steep slope we must follow to circumvent the ice-cliffs. Morshead and Somervell volunteered for this good work ; Norton and I were left to tend the cooking-pots. As we had not burdened the porters with a large supply of water, we had now to make provision both for this evening and for to-morrow morning. The Primus stoves remained at Camp III, partly because they were heavy and partly because, however carefully devised, their performance at a high altitude must always be a little uncertain. They had served us well up to 21,000 feet, and we had no need to trust them further. With our aluminium cooking sets we could use either absolute alcohol in the spirit-burner or "Meta," a French sort of solidified spirit, especially prepared in cylindrical shape and extremely efficient; you have only to put a match to the dry white cylinders and they burn without any trouble, and smokelessly, even at 23,000 feet, for not less than forty minutes. The supply of "Meta" was not very large, and it was considered rather as an emergency fuel. The alcohol was to do most of our heating at Camp IV, and all too rapidly it seemed to burn away as we kept filling and refilling our pots with snow. In the end six large thermos flasks were filled with tea or water for the use of all in the morning, and we had enough for our present needs besides.

Morshead and Somervell had not long returned, after duly fixing the rope, before our meal was ready. As I have already referred to our table manners, the more delicate-minded among my readers may not relish the spectacle of us four feasting around our cooking-pots—in which case I caution them to omit this paragraph, for now, living up to my own standard of faithful narrative, I must honestly and courageously face the subject of victuals. As mankind is agreed that the pleasures of the senses, when it is impossible they should be actually experienced, can most nearly be tasted by exercising an artistic faculty in choosing the dishes of imaginary repasts, so it might be supposed that the state of affairs, when those pleasures were thousands of feet below in other worlds, might more easily be brought to mind by reconstructing the associated menus. But such a practice was unfortunately out of the question, for it would have involved assigning this, that, and the other to breakfast, lunch, and supper; and when, calling to mind what we ate, I try to distinguish between one meal and another, I am altogether at a loss. I can only suppose they were interchangeable. The nature of our supplies confirms my belief that this was the case. Practically speaking, we hardly considered by which name our meal should be called, but only what would seem nice to eat or convenient to produce, when we next wanted food and drink. Among the supplies I classify some as "standard pattern"—such things as we knew were always to be had in abundance, the "pièce," as it were, of our whole ménage—three solid foods, two liquid foods, and one stimulant.

The stimulant, in the first place, as long as we remained at Camp III, was amazingly satisfactory, both for its kind, its quality, and especially for its abundance. We took it shamelessly before breakfast, and at breakfast again; occasionally with or after lunch, and most usually a little time before supper, when it was known as afternoon tea. The longer we stayed at this camp, the deeper were our potations. So good was the tea that I came almost to disregard the objectionable flavour of tinned milk in it. I had always supposed that General Bruce would keep a special herd of yaks at the Base Camp for the provision of fresh milk ; but this scheme was hardly practicable, for the only grass at the Base Camp, grew under canvas, and no one suggested sharing his tent with a yak. The one trouble about our stimulant was its scarcity as we proceeded up the mountain. It diminished instead of increasing to the climax where it was needed most. Fortunately, the lower temperatures at which water boils as the atmospheric pressure diminishes made no appreciable difference to the quality, and the difficulty of melting snow enough to fill our saucepans with water was set off to some extent by increasing the quantity of tea-leaves.

The two liquid foods, cocoa and pea-soup, though not imbibed so plentifully as tea, were considered no less as the natural and fitting companions of meat on any and every occasion. At Camp III it was not unusual to begin supper with pea-soup and end it with cocoa, but such a custom by no means precluded their use at other times. Cocoa tended to fall in my esteem, though it never lost a certain popularity. Pea-soup, on the other hand, had a growing reputation, and, from being considered an accessory, came to be regarded as a principal. However, before I describe its dominating influence in the whole matter of diet, I must mention the solid foods. The three of "standard pattern" were ration biscuits, ham, and cheese. It was no misfortune to find above the Base Camp that we had left the region of fancy breads; for while the chupatis and scones, baked by our cooks with such surprising skill and energy, were usually palatable, they were probably more difficult of digestion than the biscuits, and our appetite for these hard whole-meal biscuits increased as we went upwards, possibly to the detriment of teeth, which became ever more brittle. Ham, of all foods, was the most generally acceptable. The quality of our "Hunter's hams" left nothing to be desired, and the supply, apparently, was inexhaustible. A slice of ham, or several slices, either cold or fried, was fit food for any and almost every meal. The cheese supplied for our use at these higher camps, and for expeditions on the mountains besides, were always delicious and freely eaten. We had also a considerable variety of other tinned foods. Harris's sausages, sardines, herrings, sliced bacon, soups, ox tongues, green vegetables, both peas and beans, all these I remember in general use at Camp III. We were never short of jam and chocolate. As luxuries we had "quails in truffles," besides various sweet-stuffs, such as mixed biscuits, acid drops, crystallized ginger, figs and prunes (I feel greedy again as I name them), and, reserved more or less for use at the highest camps, Heinz's spaghetti. More important, perhaps, than any of these was "Army and Navy Rations," from the special use we made of it. I never quite made out what these tins contained; they were designed to be, when heated up, a rich stew of mutton or beef, or both. They were used by us to enrich a stew which was the peculiar invention of Morshead. He called it "hoosch." Like a trained chef, he was well aware that "the foundation of good cooking is the stock-pot." But such a maxim was decidedly depressing under our circumstances. Instead of accepting and regretting our want of a "stock-pot," Morshead, with the true genius that penetrates to the inward truth, devised a substitute and improved the motto: "The foundation of every dish must be pea-soup." Or if these were not his very words, it was easy to deduce that they contained the substance of his culinary thoughts. It was a corollary of this axiom that any and every available solid food might be used to stew with pea-soup. The process of selection tended to emphasise the merits of some as compared with other solids until it became almost a custom, sadly to the limitation of Morshead's art, to prefer to "sliced bacon," or even sausages, for the flotsam and jetsam of "hoosch," Army and Navy Rations. It was "hoosch" that we ate at Camp IV, about the hour of an early afternoon tea on May 19.

We had hardly finished eating and washing up—it was a point of honour to wash up, and much may be achieved with snow—when the shadow crept over our tents and the chill of evening was upon us. We lingered a little after everything was set in order to look out over the still sunlit slopes of Mount Everest between us and the Rapiu La, and over the undulating basin of snow towards the Lhakpa La and Camp IV, and to pass some cheerful remarks with the porters, already seeking shelter, before turning in ourselves for the night. It had been, so far as we could tell, a singularly windless day. Such clouds as we had observed were seemingly innocent; and now, as darkness deepened, it was a fine night. The flaps of our two tents were still reefed back so as to admit a free supply of air, poor and thin in quality but still recognisable as fresh air; Norton and I and, I believe, Morshead and Somervell also lay with our heads towards the door, and, peering out from the mouths of our eiderdown bags, could see the crest above us sharply defined. The signs were favourable. We had the best omen a mountaineer can look for, the palpitating fire, to use Mr. Santayana's words, of many stars in a black sky. I wonder what the others were thinking of between the intervals of light slumber. I daresay none of us troubled to inform himself that this was the vigil of our great adventure, but I remember how my mind kept wandering over the various details of our preparations without anxiety, rather like God after the Creation seeing that it was good. It was good. And the best of it was what we expected to be doing these next two days. As the mind swung in its dreamy circle it kept passing and repassing the highest point, always passing through the details to their intention. The prospects emerging from this mental movement, unwilled and intermittent and yet continually charged with fresh momentum, were wonderfully, surprisingly bright, already better than I had dared to expect. Here were the four of us fit and happy, to all appearances as we should expect to be in a snug alpine hut after a proper nightcap of whisky punch.

We had confidence in our porters, nine strong men willing and even keen to do whatever should be asked of them; surely these men were fit for anything. And we planned to lighten their burdens as far as possible; only four loads, beyond the warm things which each of us would carry for himself, were to go on to our next camp—two tents weighing each 15 lb., two double sleeping-bags, and provisions for a day and a half besides the minimum of feeding utensils. The loads would not exceed 20 lb. each, and we should have two men to one load, and even so a man in reserve. To provide a considerable excess of porters had for long been a favourite scheme of mine. I saw no other way of making sure that all the loads would reach their destination. As it was, we should start with the knowledge that so soon as any man at any moment felt the strain too great he could be relieved of his load, and when he in his turn required to be relieved the other would presumably be ready to take up his load again. Proceeding in this way we should be free of all anxiety lest one of the loads should be left on the mountain-side or else put on to a climber's back, with the chance of impairing his strength for the final assault. *Ceteris paribus*, we were going to succeed at least in establishing another camp. This was no mere hope wherein judgment was sacrificed to promote the lesser courage of optimism, but a reasonable conviction. It remained but to ask, Would the Fates be kind?

CHAPTER VI

THE HIGHEST POINT

My first recollection of the morning of May 20 is of shivering outside the porters' tents. It is not an enviable task at 23,000 feet, this of rousing men from the snugness of their sleeping-bags between 5 and 6 a.m. One may listen in vain for a note of alertness in their response; the heard notes will not echo the smallest zest for any enterprise. On this occasion the replies made to my tender inquiries and encouragements were so profoundly disappointing that I decided to untie the fastenings of the tent, which were as nearly as might be hermetically sealed. In the degree of somnolence and inertia prevailing I suspected the abnormal. Soon I began to make out a tale of confused complaints; the porters were not all well. The cause was not far to look for; they had starved themselves of air during the night. The best chance of a remedy was fresh air now and a brew of tea, which could easily be managed.

Meanwhile Norton had been stirring, and while I retired to "dress" he began to busy himself with preparations for our own breakfast. Tea of course was intended for us too, and further two tins of spaghetti had been reserved to give us the best possible start for the day. But one small thing had been forgotten. Those precious tins had lain all night in the snow; they should have been cuddled by human bodies, carefully nursed in the warmth of sleeping-bags. Now their contents were frozen stiff and beyond extraction even by an ice-axe. Even so it might be supposed a little boiling water would put all to rights. Had a little sufficed I should omit to tell the doleful tale. Only very gradually were the outer surfaces thawed, permitting the scarlet blocks (tomato sauce was an ingredient) to be transferred to another saucepan, where they had still to be thawed to homogeneous softness and afterwards heated to the point required for doing justice to the genius of Mr. Heinz. As the expenditure of treasured hot water merely for thawing spaghetti involved more melting of snow to water and boiling of water for indispensable tea, the kitchen-maid's task was disagreeably protracted; and the one among us, Norton, who most continuously and stubbornly played the man's part of kitchen-maid, sitting upon the snow in the chill early morning became a great deal colder than anyone should be with a day's mountaineering in front of him.

Of our nine porters it was presently discovered that five were mountain-sick in various degrees; only four were fit to come on and do a full day's work carrying up our camp. The whole of our reserve was already exhausted before we had advanced a single step up the North Ridge.

But pessimism was not in the air this morning. We had won through our various delays and difficulties, we had eaten and enjoyed our wonderful breakfast, and after all we were able to make a start about 7.30 a.m. The reserve had already been of use; without it we should have been obliged to remain in camp, waiting for sick porters to recover, and counting our stores. Morshead, who by the testimony of good spirits seemed the fittest of us all, was set to lead the party; I followed with two porters, while Norton and Somervell shepherded the others on a separate rope. In a short half-hour we were on the North Col itself, the true white neck to the South of those strange blocks of ice, and looking up the North Ridge from its foot.

The general nature of what lay ahead of us can readily be appreciated from this point of view. To the right, as you look up, the great Northern slopes of Mount Everest above the main Rongbuk Glacier are slightly concave; the North-eastern facet to the left is also concave, but much more deeply, and especially more deeply in a section of about 1,500 feet above the North Col. Consequently the ground falls away more suddenly on that side below the ridge. The climber may either follow the crest itself or find a parallel way on the gently receding face to right of it. The best way for us, we soon saw, was not to follow the crest of snow or even the snow-slopes immediately to the right; for these were merged after a little interval in the vast sweep of broken rocks forming the North face of the mountain, and at the junction between snow and rocks was an edge of stones stretching upwards for perhaps 1,500 feet at a convenient angle. Loose stones that slip as he treads on them are an abomination to the climber's feet and only less fatiguing than knee-deep sticky snow. We presently found those stones agreeably secure; enough snow lay among them to bind and freeze all to the slope; we were able to tread on firm, flat surfaces without the trouble of kicking our feet into snow; no sort of ground could have taken us more easily up the mountain. The morning, too, was calm and fine. Though it can hardly be said that we enjoyed the exercise of going up Mount Everest, we were certainly able to enjoy the sensation so long as our progress was satisfactory. But the air remained perceptibly colder than we could have wished; the sun had less than its usual power; and in the breeze which sprang up on our side, blowing across the ridge from the right, we recognized an enemy, "the old wind in the old anger," the devastating wind of Tibet. The wolf had come in lamb's clothes. But we were not deceived. Remembering bitter experiences down in the plains now 10,000 feet below us, we expected little mercy here, we only hoped for a period of respite; so long as this gentle mood should last we could proceed happily enough until we should be obliged to fight our way up.

We had risen about 1,200 feet when we stopped to put on the spare warm clothes which we carried against such a contingency as this. For my part, I added a light shetland "woolly" and a thin silk shirt to what I was wearing before under my closely woven cotton coat. As this outer garment, with knickers to match, was practically windproof, and a silk shirt too is a further protection against wind, with these two extra layers I feared no cold we were likely to meet. Morshead, if I remember right, troubled himself no more at this time than to wrap a woollen scarf round his neck, and he and I were ready and impatient to get off before the rest. Norton was sitting a little way below with his rucksack poised on his lap. In gathering up our rope so as to have it free when we should move on I must have communicated to the other rope some small jerk—sufficient, at all events, to upset the balance of Norton's rucksack. He was unprepared, made a desperate grab, and missed it. Slowly the round, soft thing gathered momentum from its rotation, the first little leaps down from one ledge to another grew to excited and magnificent bounds, and the precious burden vanished from sight. For a little interval, while we still imagined its fearful progress until it should rest for who knows how long on the snow at the head of the Rongbuk Glacier, no one spoke. "My rucksack gone down the kudh!" Norton exclaimed with simple regret. I made a mental note that my warm pyjama-legs which he had borrowed were inside it, so if I were to blame I had a share in the loss. A number of offers in woollen garments for the night were soon made to Norton; after which we began to explain what each had brought for comfort's sake, and I wondered whether my companions' system of selection resembled mine;—as I never can resolve in cold blood to leave anything behind, when each article presents itself as just the one I may particularly want, I pack them all into a rucksack and then pull out this and that more or less at random until the load is not greater than I can conveniently carry; even so I almost invariably find that I have more clothing in reserve than I actually use.

However, we had no time to spare for discussing the dispensation of absolute justice between the various claims of affection and utility among a man's equipment. We were soon plodding upwards again, and had we been inclined to tarry the bite of the keen air would have hurried us along. The respite granted us was short enough. The sun disappeared behind a veil of high clouds; and before long grey tones to match the sky replaced the varied brightness of snow and rocks, and soon now we were struggling to keep our breath and leaning our bodies against a heavy wind. We had not the experience to reckon exactly the dangers associated with these conditions. We could only look to our senses for warning, and their warning soon became obvious enough. Finger-tips and toes and ears all began to testify to the cold. By continuing on the windward flank of the ridge just where we were most exposed we should incur a heavy risk of frostbite and the whole party might be put out of action. It was clear that something must be done, and without delay. The best chance was to change our direction. Very likely we should find less wind, as is often the case, on the crest itself, and in any case we must reach shelter on the leeward side at the earliest possible moment.

While Morshead stopped, at last submitting so far as to put on a sledging suit, which is reputed to be the best possible protection, I went ahead, abandoned the rocks, and steered a slanting course over the snow to the left. Unlike the softer substance we had met in the region of the North Col, the surface here was hard; on this smooth slope the blown snow can find no lodgment, cannot stay to be gathered into drifts, and the little that falls there is swept clean away. The angle soon became steeper, and we must have steps to tread in. A strong kick was required to make the smallest impression in the snow. It was just the place where we could best be served by crampons and be helped up by their long steel points without troubling ourselves at all about steps. Crampons of course had been provided among our equipment, and the question of taking them with us above Camp IV had been considered. We had decided not to bring them: we sorely needed them now. And yet we had been right to leave them behind; for with their straps binding tightly round our boots we should not have had the smallest chance of preserving our toes from frostbite. The only way was to set to work and cut steps. The proper manner of cutting one in such a substance as this is to take but one strong blow, tearing out enough snow to allow the foot to finish the work as it treads in the hole. Such a practice is not beyond the strength and skill of an amateur in the Alps. But even if he can muster the power for this sort of blow at a great altitude, he will soon discover the inconvenience of repeating it frequently; he will be out of breath and panting and obliged to wait, so that no time has been gained after all. The alternative is to apply less force; three gentle strokes, as a rule, will be required for each step. To cut a staircase in this humble manner was by no means impossible, as was proved again on the descent, up to 25,000 feet. But the same rules and limitations determine this labour as every other up here. The work can be done and the worker will endure it provided sufficient time is allowed. It is haste that induces exhaustion. On this occasion we were obliged to hurry; our object was to reach shelter as soon as possible. In a wind like that on a bare snow-slope a man must take his axe in both hands to meet the present need; future contingencies will be left to take care of themselves. The slope was never steep; the substance was not obdurate; but when at length we lay on the rocks and out of the wind I computed our staircase to be 300 feet, and at least one of us was very tired.

I cannot say precisely how much time passed on this arduous section of our ascent. It was now 11.30 a.m. The aneroid was showing 25,000 feet compared with a reading of 23,000 on the North Col; the rise of 2,000 feet had taken us in all 3½ hours. For some reason Morshead had been delayed with two or three of the porters, and as the rest of us now sat waiting for them we began to discuss what should be done about fixing our camp. It had been our intention to reach 26,000 feet before pitching the tents. But it was evident that very few places would accommodate them. We had already seen enough to realise how steeply the rocks of this mountain dip towards the North, with the consequence that even where the ground is broken the ledges are likely to prove too steep for camping. We must pass the night somewhere on this leeward side, and we had little hopes of finding a place above us. However, at about our present level, well marked as the point of junction between snow and rocks, we had previously observed from Camp III some ground which appeared less uncompromising than the rest. A broken ledge offered a practicable line towards this same locality.

Whether the decision we came to at this crisis of our fortunes were right or wrong, I cannot tell, and I hardly want to know. I have no wish to excuse our judgment. Who can tell what might have happened had we decided otherwise? And who can judge? Then why should I be at the pains to analyse the thoughts which influenced our decision? It is perhaps a futile inquiry. Nevertheless it is such decisions that determine the fate of a mountaineering enterprise, and the operative motives or contending points of view may have an interest of their own. Among us there was deliberation often enough, but never contention. There never was a dissentient voice to anything we resolved to do, partly, I suppose, because we had little choice in the matter, more because we were that sort of party. We had a single aim in common and regarded it from common ground. We had no leader within the full meaning of the word, no one in authority over the rest to command as captain. We all knew equally what was required to be done from first to last, and when the occasion arose for doing it one of us did it. Some one, if only to avoid delay in action, had to arrange the order in which the party or parties should proceed. I took this responsibility without waiting to be asked; the rest accepted my initiative, I suppose, because I used to talk so much about what had been done on the previous Expedition. In practice it amounted only to this, that I would say to my companions, "A, will you go first? B, will you go second?" and we roped up in the order indicated without palaver. Apart from this I never attempted to inflict my own view on men who were at least as capable as I of judging what was best. Our proceedings in any crisis of our fortunes were informally democratic. They were so on the occasion from which I have so grievously digressed.

It must not be forgotten that we had just come through a trying ordeal. Nothing is more demoralising than a severe wind, and it may be that our *morale* was affected.

But I don't think we were demoralised, or not in any degree so as to affect our judgment. The impression I retain from that remote scene where we sat porched in discussion crowding under a bluff of rocks is of a party well pleased with their performance, rejoicing to be sheltered from the wind, and every one of them quite game to go higher. Perhaps the deciding influence was the weather. A mountaineer judges of the weather conditions almost by instinct; and apart from our experience of the wind, which had already been sufficiently menacing, we knew, so far as such things can be known, that the weather would get worse before it got better. But we could not imagine what might be coming without thinking definitely about the porters. It would be their lot, wherever our new camp was fixed, to return this same day to Camp IV. It was no part of our design to risk even the extremities of their limbs, let alone their lives; apart from any consideration of ethics it would not be sensible; no one supposed that this attempt on Mount Everest would be the last of the season, even for ourselves, and if the porters who first completed this stage were to suffer nothing worse than severe frostbite the moral effect of that injury alone might be an irreparable disaster. The porters must be sent down before the weather grew worse, and the less they were exposed to the cold wind the better. It was 12.30 p.m. before the stragglers who had joined us had rested sufficiently to go on. To fix a camp 1,000 feet higher would probably require, granted reasonably good fortune in finding a site, another three hours; and if snow began to fall or the ridge were enveloped in mist it would be necessary to provide an escort for the porters. Had we supposed a place might be found anywhere above us within range on this lee-side of the ridge, we might conceivably have accepted these hard conditions and pushed on. Deliberately to choose a site on the ridge with such a wind blowing and in defiance of every threat in the sky was a folly not to be contemplated, and our suppositions as to the lee side above us (they were afterwards proved correct) were all unfavourable to going higher. The plan of encamping somewhere near at hand, not lower than 25,000 feet, still left plenty to hope for this time besides building the best foundation for a second attempt. In my opinion no other alternative was sanely practicable; and I believe this conviction was shared by all when at length we left our niche, having conceded so much already to the mountain.

As the broken ledges we now followed presented no special difficulties the party was able to explore more than one level in search of some place sufficiently flat and sufficiently commodious. The nature of the ground and the presence of cloud, though we were never thickly enveloped, prevented any sort of extensive view. Many suggestions were mooted and rejected; a considerable time elapsed and still we had found no site that would serve. At about 2 p.m. Somervell and some porters shouted the news that one tent could be pitched in the place where they were. On the far side of a defined rib slanting up to the ridge we had left they had discovered some sort of a platform. It was evident that work would be required to extend and prepare it for the tent, and they at once set about building a supporting wall and levelling the ground. It remained to find a place near at hand for the other tent. We could see no obvious shelf, but the constructional works undertaken by Somervell seemed to contain such a promising idea that Norton and I in separate places each started works of our own. Each of us very soon reached the same conclusion, that nothing could be done where he was. We moved away and tried again; but always with the same result; the ground was everywhere too steep and too insecure. One soon tires of heaving up big stones when no useful end is served. Eventually coming together, we resolved to agree on the least unlikely site and make the best of it. We chose the foot of a long sloping slab—at all events it was part of the mountain and would not budge—and there built up the ground below it with some fine stones we found to hand. Our tent was pitched at last with one side of the floor lying along the foot of the sloping slab and the other half on the platform we had made. It was not a situation that promised for either of us a bountiful repose, for one would be obliged to lie along the slope and the only check to his tendency to slip down would be the body of the other. However, there it was, a little tent making a gallant effort to hold itself proudly and well.

Before we had concluded these operations the porters had been sent down about 3 p.m. and kitchen had been instituted, and a meal was already being prepared. Presumably because their single tent would have to accommodate the four of us (ours was too far away), when we set ourselves down to eat and be warm, Somervell and Morshead had arranged the kitchen outside it. Somervell had appointed himself chief in this department and it remained only for the rest of us to offer menial service. But so great had been his energy and perseverance, sheltering the flame from the cold draught and by every device encouraging the snow to melt, that almost all such offers were rejected. Like a famous pretender, I would have gladly been a scullion, but I was allowed only to open one or two tins and fill up a pot with snow. I have no recollection of what we ate; I remember only a hot and stimulating drink, Brand's essence or bovril or something of the sort. We did not linger long over this meal. We wanted to go to bed still warm. Norton and I soon left the others in possession of their tent and began to make our dispositions for the night.

To the civilised man who gets into bed after the customary routine, tucks himself in, lays his head on the pillow, and presently goes to sleep with no further worry, the dispositions in a climber's tent may seem to be strangely intricate. In the first place, he has to arrange about his boots. He looks forward to the time when he will have to start next morning, if possible with warm feet and in boots not altogether frozen stiff. He may choose to go to bed in his boots, not altogether approving the practice, and resolving that the habit shall not be allowed to grow upon him. If his feet are already warm when he turns in, it may be that he can do no better; his feet will probably keep warm in the sleeping-bag if he wears his bed-socks over his boots, and he will not have to endure the pains of pulling on and wearing frozen boots in the morning. At this camp I adopted a different plan—to wear moccasins instead of boots during the night and keep them on until the last moment before starting. But if one takes his boots off, where is he to keep them warm? Climbing boots are not good to cuddle, and in any case there will be no room for them with two now inside a double sleeping-bag. My boots were happily accommodated in a rucksack and I put them under my head for a pillow. It is not often that one uses the head for warming things, and no one would suspect one of a hot head; nevertheless my boots were kept warm enough and were scarcely frozen in the morning.

It was all-important besides to make ourselves really comfortable, if we were to get to sleep, by making experiments in the disposition of limbs, adjusting the floor if possible and arranging one's pillow at exactly the right level—which may be difficult, as the pillow should be high if one is to breathe easily at a great altitude. I had already found out exactly how to be comfortable before Norton was ready to share the accommodation. I remarked that in our double sleeping-bag I found ample room for myself but not much to spare. Norton's entrance was a grievous disturbance. It was doubtful for some time whether he would be able to enter; considering how long and slim he is, it is astonishing how much room he requires. We were so tightly pressed together that if either was to move a corresponding manœuvre was required of the other. I soon discovered, as the chief item of interest in the place where I lay, a certain boulder obstinately immovable and excruciatingly sharp which came up between my shoulder-blades. How under these circumstances we achieved sleep, and I believe that both of us were sometimes unconscious in a sort of light, intermittent slumber, I cannot attempt to explain. Perhaps the fact that one was often breathless from the exhaustion of discomfort, and was obliged to breathe deeply, helped one to sleep, as deep breathing often will. Perhaps the necessity of lying still because it was so difficult to move was good for us in the end. Norton's case was worse than mine. One of his ears had been severely frostbitten on the way up; only one side was available to lie on; and yet the blessed sleep we sometimes sigh for in easy beds at home visited him too.

The party had suffered more than at first we realized from exposure in the wind on the way up. The damage to Norton's ear was not all. I noticed when my hands got warm in bed that three finger-tips appeared to be badly bruised; the symptom could only point to one conclusion, and I soon made out how they had come to be frost-bitten. At the time when the step-cutting began I had been wearing a pair of lined leather gloves, motor-drivers' gloves well suited to the occasion, and my hands had been so warm that I thought it safe to change the glove on my right hand for a woollen one with which it was easier to grasp the axe. But wool is not a good protection against wind, and in grasping the axe I must have partially stopped the circulation in these finger-tips. The injury, though not serious, was inconvenient. And Morshead had felt the cold far more than I. It is still uncertain whether he had yet been frostbitten in toes and fingers, but though he made no complaint about them until much later I have little doubt they were already touched, if not severely frozen. At all events, he had been badly chilled on the way up; he was obliged to lie down when we reached our camp and was evidently unwell.

When all is said about our troubles and difficulties, the night, in spite of everything, was endurable. For distraction to pass the sleepless intervals engaging thoughts were not far to seek; we had still our plans for to-morrow; the climax was to come; and, might we not get so high by such a time? Then, might not the remaining hours be almost, even quite enough? Besides, we had accomplished something, and though the moments following achievement are occupied more often in looking forward than in looking back, we perhaps deliberately encouraged in ourselves a certain complacency on the present occasion; we were able to feel some little satisfaction in the mere existence of this camp, the two small tents perched there on the vast mountain-side of snow-bound rocks and actually higher, at 25,000 feet, than any climbing party had been before. "Hang it all!" we cooed, "it's not so bad."

The worst of it in dimly conscious moments was still the weather. The wind had dropped in the evening, as it often does, and nothing was to be deduced from that; but the hovering clouds had not cleared off and the night was too warm. I'm not meaning that we complained of the warmth; but for fine weather we must have a cold night, and it was no colder here than we had often known it at Camp III.[1] Occasionally stars were visible during the night; but they shone with a feeble, watery light, and in the early morning we were listening to the musical patter of fine, granular snow on the roofs of our tents. A thick mist had come up all about us, and the stones outside were white with a growing pall of fresh snow. We were greatly surprised under these conditions when, at about 6.30 a.m., a perceptible break appeared in the clouds to the East of us, the "weather quarter," and this good sign developed so hopefully that we were soon encouraged to expect a fair day. It was even more surprising perhaps that some one among us very quickly discovered his conscience: "I suppose," he said with a

[1] The thermometer confirmed our senses and showed a minimum reading for the night of 7° F.

stifled yawn, in a tone that reminded one of Mr. Saltena rolling over in his costly bed, "it's about time we were getting up." No one dissented—how could one dissent? "I suppose we ought to be getting up," we grunted in turn, and slowly we began to draw ourselves out from the tight warmth of those friendly bags.

I do not propose to emphasise the various agonies of an early-morning start or to catalogue all that may be found for fumbling fingers to do; but one incident is worth recording. A second rucksack escaped us, slipping from the ledge where it was perched, and went bounding down the mountain. Its value, even Norton will agree, was greater than that of the first; it contained our provisions; our breakfast was inside it. From the moment of its elusion I gave it up for lost. What could stop its fatal career? What did stop it unless it were a miracle? Somehow or another it was hung up on a ledge 100 feet below. Morshead volunteered to go and get it. By slow degrees he dragged up the heavy load, and our precious stores were recovered intact.

At 8 a.m. we were ready to start and roped up, Norton first, followed by myself, Morshead and Somervell. This bald statement of fact may suggest a misleading picture; the reader may imagine the four of us like runners at the start of a race, greyhounds straining at the leash, with nerves on the stretch and muscles aching for the moment when they can be suddenly tight in strong endeavour. It was not like that. I suppose we had all the same feelings in various degrees, and even our slight exertions about the camp had shown us something of our physical state. In spite of the occasional sleep of exhaustion it had been a long, restless night, scarcely less wearisome than the preceding day; we were tired no less than when we went to bed, and stiff from lying in cramped attitudes. I was clear about my own case. Struggling across with an awkward load from one tent to the other, I had been forced to put the question, Is it possible for me to go on? Judging from physical evidence, No; I hadn't the power to lift my weight repeatedly step after step. And yet from experience I knew that I should go on for a time at all events; something would set the machinery going and somehow I should be able to keep it at work. And when the moment of starting came I felt some little stir of excitement. If we were not going to experience "the wild joy of living, the leaping from rock up to rock," on the other hand this was not to be a sort of funeral procession. A certain keenness of anticipation is associated merely with tying on the rope. We tied it on now partly for convenience, so that no one would be obliged to carry it on his back, but no less for its moral effect: a roped party is more closely united; the separate wills of individuals are joined into a stronger common will. Our roping-up was the last act of preparation. We had "got ourselves ready," lacing up our boots so as to be just tight enough but not too tight, disposing puttees so that they would not slip down, attending to one small thing or another about our clothing for warmth and comfort's sake, possibly even tightening a buckle or doing up a button simply for neatness, and not forgetting to arrange the few things we wanted to take with us, some in rucksacks, some nearer to hand in pockets. Two of us, Norton and I, as Somervell's photograph proves, appeared positively dainty; the word seems hardly applicable to Somervell himself: but at all events we were all ready; we felt ready; and when all these details of preparation culminated in tying on the rope we felt something more, derived from the many occasions in the past when readiness in mind and body contained the keen anticipation of strenuous delights.

How quickly the physical facts of our case asserted their importance! We had only moved upwards a few steps when Morshead stopped. "I think I won't come with you any farther," he said. "I know I should only keep you back." Considering his condition on the previous day I had not supposed Morshead would get very much higher; but this morning he had so made light of his troubles, and worn so cheerful a countenance, that we heard his statement now with surprise and anxiety. We understood very well the spirit of the remark; if Morshead said that, there could be no longer a question of his coming on, but we wondered whether one of us should not stay behind with him. However, he declared that he was not seriously unwell and was perfectly capable of looking after himself. Somervell's judgment as a doctor confirmed him, and it was decided he should remain in camp while we three went on without him.

Our first object was to regain the crest of the North ridge, not by retracing our steps to the point where we had left it yesterday, but slanting up to meet it perhaps 800 feet above us. Ascent is possible almost everywhere on these broken slopes; a steeper pitch can usually be avoided, and the more difficult feats of climbing need not be performed. In fact, the whole problem for the mountaineer is quite unlike that presented by the ridge of any great mountain in the Alps, which, if it is not definitely a snow ridge like that from the Dômedu Gouter to the summit of Mont Blanc, will almost invariably present a sharper edge and a more broken crest. On the North ridge of Everest one has the sensations rather of climbing the face than the ridge of a mountain; and it is best thought of as a face-climb, for one is actually on the North face, though at the edge of it. I can think of no exact parallel in the Alps—the nearest perhaps would be the easier parts on the Hornli ridge of the Matterhorn, if we were to imagine the stones to be fewer, larger and more secure. Somervell's photographs will convey more to the trained eye of a mountaineer than any words of mine, and it will readily be understood that there was no question for us of gymnastic struggles and strong arm-pulls, wedging ourselves in cracks and hanging on our finger-tips. We should soon have been turned back by difficulties of that sort. We could allow ourselves nothing

Mallory and Norton approaching their highest point, 26,985 ft.

in the nature of a violent struggle. We must avoid any hasty movement. It would have exhausted us at once to proceed by rushing up a few steps at a time. We wanted to hit off just that mean pace which we could keep up without rapidly losing our strength, to proceed evenly with balanced movements, saving effort, to keep our form, as oarsmen say, at the end of the race, remembering to step neatly and transfer the weight from one leg to the other by swinging the body rhythmically upwards. With the occasional help of the hands we were able to keep going for spells of twenty or thirty minutes before halting for three or four or five minutes to gather potential energy for pushing on again. Our whole power seemed to depend on the lungs. The air, such as it was, was inhaled through the mouth and expired again to some sort of tune in the unconscious mind, and the lungs beat time, as it were, for the feet. An effort of will was required not so much to induce any movement of the limbs as to set the lungs to work and keep them working. So long as they were working evenly and well the limbs would do their duty automatically, it seemed, as though actuated by a hidden spring. I remember one rather longer halt. In spite of all my care I found that one of my feet was painfully cold, and fearing frostbite I took off my boot. Norton rubbed my foot warm. I had been wearing four thick socks, and now put back on this foot only three. As it remained warm for the rest of the day I have no doubt that the boot was previously too tight. Once again I learned the futility of stopping the circulation by wearing one layer of wool too many.

It was our intention naturally in setting out this day to reach the summit of Mount Everest. Provided we were not stopped by a mountaineering difficulty, and that was unlikely, the fate of our Expedition would depend on the two factors, time and speed. Of course, we might become too exhausted to go farther before reaching our goal; but the consideration of speed really covers that case, for provided one were capable of moving his limbs at all he would presumably be able to crawl a few steps only so slowly that there would be no point in doing so. From the outset we were short of time; we should have started two hours earlier; the weather prevented us. The fresh snow was an encumbrance, lying everywhere on the ledges from 4 inches to 8 inches deep; it must have made a difference, though not a large one. In any case, when we measured our rate of progress it was not satisfactory, at most 400 feet an hour, not counting halts, and diminishing a little as we went up. It became clear that if we could go no farther—and we couldn't without exhausting ourselves at once—we should still at the best be struggling upwards after night had fallen again. We were prepared to leave it to braver men to climb Mount Everest by night.

By agreeing to this arithmetical computation we tacitly accepted defeat. And if we were not to reach the summit, what remained for us to do? None of us,

I believe, cared much about any lower objective. We were not greatly interested then in the exact number of feet by which we should beat a record. It must be remembered that the mind is not easily interested under such conditions. The intelligence is gradually numbed as the supply of oxygen diminishes and the body comes nearer to exhaustion. Looking back on my own mental processes as we approached 27,000 feet, I can find no traces of insanity, nothing completely illogical; within a small compass I was able to reason, no doubt very slowly. But my reasoning was concerned only with one idea; beyond its range I can recall no thought. The view, for instance—and as a rule I'm keen enough about the view—did not interest me; I was not "taking notice." Wonderful as such an experience would be, I had not even the desire to look over the North-east ridge; I would have gladly got to the North-east shoulder as being the sort of place one ought to reach, but I had no strong desire to get there, and none at all for the wonder of being there. I dare say the others were more mentally alive than I; but when it came to deciding what we should do, we had no lively discussion. It seemed to me that we should get back to Morshead in time to take him down this same day to Camp IV. There was some sense in this idea, and many mountaineers may think we were right to make it a first consideration. But the alternative of sleeping a second night at our highest camp and returning next day to Camp III was never mentioned. It may have been that we shrank unconsciously from another night in such discomfort; whether the thought was avoided in this way, or simply was not born, our minds were not behaving as we would wish them to behave. The idea of reaching Camp IV with Morshead before dark, once it had been accepted, controlled us altogether. It was easy to calculate from our upward speed, supposing that we could treble this on the descent, at what time we ought to turn; we agreed to start down at 2.30 p.m., but we would maintain our rate of progress as best we could until that time approached.

At 2.15 we completed the ascent of a steeper pitch and found ourselves on the edge of an easier terain, where the mountain slopes back towards the North-east shoulder. It was an obvious place for a halt: we were in need of food; and we lay against the rocks to spend the remaining fifteen minutes before we should turn for the descent according to our bond. None of us was altogether "cooked"; we were not brought to a standstill because our limbs would carry us no farther. I should be very sorry to reach such a condition at this altitude; for one would not recover easily; and a man who cannot take care of himself on the descent will probably be the cause of disaster to his companions, who will have little enough strength remaining to help themselves and him. It is impossible to say how much farther we might have gone. In the light of subsequent events it would seem that the margin of strength to deal with an emergency was already small enough. I have little doubt that we could have struggled up perhaps in two hours more to the North-east shoulder, now little more than 400 feet above us. Whether we should then have been fit to conduct our descent in safety is another matter.

While we ate such food as we had with us, chiefly sugar in one form or another, chocolate, mintcake, or acid-drops, and best of all raisins and prunes, we now had leisure to look about us. The summit of Everest, or what appeared to be the summit (I doubt if we saw the ultimate tip), lying back along the North-east ridge, was not impressive, and we were too near up under this ridge to add anything to former observations as to the nature of its obstacles. The view was necessarily restricted when Everest itself hid so much country. But it was a pleasure to look westwards across the broad North face and down it towards the Rongbuk Glacier; it was satisfactory to notice that the North Peak which, though perceptibly below us, had still held, so to speak, a place in our circle when we started in the morning, this same Changtse had now become a contemptible fellow beneath our notice. We saw his black plebeian head rising from the mists, mists that filled all the valleys, so that there was nothing in all the world as we looked from North-east to North-west but the great twins Gyachung Kang and Chö Uyo; and even these, though they regarded us still from a station of equality, were actually inferior. The lesser of them is 26,000 feet, and we could clearly afford to despise him; the greater Chö Uyo we had to regard respectfully before we could be sure; his triangulated height is 26,870, whereas our aneroid was reading only 26,800; it seemed that we were looking over his head, but such appearances are deceptive, and we were glad to have the confirmation of the theodolite later proving that we had reached 26,985 feet—higher than Chö Uyo by 100 feet and more.

The beneficent superiority with which we now regarded the whole world except Mount Everest no doubt helped us to swallow our luncheon—or was it dinner?—a difficult matter, for our tongues were hanging out after so much exercise of breathing. We had no chance of finding a trickle here as one often may in the blessed Alps; and medical opinion, which knew all about what was good for us, frowned upon the notion of alcoholic stimulant for a climber in distress at a high altitude. And so, very naturally, when one of us (Be of good cheer, my friend, I won't give you away!) produced from his pocket a flask of Brandy—each of us took a little nip. I am glad to relate that the result was excellent; it is logically certain therefore that the Brandy contained no alcohol. The non-alcoholic Brandy, then, no doubt by reason of what it lacked, had an important spiritual effect; it gave us just the mental fillip which we required to pull ourselves together for the descent.

Happily inspired by our "medical comfort," I announced that I would take the lead. Norton and I changed

SUMMIT OF MOUNT EVEREST FROM THE HIGHEST POINT OF THE FIRST CLIMB, 26,985 FEET, 21ST MAY, 1922.

places on the rope. I optimistically supposed that I should find an easier way down by a continuous snow-slope to the West of the ridge. Somervell, also moved by inspiration, suggested that he should remain behind to make a sketch and hurry down our tracks to catch us up later. He says that I found it difficult to understand that he would only require a few minutes, and that I replied irritably. I can hardly believe that my tone just then was anything but suave, but I have no doubt I was glad to have him with us to be our sheet-anchor, and particularly so a little later, for we were in difficulties almost at once. We found more snow on this new line, as I had supposed; but it was not to our liking; it lay not on a continuous slope, but covering a series of slabs and only too ready to slide off. We were obliged to work back to the ridge itself and follow it down in our morning's tracks.

At 4 p.m. we reached our camp, where Morshead was waiting. He was feeling perfectly well, he reported, and ready to come down with us to Camp IV. After collecting a few of our possessions which we did not wish to abandon to the uncertain future, we roped up once more to continue our descent. So far our pace going down had been highly satisfactory. In the Alps one usually expects to descend on easy ground twice as fast as one would go up. But we had divided our time of ascent by 4, and in an hour and a half had come down 2,000 feet. Under normal conditions at lower altitudes even this pace would be considered slow; it would not be an exceptionally fast pace for going up these slopes; and yet the image that stays in my memory is of a party coming down quite fast. It is evident that the whole standard of speed is altered. On the ascent, too, I had the sensation of moving about twice as fast as we actually were. I imagine that the whole of life was scaled down, as it were, that we were living both physically and mentally at half, or less than half, the normal rate. However that may be, we had now to descend only 2,000 feet to Camp IV, and with more than three hours' daylight left we supposed we should have no difficulty in reaching our tents before dark.

Meditating after the event about the whole of our performance this day, I have often wondered how we should have appeared at various stages to an unfatigued and competent observer. No doubt he would have noted with some misgiving the gradually diminishing pace of the party as it crawled upwards; but he would have been satisfied, I think, that each man had control of his limbs and a sure balance, and as we were moving along together over ground where the rope will very easily be caught under the points of projecting rocks and thereby cause inconvenience and delay while it is unhitched, this observer, watching the rope, would have noticed that in fact it almost never was caught up. The party at all events were "keeping their form" to the extent of managing the rope as it ought to be managed. For a moment when they were in difficulties after turning back, he might have thought them rather shaky; but even here they were able to pull themselves together and proceed with proper attention and care. Whether he would have noticed any difference when they started off again I cannot say. A certain impetus of concentration, a gathering of mental and physical energy, a reserve called up from who knows where when they turned to face the descent, had perhaps spent its force; and though the party was a stage nearer to the end of the journey, it was also a stage nearer to exhaustion and to that state where carelessness so readily slips in unperceived. It may be supposed we were a degree less alert, all the more because we foresaw no difficulty; we had not exercised the imagination to figure difficulties on the descent, and we now came upon them unexpectedly.

The fresh snow fallen during the night had so altered appearances that we could not be certain, as we traversed back towards the ridge again, that we were exactly following the line by which we had approached our camp the day before. My impression is that we went too low and missed it. We were soon working along broken ground above a broad snow slope. Fresh snow had to be cleared away alike from protruding rocks where we wished to put our feet and from the old snow where we must cut steps. It was not a difficult place and yet not easy, as the slope below us was dangerous and yet not very steep, not steep enough to be really alarming or specially to warn the climber that a slip may be fatal. It was an occasion when the need for care and attention was greater than obviously appeared, just the sort to catch a tired party off their guard. Perhaps the steps were cut too hastily, or in one way and another were taking small risks that we would not usually take. The whole party would not necessarily have been in grave danger because one man lost his footing. But we were unprepared. When the third man slipped the last man was moving, and was at once pulled off his balance. The second in the party, though he must have checked these two, could not hold them. In a moment the three of them were slipping down and gathering speed on a slope where nothing would stop them until they reached the plateau of the East Rongbuk Glacier, 3,500 feet below. The leader for some reason had become anxious about the party a minute or two earlier, and though he too was moving when the slip occurred and could see nothing of what went on behind him, he was on the alert; warned now by unusual sounds that something was wrong, he at once struck the pick of his axe into the snow, and hitched the rope round the head of it. Standing securely his position was good, and while holding the rope in his right hand beyond the hitch, he was able to press with the other on the shaft of the axe, his whole weight leaning towards the slope so as to hold the pick of the axe into the snow. Even so it would be almost impossible to check the combined momentum of three men at once. In ninety-nine cases out of a hundred either the belay will give or the rope will break. In the still moment of suspense before the matter must be put to the test nothing further could be done to prevent a disaster one way or the other. The rope suddenly tightened and tugged at the axe-head. It gave a little as it gripped the metal like a hawser on a bollard. The pick did not budge. Then the rope came taut between the moving figures, and the rope showed what it was worth. From one of the bodies which had slid and now was stopped proceeded an utterance, not in the best taste, reproaching his fate, because he must now start going up hill again when he should have been descending. The danger had passed. The weight of three men had not come upon the rope with a single jerk. The two lengths between the three as they slipped down were presumably not stretched tight, and the second man had been checked directly below the leader before the other two. Probably he also did something to check those below him, for he was partly held up by projecting rocks and almost at once recovered his footing. We were soon secure again on the mountain-side, and—not the least surprising fact—no one had been hurt.

I suppose we must all have felt rather shaken by an incident which came so near to being a catastrophe. But a party will not necessarily be less competent or climb worse on that account. At all events we had received a warning and now proceeded with the utmost caution, moving one at a time over the snow-covered ledges. It was slow work. This little distance which with fair conditions could easily be traversed in a quarter of an hour must have taken us about five times as long. However, when we reached the ridge and again looked down the snow where we had come up the day before, though it was clear enough we must waste no time, we did not feel greatly pressed. Our old tracks were, of course, covered, and we looked about for a way to avoid this slope; but it seemed better to go down by the way we knew, and we were soon busy chipping steps. It was a grim necessity at this hour of the day. I felt one might almost have slipped down checking himself with the axe. We were distinctly tempted. But after all, we were not playing with this mountain; it might be playing with us. There was a clear risk, and we were not compelled to accept it. We must keep on slowly cutting our steps. The long toil was shared among us until the slope eased off and we had nothing more to fear. We looked down to the North Col below us. No difficulty could stop our descent. We had still an hour of daylight. After all, with ordinary good fortune, we should be back in our tents before dark.

I had been aware for some time that Morshead, though he was going steadily and well, was more tired than the rest of us. His long halt at our high camp can have done him little good. He had not recovered. His strength had just served to keep him up where it was urgently necessary that he should preserve his balance; but it was now exhausted; he had quite come to the end of his resources, and at best he could move downwards a few steps at a time. It was difficult to see what could be done for him. There were places where we might sit down and rest, and we should be obliged not only to stop often for two or three minutes, but also to stay occasionally for perhaps ten minutes or a quarter of an hour. Anything like a longer halt must be avoided if possible, as the air was already cold, and an exhausted man would be particularly sensitive. Probably a longer rest would not have helped him, and we proceeded as best we could, so as to avoid delay as much as possible. One of us, and it was usually Norton, gave Morshead the support of his shoulder and an arm round his waist, while I went first, to pick out exactly the most convenient line, and Somervell was our rearguard in any steeper place. So we crawled down the mountain-side in the gathering darkness, until as I looked back from a few yards ahead my companions were distinguishable only as vague forms silhouetted against the snow. There were long hours before us yet, and they would be hours of darkness. Occasionally the flicker of lightning from distant clouds away to the West reminded us that the present calm might sometime be disturbed. Perhaps below on the col, or it might be sooner, the old unfriendly wind would meet us once again. For the present it was fortunate that the way was easy; the great thing was to keep on the snow, and we found that the edge of rocks by which we had come up, and where it was now so much more difficult to get along, could be avoided almost everywhere. With the same edge of stones to guide us, we could not miss our way, and were still stumbling on in the dark without a lantern when we reached the North Col. But we had a lantern with us, and a candle too, in Somervell's rucksack, and we should now require a light. I was reminded once again of the most merciful circumstance, for the air was still so calm that even with matches of a Japanese brand, continually execrated among us, we had no difficulty in lighting our candle.

Two hundred yards, or little more in a direct line, now separated us from our tents, with the promise of safety, repose, and warmth in our soft eiderdown bags. Looking back, I never can make out how we came to spend so long in reaching them. We had but to go along the broken saddle of snow and ice where our tracks lay, and then drop down to our camp on the shelf. But the tracks were concealed, and not to be found; crevasses lay under the snow waiting for us. With nothing to guide us, we must proceed cautiously, and once among the confusing shapes of white walls and terraces and monticules and corridors, it was the easiest thing in the world to lose our way. Somervell, who had covered the ground once each way more often than any of us, held the helm, so to speak, against a sea of conflicting opinions. Even he, now our leader, was not always right, and we had more than once to come back along our tracks and take a cast in

THE FIRST CLIMBING PARTY.

another direction. To avoid the possible trouble or disaster of having two men at once in a crevasse, we were obliged to keep our intervals on the ropes, so that Morshead had now to take care of himself. Perhaps the lower altitude had already begun to tell, for he was stronger now, and came along much better than was to be expected. At length we reached a recognisable landmark, a cliff of ice about 15 feet high, where we had jumped down over a crevasse on our first visit here in order to avoid a disagreeable long step over another crevasse on an alternative route. I was very glad we had come this way rather than the other, for though, looking down at the dimly lit space of snow which was to receive us, I boggled a little at the idea of this leap, the landing-place was sure to be soft, and it would be easy not to miss it.

I think each of us was just a little relieved when he found himself safely down, and I dimly remember congratulating, not Morshead, but Longstaff. I had already transposed the names several times, and he now protested; but it made no difference, as I could remember no other. "Longstaff" became an *idée fixe,* and though the entity of Morshead remained unconfused—I did not, for instance, give him Longstaff's beard—he was fixedly Longstaff until the following morning.

The agreeable change of finding ourselves together in that curious coign was hardly disturbed by Somervell's remark, "We're very near the end of our candle." We felt we were all very near the end of our journey, for we had dimly made out from the higher level we had just quitted the neat rank of our tents still standing on the shelf below and ready to welcome us. We had only to find the rope which had been fixed on the steep slope below us and we should be at the end of our troubles. But the rope was deeply buried, and we searched in vain, dragging the snow with our picks along the edge of the fall. We were still searching when the last of our candle burnt out. In the end we must do without the rope, and began the abrupt descent tentatively, dubiously, uncertain that we had hit off just the right place. The situation was decidedly disagreeable. Suddenly someone among us hitched up the rope from under the snow. It may be imagined we were not slow to grasp it. The blessed security of feeling the frozen but helpful thing firmly in our hands! We positively made some sort of a noise; unrecognisable, perhaps, it would have been to sober daylight beings who know how to produce the proper effect, but if a dim bat of the night were asked what this noise resembled, he might have indicated that distantly, but without mistake it was like a cheer. A few minutes more and then—then, at 11.30 p.m., and there on the good flat snow as we fumbled at the tent-doors, then and there at last we began to say, "Thank God."

Had we known what was yet in store for us, or rather what was not in store, we might have waited a little longer for so emphatic an exclamation. We were in need of food, and no solid food could be eaten until something had been done towards satisfying our thirst. It was not that one felt, at least I did not feel, a desire to drink; but the long effort of the lungs during the day in a rarefied atmosphere where evaporation is so rapid had deprived the body of moisture to such an extent that it was impossible to swallow, for instance, a ration biscuit. We must first melt snow and have water. But where were the cooking-pots? We searched the tents without finding a trace of them. Presumably the porters whom we had expected to find here had taken them down to Camp III in error. As we sat slowly unlacing our boots within the tents, it was impossible to believe in this last misfortune. We waited for a brain-wave; but no way could be devised of melting the snow without a vessel. Still supperless, we wriggled into our sleeping-bags. And then something happened in Norton's head. In his visions of all that was succulent and juicy and fit to be swallowed with ease and pleasure there had suddenly appeared an ice-cream. It was this that he now proposed to us; we had the means at hand to make ice-creams, he said. A tin of strawberry jam was opened; frozen Ideal Milk was hacked out of another; these two ingredients were mixed with snow, and it only remained to eat the compound. To my companions this seemed an easy matter; their appetite for strawberry cream ice was hardly nice to watch. I too managed to swallow down a little before the deadly sickliness of the stuff disgusted me. My gratitude to Norton was afterwards cooled by disagreeable sensations. In the last drowsy moments before complete forgetfulness I was convulsed by shudderings which I was powerless to control; the muscles of my back seemed to be contracted with cramp; and, short of breath, I was repeatedly obliged to raise myself on my elbows and start again that solemn exercise of deep-breathing as though the habit had become indispensable.

The last stage of our descent to Camp III had still to be accomplished on the following morning of May 22. I imagine that a fresh man with old tracks to help him might cover the distance from Camp IV in about an hour and a quarter. But no sign was left of our old tracks, and the snow was deeper here than higher up. Only in the harder substance below the fresh surface could new steps be cut wherever the slope was steep; and as we began to understand that the way would be long and toilsome, another thought occurred to us—our sleeping-bags at Camp IV would now be required at Camp III, and porters must be sent to fetch them. Our tracks, therefore, must be made safe for them. Half our labour was in hewing so fine a staircase that the porters would be able to go up and down unescorted without danger. The wearisome descent, which began at 6 a.m., continued far into the morning; the sun pierced the vapoury mists and the heat was immoderate now as the cold had been higher up. The fatigued party regarded the conventions until the first man reached the snow at the foot of the final ice-slope. There, so far as I could understand, the van became possessed of the idea that it would be more companionable for all to finish together. I found myself deliberately pulled from my steps and slid

Frostbitten climber being helped down to Camp II.

about 80 feet down the ice until the pick of my axe pulled me up at the foot of the slope. I could have borne the ignominy of my involuntary glissade had I not found Finch at the foot of the slope taking advantage of my situation with a kodak.

The presence of Finch was easily explained. Reinforcements had arrived at Camp III in our absence, and the transport had worked with such wonderful speed that the oxygen cylinders were already in action. Finch, whom we had last heard of in bed with dysentery at the Base Camp, had shown such energy that he was now testing the oxygen apparatus with Wakefield and Geoffrey Bruce. They were bound for the North Col with a party of porters, so the return of our sleeping-bags was easily arranged. The lesser injustices of fate are hard to forgive, and we regretted labour that might have been left to others. However, Wakefield now took us in charge, and at noon we were at Camp III once more. Strutt and Morris had come out to meet us. Noel had stayed in camp, and, like a tormentor waiting for his disarmed victim, there we found the "movie" camera and him winding the handle.

However, our welcome in camp is a pleasing memory. The supply of tea was inexhaustible. Somervell confesses to having drunk seventeen mugfuls; he can hardly have been so moderate. Morshead probably needed to drink more than any of us; he ascribed his exhaustion on the mountain to want of liquid, and medical opinion was inclined to agree with the suggestion. However that may be, the night's rest at a lower elevation had largely restored his strength, and Morshead arrived at Camp III no more fatigued to all appearances than the rest of us. But he bore the marks of his painful ordeal. His condition had made him a prey to the cold, and we only began to realise how badly he had been frost-bitten as we sat in camp while Wakefield bound up the black swollen fingers.

THE ATTEMPT WITH OXYGEN

By

CAPTAIN GEORGE FINCH

CHAPTER VII

THE SECOND ATTEMPT

With the departure of the last of our companions on March 27, Crawford and I found ourselves left behind in Darjeeling impatiently awaiting the arrival of the oxygen equipment from Calcutta. A week elapsed before we were able to set out for Kalimpong, where we picked up the oxygen stores on April 4. On the evening of our second march out from Kalimpong, suspicious rattlings were heard in the cases containing the oxygen cylinders. On investigation, it transpired that they had been packed metal to metal, and the continual chafing caused by the rough mule transport had already resulted in considerable wear in the steel. This dangerous state of affairs, which, if not speedily remedied, would undoubtedly soon have led to the bursting of some of the cylinders, with consequent demoralisation of our transport, let alone possible casualties, called for immediate attention; so throughout the night of April 5–6, Crawford and I, aided by our porters, worked steadily at grumetting the cylinders with string and repacking them in such a manner as would render impossible any recurrence of the trouble.

On April 8, in a snowstorm, we crossed the Jelep

La; thence, proceeding viâ the Chumbi Valley and Phari, we ultimately rejoined the main body of the Expedition in Kampa Dzong on the 13th. The rest of our journey across Tibet to the Base Camp has already been described elsewhere, but perhaps I may be permitted to give a few of my own impressions of the country and its inhabitants.

In recollection, the strange land of Tibet stretches itself out before me in an endless succession of vast, dreary plains, broken by chains of mountains that, in relation to the height of their surroundings, sink into the insignificance of hills. Arid and stony desert wastes, almost totally unblessed by the living green of vegetation; interminable tracts of sand that shift unceasingly under the restless feet of an ever-hurrying, pitilessly cruel wind; bleak, barren, and unbeautiful of form, but fair and of indescribable appeal in the raiment of soft glowing rainbow hues with which distance, as in compensation, clothes all wide open spaces. Sunsets provided many a wondrous picture, while towards the South a glistening array of white-capped excrescences marked the main chain of the Himalaya. The honour of being the most poignant of my memories of Tibet, however, remains with the wind. It blew unceasingly, and its icy blasts invariably met one straight in the face. The pre-monsoon wind is westerly; the post-monsoon wind blows from the East. Our journey towards the Base Camp led us towards the West; homeward bound, during the monsoon, we travelled East. Both going and returning, therefore, we marched in the teeth of a wind, that gnawed even at our weather-beaten, hardened skins, and was the most generous contributor in the quota of discomforts that Tibet meted out to us.

And what of the dwellers in these inhospitable plains ? Like all humankind, the Tibetans have their bad as well as their good points. The former are easily told. If one wishes to converse with a Tibetan, it is always advisable to stand on his windward side. A noble Tibetan once boasted that during his lifetime he had had two baths—one on the occasion of his birth, the other on the day of his marriage. Those of us honoured by his presence found the statement difficult to believe. Apart from this rather penetrating drawback, the Tibetans are a most likeable people ; cheery, contented, good-natured, and hard-working ; slow to give a promise, but punctilious to a degree in carrying it out ; truthful and scrupulously honest. As testimony of this last-mentioned trait, be it said that during the whole of our long wanderings through Tibet, when it was quite impossible to keep a strong guard over our many stores, we never lost so much as a single ration biscuit through theft. Old age is seldom met with ; it is exceptional to see a Tibetan whose years number more than fifty-five or sixty. Presumably living in so severe a climate, at an altitude of 14,000 feet or more above sea-level, proves too great a strain upon the human heart. The priests, or "Lamas," as they are called in Tibet, constitute the governing class. They represent the educated section of the community ; the monasteries are the seats of learning, and, as such, are well-nigh all-powerful. I regret to state that I did not like the priests as much as the laity. The reason is not far to seek. If you wish to hold converse with a Lama, it is advisable not only to stand on his windward side, but also to take care that the wind is exceptionally strong. The Lamas do not marry. As two-fifths of the able-bodied population of Tibet lead a monastic life, it will be readily understood that the odour of sanctity is all-pervading. In other respects the monks proved as attractive as their simpler countrymen. Inquisitive with the direct and pardonable inquisitiveness of children, they are nevertheless men of a distinctly high order of intelligence. Kindly, courteous, and appreciative of little attentions, they were always ready to lend assistance and to give information concerning their religion and the manners and customs of their country.

These few of the more lasting of my impressions would be incomplete without mention of Tibetan music. On the assumption that whatever is, is beautiful, Tibetan music is beautiful—to the Tibetan. To the Western ear it is elementary in the extreme, and, in point of view of sheer ugliness of sound, competes with the jarring, clashing squeaks, bangs, and hoots of the jazz-bands that were so fashionable at home at the time of our departure for India.

On May 2, the day after our arrival at the Base Camp, Strutt, Norton, and I were sent off by the General to reconnoitre for a suitable first camping site near the exit of the East Rongbuk Valley. Gaining the latter by the so-called terrace route which leads over the tremendous moraines on the right bank of the main Rongbuk Glacier, we had no difficulty in finding on the right bank of the East Rongbuk Stream, but a few hundred yards West of the end of the East Rongbuk Glacier, a favourable position for Camp No. I. We returned that afternoon, descending down the snowed-over and frozen-up stream to the main Rongbuk Glacier, making our way thence to the Base Camp through the trough leading down between the glacier and the moraines. With this little excursion my climbing activities ceased for the time being. Soon afterwards I was beset by a troublesome stomach complaint, which had already claimed as victims the majority of the other members of the Expedition, and it was not until May 16 that I was sufficiently restored from the wearing effects of my illness to resume climbing. In spite of this, my time at the Base Camp was fully occupied. Frequent oxygen drills were held, and all the oxygen stores overhauled and tested. Various members of the Expedition were instructed in the use of Primus stoves. There were many small repairs of different natures to be done, and in my leisure moments I was kept busy with matters photographic. In addition, Mount Everest and the weather conditions prevalent thereon became objects of the keenest study and interest. The remark, "I suppose Mont Blanc would be absolutely dwarfed into insignificance by Mount Everest," has frequently been made to me in one form or another, and, to my questioners' amazement, my answer has always been a decided "No." As a matter of fact, Mont Blanc, as seen from the Brévant or the Flégère, excels in every way any view I have ever enjoyed of Mount Everest. It is true that I have seen the latter only from a tableland which is itself from 14,000 to 16,000 feet above sea-level, and that I know nothing of the wonderful sight that Mount Everest probably presents to the observer from the Southern (Nepalese) side. The grandeur of a mountain depends very largely upon the extent to which it is glaciated. Mont Blanc is nearly 16,000 feet high, and its glaciers descend to within 4,000 feet of sea-level—a vertical zone of 12,000 feet of perpetual ice and snow. Those glaciers of Mount Everest which flow North, and thus the only ones with which we are concerned, descend to a point about 16,500 feet above sea-level—a vertical zone of 12,500 feet of perpetual ice and snow. Thus it is evident that, from the point of view of vertical extent of glaciation, there is little difference between the monarch of the Alps and the Northern side of the highest summit in the world. From the point of view of beauty there can be no comparison. Seen from one quarter, Mont Blanc rises in a series of snowy domes piled one against the other in ever-increasing altitude to a massive yet beautifully proportioned and well-balanced whole. From another side we see great converging granite columns, breathing the essence of noble purpose, proudly supporting and lifting aloft to the sun the gleaming, snowy-capped splendour of the summit dome. Another view-point, though revealing perhaps a less beautiful Mont Blanc, lacking much of the graceful symmetry and strong, purposeful design of the

Mount Everest from Base Camp.

other views, is redeemed by the fact that the observer is forced in so close to the mountain that the rattling din of stonefalls and the loud crash of the ice-avalanche are always in his ears. Mont Blanc asserts her authority with no uncertain voice. In the Mount Everest as we of this Expedition know it, revealed in the full glare of the tropical sun, all this is lacking. Symmetry and beauty cannot truthfully be read out of the ponderous, ungainly, ill-proportioned lump which carries, as if by chance, on its Western extremity a little carelessly truncated cone to serve as a summit. Avalanches are neither seen nor heard. Falling stones there are without doubt, but one is too far off to hear them. Yet Everest had her moments. Diffused with the borrowed glory of sunrise or sunset, and clad in a mantle of fresh snow, the harsh clumsiness of her form would be somewhat softened and concealed; bathed in the yellow-blue light of dawn, as yet unkissed by the sun, but whipped into wakefulness by a driving westerly wind that tore from head and shoulders the snowy veil which she had donned during the night, rending it into long, spun-out living streamers, no beholder could gainsay her beauty.

Weather conditions naturally proved of the greatest interest. On consulting my diary, I find that during the period from May 1 to June 5, there were two days when the weather was fine and settled, and that these two days succeeded snowstorms which had thickly powdered the mountain with fresh snow. On both days the sky was cloudless, or nearly so, and, judging from the absence of driven snow-dust about the summit, Mount Everest appeared to be undisturbed by wind. Apart from these two occasions, however, the weather was never absolutely fine. Cloudless skies there were, but the great streamers of snow smoking away from the highest ridges of the mountain testified to the existence of the fierce and bitter wind against which a mountaineer would have to fight his way. On four occasions there were periods of snowstorms lasting from but a single night to three days and three nights.

On May 10, Mallory and Somervell set out for Camp III, to make ready for a first attempt to climb Mount Everest. I had practically recovered from my stomach trouble, and expected to be able to leave the Base in the course of a day or two, in order to follow up the first attempt with a second attack, in which oxygen was to be used. Norton was to be my companion. Unfortunately, however, I suffered a relapse, and Strutt, Norton, and Morshead left to join Mallory and Somervell, whereas I had to resign myself to several more days at the Base. At length, on May 15, I was ready and eager to think about doing something. My climbing companions were Geoffrey Bruce and Lance-Corporal Tejbir, the most promising of the Ghurkas. Wakefield was to accompany us as far as Camp III, in order to give us a clean bill of health from there onwards. Leaving the Base on the 16th, we proceeded to Camp I, where the following day was spent attending to our oxygen apparatus and transport arrangements. Soon after midday on the 18th, we arrived at Camp II, where the greater part of the afternoon was devoted to giving Geoffrey Bruce, Tejbir, and several of the porters, a lesson in the elements of mountaineering and of ice-craft. On the 19th we reached Camp III, where we learned from Colonel Strutt that Mallory, Norton, Somervell, and Morshead had gone up to the North Col in the morning. Geoffrey Bruce and I immediately set about overhauling our equipment, in particular our oxygen stores, and as we worked we could see the first party making their way through the séracs, and climbing the ice-cliffs of the lofty depression of the North Col.

The cylinders containing our oxygen were found to be in good condition; but the apparatus—through no fault of the makers, who had, indeed, done their work admirably—leaked very badly, and to get them into satisfactory working order, four days of hard toil with soldering-iron, hacksaw, pliers, and all the other paraphernalia of a fitter's shop were necessary. Our workshop was in the open. The temperature played up and down round about 0° F., but inclined more to the negative side of that irrational scale. The masks from which the oxygen was to be breathed proved useless, but by tackling the problem with a little thought and much cheerfulness a satisfactory substitute was eventually evolved, making it possible to use the oxygen apparatus in an efficient manner. Without this new mask no real use could have been made of our oxygen supplies; oxygen would have been misjudged as being useless, and the solution of the problem of climbing Mount Everest would have been as distant as ever.

Preparatory to embarking on the climb itself, we went for several trial walks—one over to the Rapiu La, a pass 21,000 feet high, at the foot of the North-east ridge of Everest, from which we hoped to obtain views of the country to the south. But only part of the North-east ridge showed hazily through drifting mists. Towards the north and looking down the East Rongbuk Glacier, views were clearer, though partially obscured by rolling banks of cloud. Colonel Strutt and Dr. Wakefield, unoxygenated, accompanied us on this little expedition, and oxygen at once proved its value, so easily did Bruce and I outpace them. On May 22, acting on instructions from Colonel Strutt, Geoffrey Bruce, Wakefield, Tejbir, and I, with a number of porters, set out for the North Col to meet and afford any required assistance to the members of the first climbing party who were on their way down from the mountain. It was also our intention to bring stores up into the North Col as well as give the oxygen apparatus a final severe try-out prior to embarking upon an attack upon Mount Everest itself. We met the first climbing party just above the foot of the final steep slopes leading up to the North Col. They were more or less in the last stage of exhaustion, as, indeed, men who have done their best on such a mountain should be. After supplying them with what liquid nourishment was available, and leaving Wakefield and two porters to see them back to Camp III, we carried on up to the North Col. In

East Rongbuk Glacier near Camp II.

the afternoon we returned to Camp III. There had been a considerable amount of step-cutting, for fresh snow had fallen, compelling us to deviate from the usual route; but even so, oxygen had made a brief Alpine ascent of what is otherwise a strenuous day's work. We took three hours up and fifty minutes down, with thirty-six photographs taken *en route*.

On May 24, Captain Noel, Tejbir, Geoffrey Bruce, and I, all using oxygen, went up to the North Col (23,000 feet). Bent on a determined attack, we camped there for the night. Morning broke fine and clear though somewhat windy, and at eight o'clock we sent off up the long snow-slopes leading towards the North-east shoulder of Mount Everest, twelve porters carrying oxygen cylinders, provisions for one day, and camping gear. An hour and a half later, Bruce, Tejbir, and I followed, and, in spite of the fact that each bore a load of over 30 lb., which was much more than the average weight carried by the porters, we overtook them at a height of about 24,500 feet. They greeted our arrival with their usual cheery, broad grins. But no longer did they regard oxygen as a foolish man's whim; one and all appreciated the advantages of what they naïvely chose to call "English air." Leaving them to follow, we went on, hoping to pitch our camp somewhere above 26,000 feet. But shortly after one o'clock the wind freshened up rather offensively, and it began to snow. Our altitude was 25,500 feet, some 500 feet below where we had hoped to camp, but we looked round immediately for a suitable camping site, as the porters had to return to the North Col that day, and persistence in proceeding further would have run them unjustifiably into danger. This I would under no circumstances do, for I felt responsible for these cheerful, smiling, willing men, who looked up to their leader and placed in him the complete trust of little children. As it was, the margin of safety secured by pitching camp where we did instead of at a higher elevation was none too wide; for before the last porter had departed downwards the weather had become very threatening. A cheerful spot in which to find space to pitch a tent it was not; but though I climbed a couple of hundred feet or so further up the ridge, nothing more suitable was to be found. Remembering that a wind is felt more severely on the windward side of a ridge than on the crest, a possible position to the West of the ridge was negatived in favour of one on the very backbone. The leeside was bare of any possible camping place within reasonable distance. Our porters arrived at 2 p.m., and at once all began to level off the little platform where the tent was soon pitched, on the very edge of the tremendous precipices falling away to the East Rongbuk and Main Rongbuk Glaciers, over 4,000 feet below. Within twenty minutes the porters were scurrying back down the broken, rocky ridge towards the snow-slopes leading to the North Col, singing, as they went, snatches of their native hillside ditties. What splendid men! Having seen the last man safely off, I looked to the security of the guy-ropes holding down the tent, and then joined Bruce and Tejbir inside.

It was snowing hard. Tiny, minute spicules driven by the wind penetrated everywhere. It was bitterly cold, so we crawled into our sleeping-bags, and, gathering round us all available clothing, huddled up together as snugly as was possible.

With the help of solidified spirit we melted snow and cooked a warm meal, which imparted some small measure of comfort to our chilled bodies. A really hot drink was not procurable, for the simple reason that at such an altitude water boils at so low a temperature that one can immerse the hand in it without fear of being scalded. Over a *post-prandium* cigarette, Bruce and I discussed our prospects of success. Knowing that no man can put forward his best effort unless his confidence is an established fact, the trend of my contribution to the conversation was chiefly, "Of course, we shall get to the top." After sunset, the storm rose to a gale, a term I use deliberately. Terrific gusts tore at our tent with such ferocity that the ground-sheet with its human burden was frequently lifted up off the ground. On these occasions our combined efforts were needed to keep the tent down and prevent its being blown away. Although we had blocked up the few very small openings in the tent to the best of our powers, long before midnight we were all thickly covered in a fine frozen spindrift that somehow or other was blown in upon us, insinuating its way into sleeping-bags and clothing, there to cause acute discomfort. Sleep was out of the question. We dared not relax our vigilance, for ever and again all our strength was needed to hold the tent down and to keep the flaps of the door, stripped of their fastenings by a gust that had caught us unawares, from being torn open. We fought for our lives, realising that once the wind got our little shelter into its ruthless grip, it must inevitably be hurled, with us inside it, down on to the East Rongbuk Glacier, thousands of feet below.

And what of my companions in the tent? To me, who had certainly passed his novitiate in the hardships of mountaineering, the situation was more than alarming. About Tejbir I had no concern; he placed complete confidence in his sahibs, and the ready grin never left his face. But it was Bruce's first experience of mountaineering, and how the ordeal would affect him I did not know. I might have spared myself all anxiety. Throughout the whole adventure he bore himself in a manner that would have done credit to the finest of veteran mountaineers, and returned my confidence with a cheerfulness that rang too true to be counterfeit. By one o'clock on the morning of the 26th the gale reached its maximum. The wild flapping of the canvas made a noise like that of machine-gun fire. So deafening was it that we could scarcely hear each other speak. Later, there came interludes of comparative lull, succeeded by bursts of storm more furious than ever. During such lulls we took it in turn to go outside to tighten up slackened guy-ropes, and also succeeded in tying down the tent more firmly with our Alpine rope. It was impossible to work in the open for more than three or four minutes at a stretch, so profound was the exhaustion induced by this brief exposure to the fierce cold wind. But with the Alpine rope taking some of the strain, we enjoyed a sense of security which, though probably only illusory, allowed us all a few sorely needed moments of rest.

Dawn broke bleak and chill; the snow had ceased to fall, but the wind continued with unabated violence. Once more we had to take it in turns to venture without and tighten up the guy-ropes, and to try to build on the windward side of the tent a small wall of stones as an additional protection. The extreme exhaustion and the chill produced in the body as a result of each of these little excursions were sufficient to indicate that, until the gale had spent itself, there could be no hope of either advance or retreat. As the weary morning hours dragged on, we believed we could detect a slackening off in the storm. And I was thankful, for I was beginning quietly to wonder how much longer human beings could stand the strain. We prepared another meal. The dancing flames of the spirit stove caused me anxiety bordering on anguish lest the tent, a frail shelter between life and death, should catch fire. At noon the storm once more regained its strength and rose to unsurpassed fury. A great hole was cut by a stone in one side of the tent, and our situation thus unexpectedly became more desperate than ever.

But we carried on, making the best of our predicament until, at one o'clock, the wind dropped suddenly from a blustering gale to nothing more than a stiff breeze. Now was the opportunity for retreat to the safety of the North Col camp. But I wanted to hang on and try our climb on the following day. Very cautiously and tentatively I broached my wish to Bruce, fearful lest the trying experience of the last twenty-four hours had undermined his keenness for further adventure. Once again might I have spared myself all anxiety. He jumped at the idea, and when our new plans were communicated to Tejbir, the only effect upon him was to broaden his already expansive grin.

It was a merry little party that gathered round to a scanty evening meal cooked with the last of our fuel. The meal was meagre for the simple reason that we had catered for only one day's short rations, and we were now very much on starvation diet. We had hardly settled down for another night when, about 6 p.m., voices were heard outside. Our unexpected visitors were porters who, anxious as to our safety, had left the North Col that afternoon when the storm subsided. With them they brought thermos flasks of hot beef-tea and tea provided by the thoughtful Noel. Having accepted these most gratefully, we sent the porters back without loss of time.

That night began critically. We were exhausted by our previous experiences and through lack of sufficient food. Tejbir's grin had lost some of its expanse. On the face of Geoffrey Bruce, courageously cheerful as ever, was a strained, drawn expression that I did not like. Provoked, perhaps, by my labours outside the tent, a dead, numbing cold was creeping up my limbs—a thing I had only once before felt

OXYGEN APPARATUS.

CAPTAIN NOEL KINEMATOGRAPHING THE ASCENT OF MOUNT EVEREST FROM THE CHANG LA.

and to the seriousness of which I was fully alive. Something had to be done. Like an inspiration came the thought of trying the effect of oxygen. We hauled an apparatus and cylinders into the tent, and, giving it the air of a joke, we took doses all round. Tejbir took his medicine reluctantly, but with relief I saw his face brighten up. The effect on Bruce was visible in his rapid change of expression. A few minutes after the first deep breath, I felt the tingling sensation of returning life and warmth to my limbs. We connected up the apparatus in such a way that we could breathe a small quantity of oxygen throughout the night. The result was marvellous. We slept well and warmly. Whenever the tube delivering the gas fell out of Bruce's mouth as he slept, I could see him stir uneasily in the uric, greenish light of the moon as it filtered through the canvas. Then half unconsciously replacing the tube, he would fall once more into a peaceful slumber. There is little doubt that it was the use of oxygen which saved our lives during this second night in our high camp.

Before daybreak we were up, and proceeded to make ready for our climb. Putting on our boots was a struggle. Mine I had taken to bed with me, and a quarter of an hour's striving and tugging sufficed to get them on. But Bruce's and Tejbir's were frozen solid, and it took them more than an hour to mould them into shape by holding them over lighted candles. Shortly after six we assembled outside. Some little delay was incurred in arranging the rope and our loads, but at length at 6.30 a.m., soon after the first rays of the sun struck the tent, we shouldered our bundles and set off. What with cameras, thermos bottles, and oxygen apparatus, Bruce and I each carried well over 40 lb.; Tejbir with two extra cylinders of oxygen shouldered a burden of about 50 lb.

Our scheme of attack was to take Tejbir with us as far as the North-east shoulder, there to relieve him of his load and send him back. The weather was clear. The only clouds seemed so far off as to presage no evil, and the breeze, though intensely cold, was bearable. But it soon freshened up, and before we had gone more than a few hundred feet the cold began to have its effect on Tejbir's sturdy constitution, and he showed signs of wavering. Bruce's eloquent flow of Gurumuki, however, managed to boost him up to an altitude of 26,000 feet. There he collapsed entirely, sinking face downwards on to the rocks and crushing beneath him the delicate instruments of his oxygen apparatus. I stormed at him for thus maltreating it, while Bruce exhorted him for the honour of his regiment to struggle on; but it was all in vain. Tejbir had done his best; and he has every right to be proud of the fact that he has climbed to a far greater height than any other native. We pulled him off his apparatus and, relieving him of some cylinders, cheered him up sufficiently to start him with enough oxygen on his way back to the high camp, there to await our return. We had no compunction about letting him go alone, for the ground was easy and he could not lose his way, the tent being in full view below.

After seeing him safely off and making good progress, we loaded up Tejbir's cylinders, and, in view of the easy nature of the climbing, mutually agreed to dispense with the rope, and thus enable ourselves to proceed more rapidly. Climbing not very steep and quite easy rocks, and passing two almost level places affording ample room for some future high camp, we gained an altitude of 26,500 feet. By this time, however, the wind, which had been steadily rising, had acquired such force that I considered it necessary to leave the ridge and continue our ascent by traversing out across the great northern face of Mount Everest, hoping by so doing to find more shelter from the icy blasts. It was not easy to come to this decision, because I saw that between us and the shoulder the climbing was all plain sailing and presented no outstanding difficulty. Leaving the ridge, we began to work out into the face. For the first few yards the going was sufficiently straightforward, but presently the general angle became much steeper, and our trials were accentuated by the fact that the stratification of the rocks was such that they shelved outward and downward, making the securing of adequate footholds difficult. We did not rope, however. I knew that the longer we remained unroped, the more time we should save—a consideration of vital importance. But as I led out over these steeply sloping, evilly smooth slabs, I carefully watched Bruce to see how he would tackle the formidable task with which he was confronted on this his first mountaineering expedition. He did his work splendidly and followed steadily and confidently, as if he were quite an old hand at the game. Sometimes the slabs gave place to snow—treacherous, powdery stuff, with a thin, hard, deceptive crust that gave the appearance of compactness. Little reliance could be placed upon it, and it had to be treated with great care. And sometimes we found ourselves crossing steep slopes of scree that yielded and shifted downwards with every tread. Very occasionally in the midst of our exacting work we were forced to indulge in a brief rest in order to replace an empty cylinder of oxygen by a full one. The empty ones were thrown away, and as each bumped its way over the precipice and the good steel clanged like a church bell at each impact, we laughed aloud at the thought that "There goes another 5 lb. off our backs." Since leaving the ridge we had not made much height although we seemed to be getting so near our goal. Now and then we consulted the aneroid barometer, and its readings encouraged us on. 27,000 feet; then we gave up traversing and began to climb diagonally upwards towards a point on the lofty North-east ridge, midway between the shoulder and the summit. Soon afterwards an accident put Bruce's oxygen apparatus out of action. He was some 20 feet below me, but struggled gallantly upwards as I went to meet him, and, after connecting him on to my apparatus and so renewing his supply of oxygen, we soon traced the trouble and effected a satisfactory repair. The barometer here recorded a height 27,300 feet. The highest mountain visible was Chö Uyo, which is just short of 27,000 feet. We were well above it and could look across it into the dense clouds beyond. The great West Peak of Everest, one of the most beautiful sights to be seen from down in the Rongbuk Valley, was hidden, but we knew that our standpoint was nearly 2,000 feet above it. Everest itself was the only mountain top which we could see without turning our gaze downwards. We could look across into clouds which lay at some undefined distance behind the North-east shoulder, a clear indication that we were only a little, if any, below its level. Pumori, an imposing ice-bound pyramid, 23,000 feet high, I sought at first in vain. So far were we above it that it had sunk into an insignificant little ice-hump by the side of the Rongbuk Glacier. Most of the other landmarks were blotted out by masses of ominous, yellow-hued clouds swept from the West in the wake of an angry storm-wind. The point we reached is unmistakable even from afar. We were standing on a little rocky ledge, just inside an inverted V of snow, immediately below the great belt of reddish-yellow rock which cleaves its way almost horizontally through the otherwise greenish-black slabs of the mountain. Though 1,700 feet below, we were well within half a mile of the summit, so close, indeed, that we could distinguish individual stones on a little patch of scree lying just underneath the highest point. Ours were truly the tortures of Tantalus; for, weak from hunger and exhausted by that nightmare struggle for life in our high camp, we were in no fit condition to proceed. Indeed, I knew that if we were to persist in climbing on, even if only for another 500 feet, we should not both get back alive. The decision to retreat once taken, no time was lost, and, fearing lest another accidental interruption in the oxygen supply might lead to a slip on the part of either of us, we roped together. It was midday. At first we returned in our tracks, but later found better going by aiming to strike the ridge between the North-east shoulder and the North Col at a point above where we had left it in the morning. Progress was more rapid, though great caution was still necessary. Shortly after 2 p.m., we struck the ridge and there reduced our burdens to a minimum by dumping four oxygen cylinders. The place will be easily recognised by future explorers; those four cylinders are perched against a rock at the head of the one and only large snow-filled couloir running right up from the head of the East Rongbuk Glacier to the ridge. The clear weather was gone. We plunged down the easy, broken rocks through thick mists driven past us from the West by a violent wind. For one small mercy we were thankful—no snow fell. We reached our high camp in barely half an hour, and such are the vagaries of Everest's moods that in this short time the wind had practically dropped. Tejbir lay snugly wrapped up in all three sleeping-bags, sleeping the deep sleep of exhaustion. Hearing the voices of the porters on their way up to bring down our kit, we woke him up, telling him to await their arrival and to go down with them. Bruce and I then proceeded on our way, met the ascending porters and passed on, greatly cheered by their bright welcomes and encouraging smiles.

THE BRITISH MEMBERS OF THE SECOND CLIMBING PARTY.

But the long descent, coming as it did on the top of a hard day's work, soon began to find out our weakness. We were deplorably tired, and could no longer move ahead with our accustomed vigour. Knees did not always bend and unbend as required. At times they gave way altogether and forced us, staggering, to sit down. But eventually we reached the broken snows of the North Col, and arrived in camp there at 4 p.m. A craving for food, to the lack of which our weakness was mainly due, was all that animated us. Hot tea and a tin of spaghetti were soon forthcoming, and even this little nourishment refreshed us and renewed our strength to such an extent that three-quarters of an hour later we were ready to set off for Camp III. An invaluable addition to our little party was Captain Noel, the indefatigable photographer of the Expedition, who had already spent four days and three nights on the North Col. He formed our rearguard and nursed us safely down the steep snow and ice slopes on to the almost level basin of the glacier below. Before 5.30 p.m., only forty minutes after leaving the col, we reached Camp III. Since midday, from our highest point we had descended over 6,000 feet; but we were quite finished.

That evening we dined well. Four whole quails truffled in *pâté-de-foie gras*, followed by nine sausages, left me asking for more. The last I remember of that long day was going to sleep, warm in the depths of our wonderful sleeping-bag, with the remains of a tin of toffee tucked away in the crook of my elbow.

Next morning showed that Bruce's feet were sorely frostbitten. I had practically escaped; but the cold had penetrated the half-inch-thick soles of my boots and three pairs of heavy woollen socks, and four small patches of frostbite hampered me at first in my efforts to walk. Bruce was piled on to a sledge, and I journeyed with him as his fellow-passenger. Willing porters dragged us down until the surface of the glacier became so rough as to impose too great a strain on our slender conveyance with its double burden.

Our attack upon Mount Everest had failed. The great mountain with its formidable array of defensive weapons had won; but if the body had suffered, the spirit was still whole. Reaching a point whence we obtained our last close view of the great unconquered Goddess Mother of the Snows, Geoffrey Bruce bade his somewhat irreverent adieux with "Just you wait, old thing, you'll be for it soon!"—words that still are expressive of my own sentiments.

CHAPTER VIII

CONCLUSIONS

Geoffrey Bruce and I arrived back at the Base Camp early in the afternoon of May 29. The next few days were spent in resting, and I then underwent the same experience as the members of the first climbing party; that is, instead of recovering my strength rapidly during the first three or four days, if anything a further decline took place. However, as the weather appeared fine, and there seemed promise of a bright spell prior to the breaking of the monsoon, it was decided to make another attempt on the mountain. Of the remaining climbing members of the Expedition, Somervell was undoubtedly the fittest, with Mallory a good second. Both had enjoyed some ten days' rest since their first assault upon Mount Everest, and therefore had a chance of recovering from the abnormal strain to which they had been submitted. Medical opinion as to my condition after so brief a rest was somewhat divided, but in the end I was passed as sufficiently fit to join in the third attempt. On the 3rd of June we left the Base Camp. The party consisted of Wakefield as M.O., Crawford, and later Morris, as transport officers, Mallory, Somervell and myself as climbers. The attempt was to be made with oxygen, and I was placed in command. It required a great effort for me to get as far as Camp I, and I realised there that the few days' rest which I had enjoyed at the Base Camp had been quite insufficient to allow of my recuperation. During the night the weather turned with a vengeance and it snowed heavily, and I knew that there could be no object in my proceeding farther. After giving Somervell final detailed instructions regarding the oxygen apparatus, I wished them all the best of luck, and on the 4th returned to the Base Camp. As Strutt, Longstaff, and Morshead were leaving next day for Darjeeling, I was given, and availed myself of, the opportunity of accompanying them.

That return journey constitutes one of the most delightful experiences of my life. Within a week of leaving the Base Camp, I had entirely regained my strength, although a certain tenderness in the soles of my feet made itself felt for some considerable time. For the most part the weather was warm, and everywhere the eye feasted on the riotous colouring of blossoms such as we had never before seen. The only fly in the ointment was the ever-present sense of defeat coupled with the knowledge that with only a little better luck we should have won through.

In spite of our failure, however, I felt that we had learnt much; and perhaps the most important lesson of all was that we had been taught the real value of oxygen. Prior to the formation of the 1922 Expedition, the oxygen problem had already been the subject of much discussion round which two distinct schools of thought had arisen. The first, headed by Professor G. Dreyer, F.R.S., Professor of Pathology at the University of Oxford, was staunch to the belief that, without the assistance of a supply of oxygen carried in containers on the back of the climber, it would be impossible for a man to reach the summit of Mount Everest. The second body of scientific opinion held that, not only would it be possible for a man to attain the summit of Everest unaided by an artificial supply of oxygen, but that the weight of such a supply would only hamper the climber in his efforts, and thus completely counterbalance any advantages likely to accrue from its use. To arrive at an impartial conclusion as to the correctitude of these two divergent opinions, it is only necessary to give careful consideration to the results achieved on the two high climbs of May 22 and May 27 respectively. The former was made without an artificial supply of oxygen, the latter with. The first climbing party, consisting of Mallory, Morshead, Norton, and Somervell, left the North Col at 7 a.m. on the 20th of May, and that afternoon, at an altitude of 25,000 feet above sea-level, pitched a camp just off the great North ridge leading down from the shoulder. Morshead had suffered from the cold and was evidently unwell. One of Norton's ears had been badly frostbitten, and Mallory had frost-bitten finger-tips. Somervell alone was, to all intents and purposes, as yet untouched. Snow fell during the night, but they were untroubled by wind. At eight o'clock next morning they left their camp—all save Morshead, who, apparently at the end of his tether and unable to go farther, had to remain behind. After over six hours' climbing, Mallory, Norton, and Somervell succeeded in reaching an altitude of 26,985 feet; so that, since their departure from their high camp, they had gained a vertical height of 1,985 feet at a rate of ascent of 330 feet per hour. The point at which they turned back lies below the shoulder on the great North ridge, and is, in horizontal distance, about 1⅛ miles from the summit, and rather over 2,000 feet below it in vertical height. They began to retrace their steps at 2.30 in the afternoon, and regained their high camp at four o'clock; their rate of descent therefore was 1,320 feet per hour. Shortly after 4 p.m., accompanied by Morshead, they started on the return journey to the North Col, where they arrived at 11.30 that night, a rate of descent of 270 feet per hour. We had seen them on their way down from their high camp, and acting on instructions from Colonel Strutt, we went up towards the North Col on the 23rd to render them assistance. We met them just above the foot of the steep slopes leading up the col. They were obviously in the last stages of exhaustion, as, indeed, men should be who had done their best on a mountain like Mount Everest.

On the 25th of May the second party, consisting of Geoffrey Bruce, Tejbir and myself, left the North Col. Our porters, who did not use oxygen, left at eight o'clock;

we, using oxygen, left at 9.30 a.m., and in an hour and a half succeeded in overtaking them at an altitude of 24,500 feet, where, somewhat fatigued with their three hours' effort, they paused to rest. A moment's calculation will show that we had been climbing at the rate of 1,000 feet per hour. Leaving the porters to follow, we eventually gained an altitude of 25,500 feet, where, owing to bad weather, we were constrained to camp. It was not until two o'clock in the afternoon that the porters rejoined us, despite the fact that our own progress had been hindered by the necessity for much step-cutting. That night in our high camp was a night of trial and no rest, and the following day, the 26th, was little better; in addition, our supply of food was exhausted. Then followed a second night, when the advantages of using oxygen to combat fierce cold were strikingly evident. At six o'clock on the morning of the 27th, having had practically no rest for two nights and a day, half starved and suffering acutely from hunger, we set out from our high camp in full hopes of gaining the summit of Mount Everest. Half an hour later, at an altitude of 26,000 feet, Tejbir broke down—an unfortunate occurrence that may be largely attributed to his lack of really windproof clothing. On arriving at a height of 26,500 feet we were forced to leave the ridge, so violent and penetratingly cold was the wind to which we were exposed. The thousand feet from our camp up to this point had occupied one and a half hours, some twenty minutes of which had been employed in re-arranging the loads when Tejbir broke down. Our rate of progress, therefore, had been about 900 feet per hour, in spite of the fact that we each carried a load of over 40 lb. After leaving the ridge we struck out over difficult ground across the great North face of the mountain, gaining but little in altitude, but steadily approaching our goal. Eventually we decided to turn back at a point less than half a mile in horizontal distance from, and about 1,700 feet below, the summit. Thus, although we had climbed in vertical height only some 300 feet higher than the first party, nevertheless we were more than twice as close to the summit than they had been when they turned back.

To summarise the two performances. The first party established a camp at an altitude of 25,000 feet, occupied it for one night, and finally reaching a point 26,985 feet in height, and 1⅜ miles from the summit, returned without a break to the North Col. The second party established a camp at an altitude of 25,500 feet, occupied it for two nights and almost two days, and eventually reaching a point of 27,300 feet high and less than half a mile from the summit, returned without a break to Camp III. The weather conditions throughout were incomparably worse than those experienced by the first party. The difference between the two performances cannot be ascribed to superior climbing powers on the part of the second party, for the simple reason that all the members of the first party were skilled and proven mountaineers, while Geoffrey Bruce and Lance-Corporal Tejbir, though at home in the hills, had never before set foot on a snow and ice mountain. No matter how strong and willing and gallant an inexperienced climber may be, his lack of mountaineering skill and knowledge inevitably results in that prodigality of effort—much of it needless—which invariably and quickly places him at a grave disadvantage when compared with the trained mountaineer. The strength of a climbing party is no greater than that of its weakest member. Judged on this basis the second party was very weak compared with the first, and the superior results obtained by the former can only be ascribed to the fact that they made use of an artificial supply of oxygen.

The contention, therefore, that the disadvantages of its weight would more than counterbalance the advantages of an artificial supply of oxygen, may be dismissed as groundless, and the assumption may be made that on any further attempt upon Everest oxygen will form a most important part of the climber's equipment. The question next arises as to the exact stage in the proceedings at which recourse should be made to the assistance of oxygen. The strongest members of the Expedition felt fit and well, and recuperated readily from fatigue, at Camp III, 21,000 feet above sea-level, but at the North Col this was no longer the case. Thus it would seem that the upper level of true acclimatisation lies somewhere between 21,000 and 23,000 feet. I would therefore advocate commencing to use oxygen somewhere between these two levels, preferably at the foot of the steep slopes leading up to the North Col. The use of small quantities would allow the climber to reach the Col without unduly tiring himself. From the North Col to a high camp situated at an altitude of about 26,500 feet, a slightly increased quantity of oxygen would suffice to enable the climber to progress almost as rapidly as he would in the much lower levels of the Alps. We know from experience that a camp at the above-mentioned altitude can be readily established, and in all except the worst of weather conditions a party can make its way down again. Between the camp and the summit there would be a vertical height of only 2,500 feet, and it is conceivable that with a full supply of oxygen this distance could be covered in as little as four hours. I am strongly of the opinion that only one camp should be used between the North Col and the summit. No matter what precautions are taken, man's strength is rapidly sapped during the stay at these great altitudes, and the plan of campaign most likely to ensure success would appear to be leisurely and comfortable progress as far as the North Col, the establishment of a high camp at 26,500 feet, and a final dash to the summit. This last part of the programme, however, would not be feasible unless a small dump of oxygen were made at a height of about 27,500 feet. To do this it would be necessary for a specially detailed party to spend one night at the high camp, and on the following day employ their strength in making a dump somewhere above the shoulder. This done, they would then be able to return to the North Col with the satisfaction of knowing that they had made it possible for the actual climbing party to win through.

It is by no means yet certain which is the best line of approach to the North Col. The route hitherto followed, viâ the East Rongbuk Glacier, is tedious and roundabout, but it has the advantage of being well sheltered from the wind, and, except for the final steep slopes beneath the col, safe under any conditions. Much more direct, however, and probably less arduous, is the approach from over the main Rongbuk Glacier. The line of ascent thence to the summit of the col presents no real difficulty, and, provided it is not found to be too exposed to the wind, is undoubtedly much safer, even after heavy snowfalls, than that previously followed. In the light of past experience one can hardly hope to count on good weather as an ally; adequate protection in the form of windproof clothing will enable the climber to face all but actual snowstorms.

Climbing parties making the final assaults on the summit should be small, consisting of two men and no more. In the event of one man collapsing, his comrade, if at all up to scratch, should be able to get him down in safety. By so limiting the size of the parties, a number of attacks, each one as strong as if effected by a large and cumbersome team of, say, four, could be carried out. Again, in the case of small parties as suggested, mutual attention to each other's oxygen outfit is possible and any necessary repair or adjustment more expeditiously made.

The type of climber who should go farthest on Mount

Everest would appear to be similar to that which best suits the Alps. Of the physical attributes necessary, the following points, in addition to what is usually termed perfect physical fitness, may be emphasised. In the rarefied atmosphere of high altitudes the larger the vital capacity the better. By the term "vital capacity" is meant the maximum amount of air an individual is able to expel from the lungs by voluntary effort after taking the deepest possible inspiration. Compared with the lean, spare type of individual, the thickset, often muscle-bound man, though possibly equal to an immense effort provided it is of short duration, is, as a rule, at a great disadvantage. The Expedition has also shown beyond all possible doubt that the tall man is less prone to become fatigued than one of shorter stature. Again, as is well known amongst mountaineers, the long-legged, short-trunk type of body is immensely superior to the short-legged, long-trunk type.

Perhaps more important than perfect physical fitness to the would-be conqueror of Everest is the possession of the correct mentality. Absolutely essential are singleness of aim, namely, the attainment of the summit, and unswerving faith in the possibility of its achievement. Half-heartedness in even one member of the attacking party spells almost certain failure. Many a strong party in the Alps has failed to reach its objective through the depressing effect of the presence of one doubting Thomas. Like an insidious disease, a wavering, infirm belief is liable to spread and cause the destruction of the hopes of those who come into contact with it. The man who cannot face Mount Everest without at the same time proclaiming that the mountain has the odds in its favour would do better by himself and others to leave the proposition severely alone. Of almost equal importance is the possession of what may be called mental energy or will power, or simply "go." Mountaineers may be divided into two classes according to their behaviour when, tired and well-nigh exhausted, they are called upon to make yet one more supreme effort. There are those who, lacking the will power necessary to force their jaded bodies on to still further action, give in; others, possessed of an almost inexhaustible fund of mental energy, will rise to the occasion, not once, but time and again. Physical pain is the safety valve which nature has provided to prevent harm being done to the body by exhaustion. But nature's margin of safety is a wide one. On Everest, this margin must be narrowed down, if necessary, to vanishing-point; and this can only be done by the climber whose fund of mental energy is sufficient to drive his body on and on, no matter how intense the pains of exhaustion, even to destruction if need be.

CHAPTER IX

NOTES ON EQUIPMENT

Our recent experiences having shown that the greatest altitude at which acclimatisation takes place is about 22,000 feet above sea-level, it may be reasonably assumed that, from the climber's point of view, high altitude on Mount Everest begins at that height. Incidentally, also, on approaching the North Col over the East Rongbuk Glacier, the snow and ice conditions met with up to this level approximate very closely to summer conditions in the Alps. Above 22,000 feet, however, such conditions, particularly the state of the snow, resemble those met with in the Alps in mid-winter. This high-altitude zone may be further divided into two sub-zones—the first, from 22,000 feet (the foot of the steep snow and ice slopes leading up to the North Col) to 23,000 feet, in which climatic conditions are by no means severe, as the North Col affords protection from the prevailing west wind; and the second, from 23,000 feet onwards, of which extreme cold and strong wind are the predominant characteristics.

It is therefore evident that the climber must be equipped according to the zone in which he finds himself. In the first zone clothing somewhat warmer than that used in the Alps in the summer is practically sufficient. Owing to the marked intensity of the sun's rays, however, it is advisable to cover the trunk with at least one layer of sunproof material, such as a sunproof shirt with spine pad, while a solar topee and suitable snow-glasses constitute the best form of headgear. Crookes' glasses of smoke-blue colour proved superior to other varieties; they afford complete protection from glare and do not cause eye-strain and subsequent headache. As sunburn, even very superficial and involving only a small area, is invariably followed by conditions of feverishness which must impair one's fitness, a veil should be worn over the face and gloves on the hands. Oxygen should be employed from the foot of the North Col slopes onwards, for no useful purpose can be served by tiring oneself through not using it, when, as we have seen elsewhere, full recovery from fatigue is no longer possible at 23,000 feet. The second zone (from 23,000 feet onwards), where a radical change in climatic conditions is manifest, demands more complicated preparation. Wind is seldom absent, and the degree of intensity of the cold is comparable with that met with at the Poles, and indeed probably often exceeds it. Also, owing to the rarefied state of the atmosphere, the cold is felt much more severely than would be the case at sea-level. A far greater volume of air is expelled from the climber's lungs, and this air, at blood heat and under a low pressure approximating to one-third of an atmosphere, is saturated with moisture drawn from the body viâ the lungs. The result is a proportionately far greater loss of animal heat. Further, the partial pressure of oxygen contained in a normal atmosphere becomes so low at altitudes over 23,000 feet that, unless the climber has recourse to a supply of oxygen carried by himself, his climbing efficiency is enormously reduced. The climbing equipment of the mountaineer in this second zone of high altitude should therefore include, firstly, a supply of oxygen; secondly, warm and windproof clothing and footgear; thirdly, plenty of food and drink, as the use of oxygen has a most stimulating effect upon the appetite.

The oxygen equipment has already been fully described by Mr. Unna in the *Alpine Journal*, vol. xxxiv., page 235. The apparatus is, in principle, quite simple. It consists of a frame carried on the shoulders of the climber, at whose back, in a rack attached to the frame, are four steel cylinders filled with oxygen compressed to 120 atmospheres. From the cylinders the oxygen is taken by means of copper tubes over to an instrument arm in front of the climber. This instrument arm, also attached to the frame, carries the pressure gauges and so forth which indicate how much oxygen the climber is left and how rapidly the supplies are being used up. Close to the instrument arm and readily accessible are the valves necessary for controlling the rate of flow of oxygen from the apparatus. From the instrument arm the oxygen passes through a flexible rubber tubing up to a mask covering the face of the climber. The two types of mask supplied to the Expedition proved useless, partly owing to their stifling effect upon the wearer, and partly to the fact that saliva and moisture collected rapidly under them and froze. Both, therefore, had to be discarded, but fortunately I was able to make a substitute which functioned successfully. This mask consists of a rubber tube into which is let a rubber bladder by means of a glass T-piece, or by means of two straight pieces of glass tube let in at opposite ends of the bladder. One end of the rubber tube is fastened to the tube of the apparatus out of which the oxygen flows, the other end being held in the climber's mouth. On exhaling, the climber closes the rubber tube by biting upon it, and the oxygen issuing from the apparatus, instead of being wasted, is stored up in the rubber bladder. On inhaling, the pressure of the teeth is released sufficiently to allow the rubber tube to open, thus permitting the oxygen stored up in the bladder to flow into the climber's mouth, whence, mixing with the air exhaled, it is drawn into the lungs. The chief advantages of this mask are that, firstly, it economises oxygen to the greatest possible extent, and secondly, the swelling and the shrinking of the bladder during each exhalation and inhalation respectively give the climber a fair idea as to how rapidly the oxygen is flowing from the apparatus, and thus enables him to keep a check upon the readings of the flow-meter, or instrument which indicates the rate of flow of gas. In actual practice it was found that in the space of a few minutes the climber used the mask quite automatically.

The biting upon and closing the rubber tube and subsequent opening were performed without mental effort.

A certain amount of breathing takes place viâ the pores of the skin. As, however, the best clothing for a climber on Mount Everest is windproof, there is a likelihood of the air surrounding the body becoming stale, in which case the process of skin-breathing is seriously impeded. This difficulty could be easily surmounted by flushing out the stale air by means of a tube inserted inside the climber's clothes, the flushing-out process being done at intervals by temporarily fixing this tube to the orifice of the oxygen apparatus. It is not known definitely whether the advantage gained would be worth the trouble, but there is every reason for believing so. In any case it is a matter which might well be critically tested on the next Expedition.

Cigarette-smoking proved of great value at high altitudes. Geoffrey Bruce, Tejbir, and I, after pitching camp at 25,500 feet, settled down inside our little tent about 2.30 in the afternoon. From then until seven o'clock the following evening we used no oxygen at all. At first we noticed that unless one kept one's mind on the question of breathing—that is, made breathing a voluntary process unstead of the involuntary process it ordinarily is—one suffered from lack of air and a consequent feeling of suffocation—a feeling from which one recovered by voluntarily forcing the lungs to work faster than they would of their own accord. There is a physiological explanation for this phenomenon. At normal altitudes human blood holds in solution a considerable quantity of carbon dioxide, which serves to stimulate the nerve centre controlling one's involuntary breathing. At great altitudes, however, where, in order to obtain a sufficiency of oxygen, the climber is forced to breathe enormous volumes of air, much of this carbon dioxide is washed out of the blood, and the nerve centre, no longer sufficiently stimulated, fails to promote an adequately active involuntary breathing. A voluntary process must be substituted, and this throws a considerable strain upon the mind, and renders sleep impossible. On smoking cigarettes we discovered after the first few inhalations it was no longer necessary to concentrate on breathing, the process becoming once more an involuntary one. Evidently some constituent of cigarette smoke takes the place and performs the stimulating function of the carbon dioxide normally present. The effect of a cigarette lasted for about three hours.

Clothing is a most important matter. It would be difficult to exaggerate the intensity of the cold encountered at high altitudes on Mount Everest. Several layers—the innermost of which should be of silk, the others wool of moderate weight—form a much better protection against cold than one or two heavy layers. The chief item of clothing, however, should consist of a jumper and trousers made of windproof material. Two of these windproof suits should be worn one above the other, and every precaution taken to reduce the circulation of the air to the smallest possible extent. The hands must be protected in accordance with the same principles, and the head. I used a R.N.A.S. pattern flying helmet and found it most satisfactory. Helmet and snow-glasses should completely cover the head and face, leaving no skin exposed. Boots were a source of trouble to all, but fortunately we had so many different designs which we could test out thoroughly that we are now able to form a very shrewd idea as to which kind is the most suitable. Leather conducts heat too well for reliance to be placed upon it for the preservation of warmth. The uppers of the boots should be of felt, strengthened where necessary to prevent stretching, by leather straps covered by duroprened canvas. Toe and heel caps must be hard and strong, and the former especially should be high, so that the toes are given plenty of room. The sole of the boot should be composed of a layer of thin leather attached to a layer of three-ply wood, hinged in two sections at the instep. A thin layer of felt should form the inside of the sole. The boots should be large enough to accommodate in comfort two pairs of thick socks, or, even better still, two pairs of thin socks and one pair of thick socks. Nails used in the boots should penetrate through the leather into the three-ply wood, but not through the latter.

In conclusion, I should like to thank the Governing Body of the Imperial College of Science and Technology for granting me the necessary leave to enable me to take part in the 1922 Mount Everest Expedition, and also for granting me facilities for carrying out a considerable number of investigations in the laboratory of the Department of Chemical Technology upon questions relating, amongst others, to oxygen equipment, fuels, and vacuum flasks. These last were required in order to enable us to keep foods liquid at heights over 23,000 feet, and the flasks obtained on the market proved quite useless for this purpose in view of the fact that they had not been sufficiently well evacuated.

THE THIRD ATTEMPT

By

GEORGE LEIGH-MALLORY

CHAPTER X

THE THIRD ATTEMPT

The project of making a third attempt this season was mooted immediately on the return of Finch and Geoffrey Bruce to the Base Camp. There in hours of idleness we had discussed their prospects and wondered what they would be doing as we gazed at the mountain to make out the weather on the great ridge. We were not surprised to learn when they came down that the summit was still unconquered, and we were not yet prepared to accept defeat. The difficulty was to find a party. Of the six who had been already engaged only one was obviously fit for another great effort. Somervell had shown a recuperative capacity beyond the rest of us. After one day at the Base he had insisted on going up again to Camp III in case he might be of use to the others. The rest were more or less knocked out. Morshead's frostbitten fingers and toes, from which he was now suffering constant pain, caused grave anxiety of most serious consequences, and the only plan for him was to go down to a lower elevation as soon as possible. Norton's feet had also been affected; he complained at first only of bruises, but the cold had come through the soles of his boots; his trouble too was frostbite. In any case he could not have come up again, for the strain had told on his heart and he now found himself left without energy or strength.

Geoffrey Bruce's feet also were so badly frostbitten that he could not walk. Finch, however, was not yet to be counted out. He was evidently very much exhausted, but an examination of his heart revealed no disorder; it was hoped that in five or six days he would be able to start again. My own case was doubtful. Of my frostbitten finger-tips only one was giving trouble; the extremity above the first joint was black, but the injury was not very deep. Longstaff, who took an interest which we all appreciated in preventing us from doing ourselves permanent injury, pointed out the probability that fingers already touched and highly susceptible to cold would be much more severely injured next time, and was inclined to turn me down, from his medical point of view, on account of my fingers alone. A much more serious matter was the condition of my heart. I felt weak and lazy when it was a question of the least physical exertion, and the heart was found to have a "thrill." Though I was prepared to take risks with my fingers I was prepared to take none with my heart, even had General Bruce allowed me. However, I did not abandon hope. My heart was examined again on June 3, no thrill was heard, and though my pulse was rapid and accelerated quickly with exertion it was capable of satisfactory recovery. We at once arranged that Somervell, Finch, and I, together with Wakefield and Crawford, should set forth the same day.

It was already evident that whatever we were to do would now have to wait for the weather. Though the Lama at the Rongbuk Monastery had told us that the monsoon was usually to be expected about June 10, and we knew that it was late last year, the signs of its approach were gathering every day. Mount Everest could rarely be seen after 9 or 10 a.m. until the clouds cleared away in the evening; and a storm approaching from the West Rongbuk Glacier would generally sweep down the valley in the afternoon. Though we came to despise this blustering phenomenon,—for nothing worse came of it than light hail or snow, either at our camp or higher,—we should want much fairer days for climbing, and each storm threatened to be the beginning of something far more serious. However, we planned to be on the spot to take any chance that offered. The signs were even more ominous than usual as Finch and I walked up to Camp I on the afternoon of June 3; we could hardly feel optimistic; and it was soon apparent that, far from having recovered his strength, my companion was quite unfit for another big expedition. We walked slowly and frequently halted; it was painful to see what efforts it cost him to make any progress. However, he persisted in coming on.

We had not long disposed ourselves comfortably within the four square walls of our "sangar," always a pleasant change from the sloping sides of a tent, when snow began to fall. Released at last by the West wind which had held it back, the monsoon was free to work its will, and we soon understood that the great change of weather had now come. Fine, glistening particles were driven by the wind through the chinks in our walls, to be drifted on the floor or on our coverings where we lay during the night; and as morning grew the snow still fell as thickly as ever. Finch wisely decided to go back, and we charged him with a message to General Bruce, saying that we saw no reason at present to alter our plans. With the whole day to spend confined and inactive we had plenty of time to consider what we ought to do under these conditions. We went over well-worn arguments once more. It would have been an obvious and easy course, for which no one could reproach us, to have said simply, The monsoon has come; this is the end of the climbing season; it is time to go home. But the case, we felt, was not yet hopeless. The monsoon is too variable and uncertain to be so easily admitted as the final arbiter. There might yet be good prospects ahead of us. It was not unreasonable to expect an interval of fine weather after the first heavy snow, and with eight or ten fair days a third attempt might still be made. In any case, to retire now if the smallest chance remained to us would be an unworthy end to the Expedition. We need not run our heads into obvious danger; but rather than be stopped by a general estimate of conditions we would prefer to retire before some definite risk that we were not prepared to take or simply fail to overcome the difficulties.

After a second night of unremitting snowfall the weather on the morning of June 5 improved and we decided to go on. Low and heavy clouds were still flowing down the East Rongbuk Glacier, but precipitation ceased at an early hour and the sky brightened to the West. It was surprising, after all we had seen of the flakes passing our door, that no great amount of snow was lying on the stones about our camp. But the snow had come on a warm current and melted or evaporated, so that after all the depth was no more than 6 inches at this elevation (17,500 feet). Even on the glacier we went up a long way before noticing a perceptible increase of depth. We passed Camp II, not requiring to halt at this stage, and were well up towards Camp III before the fresh snow became a serious impediment. It was still snowing up here, though not very heavily; there was nothing to cheer the grey scene; the clinging snow about our feet was so wet that even the best of our boots were soaked through, and the last two hours up to Camp III were tiresome enough. Nor was it a cheering camp when we reached it. The tents had been struck for the safety of the poles, but not packed up. We found them now half-full of snow and ice. The stores were all buried; everything that we wanted had first to be dug out.

The snow up here was so much deeper that we anxiously discussed the possibility of going further. With

15 to 18 inches of snow to contend with, not counting drifts, the labour would be excessive, and until the snow solidified there would be considerable danger at several points. But the next morning broke fine; we had soon a clear sky and glorious sunshine; it was the warmest day that any of us remembered at Camp III; and as we watched the amazing rapidity with which the snow solidified and the rocks began to appear about our camp, our spirits rose. The side of Everest facing us looked white and cold; but we observed a cloud of snow blown from the North Ridge; it would not be long at this rate before it was fit to climb. We had already resolved to use oxygen on the third attempt. It was improbable that we should beat our own record without it, for the strain of previous efforts would count against us, and we had not the time to improve on our organisation by putting a second camp above the North Col. Somervell, after Finch's explanation of the mechanical details, felt perfectly confident that he could manage the oxygen apparatus, and all those who had used oxygen were convinced that they went up more easily with its help than they could expect to go without it. Somervell and I intended to profit by their experience. They had discovered that the increased combustion in the body required a larger supply of food; we must arrange for a bountiful provision. Their camp at 25,000 feet had been too low; we would try to establish one now, as we had intended before, at 26,000 feet. And we hoped for a further advantage in going higher than

Finch and Bruce had done before using oxygen; whereas they had started using it at 21,000 feet, we intended to go up to our old camp at 25,000 feet without it, perhaps use a cylinder each up to 26,000 feet, and at all events start from that height for the summit with a full supply of four cylinders. If this was not the correct policy as laid down by Professor Dryer, it would at least be a valuable experiment.

Our chief anxiety under these new conditions was to provide for the safety of our porters. We hoped that after fixing our fifth camp at 26,000 feet, at the earliest three days, hence on the fourth day of fine weather, the porters might be able to go down by themselves to the North Col in easy conditions; to guard against the danger of concealed crevasses there Crawford would meet them at the foot of the North Ridge to conduct them properly roped to Camp IV. As the supply officer at this camp he would also be able to superintend the descent over the first steep slope of certain porters who would go down from Camp IV without sleeping after carrying up their loads.

But the North Col had first to be reached. With so much new snow to contend with we should hardly get there in one day. If we were to make the most of our chance in the interval of fair weather, we should lose no time in carrying up the loads for some part of the distance. It was decided therefore to begin this work on the following day, June 7.

In the ascent to the North Col after the recent snowfall we considered that an avalanche was to be feared only in one place, the steep final slope below the shelf. There we could afford to run no risk; we must test the snow and be certain that it was safe before we could cross this slope. Probably we should be obliged to leave our loads below it, having gained, as a result of our day's work, the great advantage of a track. An avalanche might also come down, we thought, on the first steep slope where the ascent began. Here it could do us no harm, and the behaviour of the snow on this slope would be a test of its condition.

The party, Somervell, Crawford, and I, with fourteen porters (Wakefield was to be supply officer at Camp III), set out at 8 a.m. In spite of the hard frost of the previous night, the crust was far from bearing our weight; we sank up to our knees in almost every step, and two hours were taken in traversing the snowfield. At 10.15 a.m., Somervell, I, a porter, and Crawford, roped up in that order, began to work up the steep ice-slope, now covered with snow. It was clear that the three of us without loads must take the lead in turns stamping out the track for our porters. These men, after their immense efforts on the first and second attempts, had all volunteered to "go high," as they said once more, and everything must be done to ease the terrible work of carrying the loads over the soft snow. No trace was found of our previous tracks, and we were soon arguing as to where exactly they might be as we slanted across the slope. It was remarkable that the snow adhered so well to the ice that we were able to get up without cutting steps. Everything was done by trenching the snow to induce it to come down if it would; every test gave a satisfactory result. Once this crucial place was passed, we plodded on without hesitation. If the snow would not come down where we had formerly encountered steep bare ice, a fortiori, above, on the gentler slopes, we had nothing to fear. The thought of an avalanche was dismissed from our minds.

It was necessarily slow work forging our way through the deep snow, but the party was going extraordinarily well, and the porters were evidently determined to get on. Somervell gave us a long lead, and Crawford next, in spite of the handicap of shorter legs, struggled upwards in some of the worst snow we met until I relieved him. I found the effort at each step so great that no method of breathing I had formerly employed was adequate; it was necessary to pause after each lifting movement for a whole series of breaths, rapid at first and gradually slower, before the weight was transferred again to the other foot. About 1.30 p.m. I halted, and the porters, following on three separate ropes, soon came up with the leading party. We should have been glad to stay where we were for a long rest. But the hour was already late, and as Somervell was ready to take the lead again, we decided to push on. We were now about 400 feet below a conspicuous block of ice and 600 feet below Camp IV, still on the gentle slopes of the corridor. Somervell had advanced only 100 feet, rather up the slope than across it, and the last party of porters had barely begun to move up in the steps. The scene was peculiarly bright and windless, and as we rarely spoke, nothing was to be heard but the laboured panting of our lungs. This stillness was suddenly disturbed. We were startled by an ominous sound, sharp, arresting, violent, and yet somehow soft like an explosion of untamped gunpowder. I had never before on a mountain-side heard such a sound; but all of us, I imagine, knew instinctively what it meant, as though we had been accustomed to hear it every day of our lives. In a moment I observed the surface of the snow broken and puckered where it had been even for a few yards to the right of me. I took two steps convulsively in this direction with some quick thought of getting nearer to the edge of the danger that threatened us. And then I began to move slowly downwards, inevitably carried on the whole moving surface by a force I was utterly powerless to resist. Somehow I managed to turn out from the slope so as to avoid being pushed headlong and backwards down it. For a second or two I seemed hardly to be in danger as I went quietly sliding down with the snow. Then the rope at my waist tightened and held me back. A wave of snow came over me and I was buried. I supposed that the matter was settled. However, I called to mind experiences related by other parties; and it had been suggested that the best chance of escape in this situation lay in swimming. I thrust out my arms above my head and actually went through some sort of motions of swimming on my back. Beneath the surface of the snow, with nothing to inform the senses of the world outside it, I had no impression of speed after the first acceleration—I struggled in the tumbling snow, unconscious of everything else—until, perhaps, only a few seconds later, I knew the pace was easing up. I felt an increasing pressure about my body. I wondered how tightly I should be squeezed, and then the avalanche came to rest.

My arms were free ; my legs were near the surface. After a brief struggle, I was standing again, surprised and breathless, in the motionless snow. But the rope was tight at my waist ; the porter tied on next me, I supposed, must be deeply buried. To my further surprise, he quickly emerged, unharmed as myself. Somervell and Crawford too, though they had been above me by the rope's length, were now quite close, and soon extricated themselves. We subsequently made out that their experiences had been very similar to mine. But where were the rest ? Looking down over the foam of snow, we saw one group of porters some little distance, perhaps 150 feet, below us. Presumably the others must be buried somewhere betweeen us and them, and though no sign of these missing men appeared, we at once prepared to find and dig them out. The porters we saw still stood their ground instead of coming up to help. We soon made out that they were the party who had been immediately behind us, and they were pointing below them. They had travelled further than us in the avalanche, presumably because they were nearer the centre, where it was moving more rapidly. The other two parties, one of four and one of five men roped together, must have been carried even further. We could still hope that they were safe. But as we hurried down we soon saw that beneath the place where the four porters were standing was a formidable drop ; it was only too plain that the missing men had been swept over it. We had no difficulty in finding a way round this obstacle ; in a very short time we were standing under its shadow. The ice-cliff was from 40 to 60 feet high in different places ; the crevasse at its foot was more or less filled up with avalanche snow. Our fears were soon confirmed. One man was quickly uncovered and found to be still breathing ; before long we were certain that he would live. Another whom we dug out near him had been killed by the fall. He and his party appeared to have struck the hard lower lip of the crevasse, and were lying under the snow on or near the edge of it. The four porters who had escaped soon pulled themselves together after the first shock of the accident, and now worked here with Crawford and did everything they could to extricate the other bodies, while Somervell and I went down into the crevasse. A loop of rope which we pulled up convinced us that the other party must be here. It was slow work loosening the snow with the pick or adze of an ice-axe and shovelling it with the hands. But we were able to follow the rope to the bodies. One was dug up lifeless ; another was found upside down, and when we uncovered his face Somervell thought he was still breathing. We had the greatest difficulty in extricating this man, so tightly was the snow packed about his limbs ; his load, four oxygen cylinders on a steel frame, had to be cut from his back, and eventually he was dragged out. Though buried for about forty minutes, he had survived the fall and the suffocation, and suffered no serious harm. Of the two others in this party of four, we found only one. We had at length to give up a hopeless search with the certain knowledge that the first of them to be swept over the cliff, and the most deeply buried, must long ago be dead. Of the other five, all the bodies were recovered, but only one was alive. The two who had so marvellously escaped were able to walk down to Camp III, and were almost perfectly well next day. The other seven were killed.

This tragic calamity was naturally the end of the third attempt to climb Mount Everest. The surviving porters who had lost their friends or brothers behaved with dignity, making no noisy parade of the grief they felt. We asked them whether they wished to go up and bring down the bodies for orderly burial. They preferred to leave them where they were. For my part, I was glad of this decision. What better burial could they have than to lie in the snow where they fell? In their honour a large cairn was built at Camp III.

A few words must be added with regard to this accident. No one will imagine that we had pushed on recklessly disregarding the new conditions of fresh snow. Three members of the Alpine Club, with experience of judging snow for themselves, chiefly, of course, in the Alps, had all supposed that the party was safe. They had imagined that on those gentle slopes the snow would not move. In what way had they been deceived? The fact that the avalanche snow came to rest on the slope where they were proves that their calculation was not so very far wrong. But the snow cannot all have been of the quality that adhered so well to the steep ice-slope lower down. Where the avalanche started, not from the line of their steps, but about 100 feet higher, it was shaded to some extent by a broken wall of ice. There, perhaps, it had both drifted more deeply and remained more free and powdery, and the weight of this snow was probably sufficient to push the other down the slope once its surface had been disturbed. More experience, more knowledge might perhaps have warned us not to go there. One never can know enough about snow. But looking up the corridor again after the event, I wondered how I ever could be certain not to be deceived by appearances so innocent.

The regret of all members of the Expedition for the loss of our seven porters will have been elsewhere expressed. It is my part only to add this: the work of carrying up our camps on Mount Everest is beyond the range of a simple contract measured in terms of money; the porters had come to have a share in our enterprise, and these men died in an act of voluntary service freely rendered and faithfully performed.

CHAPTER XI

CONCLUSIONS

It might be supposed that, from the experience of two expeditions to Mount Everest, it would be possible to deduce an estimate of the dangers and difficulties involved and to formulate a plan for overcoming the obstacles which would meet with universal approval among mountaineers. But, in fact, though many deductions could hardly be denied, I should be surprised to find, even among us of the second party, anything like complete agreement either in our judgment of events or in our ideas for the future. Accordingly, I must be understood as expressing only my personal opinions. The reader, no doubt, will judge the book more interesting if he finds the joint authors disagreeing among themselves.

The story of the first attempt to climb the mountain in 1922 will have no doubts on one point. The final camp was too low. However strong a party may be brought to the assault, their aim, unless they are provided with oxygen, must be to establish a camp considerably higher than our camp at 25,000 feet. The whole performance of the porters encourages us to believe that this can be done. Some of them went to a height of 25,000 feet and more, not once only, but thrice; and they accomplished this feat with strength to spare. It is reasonable to suppose that these same men, or others of their type, could carry loads up to 27,000 feet. But it would be equally unreasonable to suppose that they could reach this height in one day from the camp on Chang La at 23,000 feet. No one would be so foolish as to organise an attempt on this assumption. Two camps instead of one must be placed above the Chang La; another stage must be added to the structure before the climbing party sets forth to reach the summit.

But how exactly is this to be done? It is to this question that one would wish to deduce an answer from the experience of 1922. It is very unlikely that any future party will find itself in the position to carry out any ideal plan of organisation. Ideally, they ought to start by considering what previous performances might help or hinder the aim of bringing the party of attack in the fittest possible condition to the last camp. What ought they to have done or not to have done, having regard to acclimatisation? It is still impossible to lay down the law on this head. After the first Expedition, I supposed that the limit of acclimatisation must be somewhere about 21,000 feet. It now seems probable that it is higher. One of the physiologists who has been most deeply concerned with this problem of acclimatisation considers that it would probably be desirable, from the physiological point of view, to stay four or five days at 25,000 feet before proceeding to attempt the two last stages on consecutive days. Those of us who slept at Camp V for the first attempt would certainly be agreed in our attitude towards this counsel. The desire to continue the advance and spend another night at a higher elevation, if it persisted at all for so long a time at 25,000 feet, would be chilled to tepidity, and the increasing desire to get away from Camp V might lead to retreat instead of advance. The conditions must be altogether more comfortable if the climbers are to derive any advantage from their rustication at this altitude. It would not be impossible, perhaps, if every effort were concentrated on this end, to make a happy home where the aspiring mountaineers might pass a long week-end in enjoyment of the simplest life at 25,000 feet; it would not be practicable, having regard to other ends to be served by the system of transport. But it might be well to spend a similar period for acclimatisation 2,000 feet lower on the Chang La. There a very comfortable camp, with perfect shelter from the prevailing wind and good snow to lie on, can easily be established. Noel actually spent three successive nights there in 1922, and apparently was the better rather than the worse for the experience.

No less important in this connection is the effect of exertions at high altitudes on a man's subsequent performance. We have to take into account the condition of the climbing parties when they returned to the Base Camp after reaching approximately 27,000 feet. With one exception, all the climbers were affected in various degrees by their exertions, to the prejudice of future efforts. It would seem, therefore, that they cannot have had much strength to spare for the final stage to the summit. But there was a general agreement among the climbers that it was not so much the normal exertion of climbing upwards that was in itself unduly exhausting, but the addition of anything that might be considered abnormal, such as cutting steps, contending with wind, pushing on for a particular reason at a faster pace, and the many little things that had to be done in camp. It is difficult from a normal elevation to appreciate how great is the difference between establishing a camp on the one hand and merely ascending to one already established on the other. If ever it proves possible to organise an advanced party whose business it would be to establish at 25,000 feet a much more comfortable camp than ours in 1922, and if, in addition, a man could be spared to undertake the preparation of meals, the climbers detailed for the highest section of all would both be spared a considerable fatigue and would have a better chance of real rest and sleep.

The peculiar dangers of climbing at great altitudes were illustrated by the experience of 1922. The difficulty of maintaining the standard of sound and accurate mountaineering among a party all more or less affected by the conditions, and the delays and misfortunes that may arise from the exhaustion of one of the party, are dangers which might be minimised by a supporting party. Two men remaining at the final camp and two men near Camp V watching the progress of the unit of assault along the final ridge, and prepared to come to their assistance, might serve to produce

CHANG LA AND NORTH-EAST SHOULDER OF MOUNT EVEREST

vital stimulants, hot tea or merely water, at the critical moment, and to protect the descent. It is a counsel of perfection to suggest providing against contingencies on this lavish scale; but it is well to bear in mind the ideal. And there is, besides, a precaution which surely can and will be taken: to take a supply of oxygen for restorative purposes. The value of oxygen for restoring exhausted and warming cold men was sufficiently well illustrated during the second attempt in 1922.

The question as to whether the use of oxygen will otherwise help or hinder climbers is one about which opinions may be expected to disagree. Anyone who thinks that it is impossible to get up without oxygen can claim that nothing has shown it to be impossible to get up with its aid. For my part, I don't think it impossible to get up without oxygen. The difference of atmospheric pressure between 27,000 feet and the summit is small, and it is safe to conclude that men who have exerted themselves at 27,000 feet could live without difficulty for a number of hours on the summit. As to whether their power of progress would give out before reaching 29,000 feet, it is impossible to dogmatise. I can only say that nothing in the experience of the first attempt has led me to suppose that those last 2,000 feet cannot be climbed in a day. I am not competent to sift and weigh all the evidence as to whether, how much, and with what consumption of gas it was easier to proceed up the slopes of Mount Everest with oxygen so far as Finch and Bruce went on that memorable day. But I do venture to combat the suggestion that it is necessarily easier to reach the top in that manner. I think no one will dispute the statement that the final camp for the second attempt was too low, as it had been for the first, to enable the oxygen party to reach the summit. With the same apparatus it will be necessary in this case also to provide a second camp above the North Col. And the question for the moment will ultimately be, is it possible to add to that immense burden of transport to 27,000 feet the weight of the oxygen cylinders required ?

The weather in all probability will have something to say to this problem. The Expedition of 1922 was certainly not favoured by the weather. There was no continuous spell of calm fine days, and the summer snows began a week earlier than the most usual date. One wonders what sort of weather is to be expected with the most favourable conditions on Mount Everest. It is conceivable that a series of calm fine days sometimes precede the monsoon. But when we consider the perpetual winds of Tibet at all seasons, it seems unlikely that Mount Everest is often immune from this abominable visitation. It is far more likely that the calm day is a rare exception, and only to be expected when the north-westerly current is neutralised by the monsoon from the South-east. The ill-luck of 1922 may probably be computed as no more than those seven days by which the monsoon preceded expectation. With so short a time for preparations and advance, we were indeed unfortunate in meeting an early monsoon. And it is hardly possible considerably to extend the available time by starting earlier. There was only the barest trickle of water at the Base Camp on May 1, 1922, and the complications involved by the necessity of melting snow for water, both here and at all higher stages, for any considerable time, would be a severe handicap. But it must be remembered that the second attempt was made a week before the monsoon broke. Time appeared short on the mountain chiefly from the threat of bad weather and the signs showing that the majority of days were, to say the least, extremely disagreeable for climbing high on the mountain. If others are confronted by similar conditions, they too will probably feel that each fine day must be utilised and the attack must be pressed on; for the fine days past will not come back, and ahead is the uncertain monsoon.

A final question may now be asked: What advantages will another Expedition have which we did not have in 1922? In one small and in one large matter the next Expedition may be better equipped. It was disappointing, after so much time and thought had been expended upon the problem of foot-gear, that nothing was evolved in 1922 which succeeded in taking the place of Alpine boots of well-known patterns. The great disadvantage of these sorts of boot is that one cannot wear crampons with them at these high altitudes, for the strap bound tightly round the foot will almost certainly cause frost-bite; either different boots or different spikes must be invented if the climbers are to have crampons or their equivalent. It is essential that they should be so equipped to avoid the labour of step-cutting, and the lack of this equipment might well rob them of victory on the steep final slopes below the summit. This matter of foot-gear is not so very small, after all. But a still more important one is the oxygen apparatus. It is conceivable, and I believe by no means unlikely, that a different type of cylinder may be used in the future, and capable of containing more oxygen, compared with the same weight, than those of 1922. A 50 per cent. improvement in this direction should alter the whole problem of using oxygen. With this advantage it might well be possible to go to the top and back with the four cylinders which a man may be expected to carry from a height of 25,000 feet or little higher. If a second camp above the North Col becomes unnecessary in this way, the whole effort required, and especially the effort of transport, will be reduced to the scale of what has already been accomplished, and can no doubt be accomplished again.

The further advantage of a future Expedition is simply that of experience. It amounts to something, one cannot say how much. In small ways a number of mistakes may be avoided. The provision of this and that may be more accurately calculated according to tried values. The whole organisation of life in high camps should be rather more efficient. Beyond all this, the experience of 1922 should help when the moment comes towards the making of a right plan; and a party which chooses rightly what to do and when to do it, and can so exclude other possibilities as to be certain that no better way could be chosen, has a great advantage. But, when all is said as to experience and equipment, it still remains true that success requires a quality. History repeats itself, perhaps, but in a vague and general fashion only where mountains are concerned. The problem of reaching the summit is every time a fresh one. The keen eye for a fair opportunity and resource in grave emergencies are no less necessary to the mountaineer everywhere, and not least upon Mount Everest, than determination to carry through the high project, the simple will to conquer in the struggle.

NOTES

By

T. HOWARD SOMERVELL

on

ACCLIMATISATION AT HIGH ALTITUDES

COLOUR IN TIBET

TIBETAN CULTURE

CHAPTER XII

ACCLIMATISATION AT HIGH ALTITUDES

The Everest Expedition of 1922 had no preconceived programme of scientific investigation, and was first and foremost an attempt to get up the mountain; though, as I had been connected with physiological research for some years, I was naturally anxious to make observations on the effect of altitude on the human frame. These observations were rather subjective, and were unaccompanied by any accurate data—in other words, the reader will be relieved to hear that there are no tables of figures to be reproduced. Barcroft and others were in the course of their Expedition to the Andes, and I knew full well their results would supply more accurate information on the exact process of acclimatisation at high altitudes than anything we could do with our simpler apparatus. We left it to this other Expedition, therefore, to supply the figures, while our observations were exclusively on the practical side; that is to say, we observed the rapidity and effect of acclimatisation, while not investigating exactly how it is brought about.

The first effect of altitude, in such moderate degree as we encountered it on the plains of Tibet, was almost entirely a mere breathlessness, which limited our rate of walking, and increased the popularity of our uncomfortable Tibetan saddles when travelling up-hill. A few of us had severe headaches from time to time; at the modest height of 17,000 feet I noticed Cheyne-Stokes respiration at night when lying down, though never when sitting or standing; and I remember being distinctly amused at the fact that one was unable to control it.[1] A few of the party had a single attack of vomiting, but no permanent effect was noticed, and by the time we had lived on the Tibetan Plateau for a few weeks we had lost all ill effects save only breathlessness, which, of course, persisted to some extent until we reached comparatively low elevations. Further effect at these heights was not noticed save in the case of some of the older members of the party, who suffered from a considerable loss of appetite while at the Base Camp at 16,000 feet; this effect on appetite did not improve as time went on.

It was when we began the more serious work on the mountain that we made the most interesting observations on acclimatisation, and proved both its rapidity (which was known before) and its persistence to great heights. Scientists of various schools had, before the start of the Expedition, predicted that acclimatisation would be im-

[1] For the benefit of the non-medical reader, Cheyne-Stokes breathing is the gradual alternation of shallow and deep respirations: usually about ten shallow breaths are followed by respirations which get gradually deeper; then by three or four really deep ones, which become shallower until the cycle recommences.

possible above the height of 20,000 feet. Why they had done so will always remain a mystery to me; but possibly they were misled by the fact that so many climbing expeditions in the past have failed somewhere in the region of 23,000 feet above sea-level. We were enabled, however, to prove conclusively that acclimatisation does go on to greater heights; in fact, I do not see a theoretical limit to it at any elevation below the top of Mount Everest. Our observations were largely subjective, but for that reason they are perhaps all the more to be appreciated by the general reader; and in view of their subjective nature I may perhaps be pardoned in substituting "feelings" for figures and putting information in the form of a personal experience.

When Mallory and I arrived at Camp III and established it on the site chosen by the reconnaissance party, our first concern was the preparation of another camp at the North Col. I shall never forget our first ascent up that accursed slope of snow and ice, each step a hardship, every foot a fight: until at last we lay almost exhausted on the top. After a day or two at Camp III below, we went up again to the col, this time with Strutt and Morshead, and I think Norton. The ascent of the col this time was hard work, but not more than that; and after the col had been reached Morshead and I were sufficiently cheerful to explore the way leading up to Everest. A day or two later we again ascended the North Col, and never really noticed more discomfort than was occasioned by breathlessness. Though not possessing the scientific data which explained this change in our condition, yet in those few days of life at 21,000 feet we had become acclimatised to our altitude to a very remarkable degree; what had previously been a hard struggle had now become a comparatively easy job. By this rapid change in our constitution we had not only proved the predictions of scientists to be wrong, but had gained the physical power which took us without artificial oxygen supply to 27,000 feet, and we had determined that acclimatisation is not only possible but is also quite rapid at these high altitudes.

Thus, by sojourn and exercise for a week above 20,000 feet, we obtained the physiological equipment necessary for an attempt on the mountain, and at this point some personal experiences may be of interest, though possibly of no great importance. We found that, as we ascended, we fell into an automatic rate of breathing; Mallory preferred to breathe slowly and deeply, while rapid and shallower respirations appealed to me; but we all walked upwards at almost exactly the same rate at any given height. Below the North Col, I took three breaths to a step, while at 26,000 feet I was taking five complete respirations; but as long as I was walking slowly enough I experienced no distress or discomfort. If one hurried for a short distance, one was forced to rest for a few seconds—a rest was imperative, and one felt it were impossible to do without it; but as long as an even pace was kept up, one had no desire to stop, nor to make one's admiration of the landscape an excuse for delaying one's comrades. At the height of 26,000 feet, I took my pulse (which was 180) and my respirations (which were 50 to 55 to the minute); but withal one felt perfectly comfortable even though these abnormal physiological conditions were present. No doubt the heart must be young to stand this rate of beating for many hours; yet not too young, or it will easily become enlarged and permanently damaged.

In view of our experiences it seems justifiable to predict that acclimatisation at 23,000 feet will be sufficient for the attainment of the summit of Mount Everest, if indeed a sojourn at 21,000 feet is insufficient—which is to my mind more than doubtful. The other important practical observation we made is less encouraging: namely, that we all varied in our rate of acclimatisation, and in fact some of our number (especially the older ones among us) actually seemed to deteriorate in condition while staying at a great height. But I think we proved that it is possible to climb to the summit of Everest without the use of oxygen, though the selection of men who are able to do so is very difficult until those heights are actually reached at which acclimatisation becomes established. Personally I felt perfectly well at 27,000 feet, and my condition seemed no different at that height from what it had been at 25,000 feet, or even lower; and I have no doubt there are many people, if only they can be found, who can get to the top of Everest unaided save by their own physiological reaction to a life at 21,000 feet for a few days. If a number of such people were allowed to live at a height corresponding to our Camp III for a fortnight or so, making perhaps a few minor excursions to 23,000 or 24,000 feet, then I have no doubt from the physiological point of view that they will be able to climb Mount Everest, provided the weather is fine and the wind not too violent. Without allowing time for acclimatisation to take place, it is probable that nobody—that is, unless some *lusus naturæ* exists—will reach the summit; if artificially supplied oxygen be used, the acclimatisation may not be necessary; but the danger of an attempt by non-acclimatised men with oxygen apparatus is that a breakdown of the apparatus might lead to serious consequences, while a fully acclimatised man is probably just as capable of standing a height of 29,000 feet, unaided, as you or I would be able to stand the height of Mount Blanc to-morrow. When the Expedition of 1922 started I was personally of opinion that nobody could exist at a height about 25,000 or 26,000 feet without oxygen; but since we have proved that this can be done, it seems that the chances of climbing the mountain are probably greater if oxygen be not used. For the apparatus, and the spare cylinders required, necessitate the use of a large number of coolies; while in an attempt without oxygen only three or four coolies are required for the camping equipment and the food at the highest camp. Therefore it seems that the best chance of getting to the top of Mount Everest lies in the sending out of some nine or ten climbers, who can remain at a high camp, become thoroughly acclimatised, and then make a series of expeditions up the mountain, three or so at a time, as continuously as weather conditions will allow. By adopting these tactics the number of possible attempts up the mountain can be increased; and it seems to me that the chances of climbing to the summit lie in the multiplicity of possible attempts rather than in any other direction. It were better to prepare for a number of attempts each by a small but acclimatised party, rather than to stake all on one or two highly organised endeavours, in which oxygen, and a large number of coolies, are used. It is only a small proportion of coolies who can get up to the heights of 25,000 or 27,000 feet, and they should be used for any one attempt as sparingly as possible. During the war we all had our ideas of how it should be run, and they were generally wrong; the above plan is the writer's idea of how to climb Mount Everest, and may or may not be right, but is enunciated for what it is worth.

Among subsidiary effects of extreme altitudes, were those upon appetite, temper, and mental condition generally. Most of us will admit a good deal of peevishness and irritability while at a level of 22,000 feet and more; for the altitude undoubtedly makes one lose to some extent one's mental balance, and the first way in which this appears on the surface is by a ruffling of the temper. In addition, one has a certain lack of determination, and when at a height approaching 27,000 feet I remember distinctly that I cared very little whether we reached the top of Everest or not. A good instance of this altered attitude of mind is provided by the fact that Finch and Bruce took a camera with them on their ascent, and forgot to take any photographs of their last day's climbing.

I have mentioned the deleterious effect of altitude on the appetite of some of our older members; but the same was to some extent true of us all. I have the most vivid recollection of distaste for food during our first few days at Camp III, and especially of the way one had almost to push a prune down one's throat on the way up to the North Col; but with the majority of us this distaste for food (especially for meat and the slowly-digested foods) diminished during our sojourn at great heights, though our appetites never became quite normal until we reached one of the lower camps. Those who had oxygen reported that they had large appetites above the North Col; and there is no doubt that it is the rarefaction of the air that causes this alteration of the appetite. One may perhaps be justified in assuming that the secretion of gastric juice is diminished while air that is poor in oxygen is inhaled, though it is rather hard to understand how this is brought about.

Although acclimatisation is not entirely connected with the actual increase in the number of blood corpuscles (as has been proved by Barcroft in 1922), yet this is still recognised as one of the important factors in its production.

But this increase in the concentration of the blood must be associated with a great increase in its viscosity, and when that is combined with intense cold with its accompanying constriction of all the smaller blood-vessels, there are present all the conditions necessary for the production of frostbite. Therefore acclimatisation with all its benefits probably increases the risk of frostbite ; hence one who is acclimatised must be especially careful of feet and hands and their coverings. It is hard to put on too many clothes at a great altitude, and very easy to put on too few.

The chief point still remaining to be mentioned concerns the after-effects of the climbing of Everest ; but these varied so much that they give us little or no scientific information. Some of us were tired for twenty-four hours only, some for many days ; some were reported to have enlarged hearts, while in some the heart was normal ; some were incapacitated by frostbite, though their general physical condition was very probably good. One therefore cannot generalise about after-effects, but as a medical man I felt strongly (by observation on myself and my companions on the Expedition) that if one is to "live to fight another day" and to require the minimum recuperation period after an attempt on the mountain, it is essential during the attempt to keep oneself well within one's powers. One is tempted to go too hard, and to exert one's strength to its limits ; but it is just the last few ounces of strength which call forth the greatest effort and make the maximum demands on one's resources ; and if these resources are to be used to their full extent they should be continuously conserved by an avoidance of definite hurry. Personally I am of opinion that exercise before the climbing begins is of great value. Mallory and I were the only ones whom Longstaff allowed to make two attempts on Everest; and we were probably rendered fit in this way by the subsidiary expeditions we had made on the way to Mount Everest and by our preliminary work in getting the camp ready on the North Col. It is, however, hard to generalise on a point like this, but each man knows the idiosyncrasies of his own constitution, and it should be left to individuals to a great extent to see that their condition on arrival at the foot of the mountain is the best that is possible.

CHAPTER XIII

COLOUR IN TIBET

In order to bring before the reader a vivid picture of Tibet, and especially of the region around Mount Everest, a comparison between Tibet and other better-known countries is almost inevitable. The Expedition of 1922 took with them no official artist, or no doubt he would have been deputed to write this section of the book; there were, however, two people who tried to paint pictures of the country, Major Norton and myself; and though I realise how inadequate our efforts were, perhaps those of an official artist might have been almost as bad. However, as one who looks on the world with an eye for its beauty, although lacking the ability to transfer that beauty to canvas, one may perhaps be pardoned for endeavouring to describe certain general impressions of the scenery encountered by the Expedition.

In the course of our journey we passed through a great variety of landscape; in Sikkim, for instance, we found a land of steep slopes and dense forests, while Tibet is almost a desert country. We experienced the clear air of the winter, and the mists and storm-clouds of the monsoon. While we were on the rolling plains of the Tibetan Plateau, only a few miles away were the snow-covered summits of the highest mountains in the world.

Sikkim is a country of deep valleys and of luxurious vegetation; the air is generally damp and the skies cloudy, and there is often a beautiful blue haze that gives atmosphere to the distance. Sikkim is not unlike the Italian side of the Alps, in many ways. True, its scale is larger, and it possesses some of the most beautiful and impressive peaks in the world (for no Alpine peak can vie with Siniolchum or Pandim for sheer beauty of form and surface), but on the whole the scenery of Sikkim is of the same general build as the valleys and peaks of Northern Italy. In this sense Sikkim did not offer to the new-comer anything entirely different from what he had seen before. But Tibet and Everest certainly did; and the difference between Sikkim and Tibet is twofold—first, Tibet is almost uniformly over 13,000 feet above sea-level, and therefore bears no trees at all; second, Tibet is almost free from rainfall and is, in consequence, a desert country. One's eye travelled, for mile after mile, over red-brown sand and red-brown limestone hills, finally to rest on the blue and white of the distant snows. The air, before the monsoon commences, is almost always clear—clear to an extent unimagined by a European, clearer even than the air of an Alpine winter. So peaks and ridges 30 or 40 miles away are often almost in the same visual plane as the foreground of the landscape. In some extensive views, such as we had from the hills above Tinki Dzong, one came to look upon hills 30 miles away as the middle distance of one's picture, while the background was formed of mountains a hundred miles from the point of view. It is this lack of atmosphere which makes pictorial representation of these Tibetan scenes so very difficult; the pictures I made on the course of the Expedition have all had one criticism from many different people—"there is no atmosphere." Many as are the demerits of these pictures, this is the one merit they have; and if they had an "atmosphere" they would cease to be truthful. In the Alps one has often seen mountains with extreme clearness at a great distance, but I never remember having viewed an Alpine landscape in which there was practically no effect of distance, and practicallly no blueness of the more distant shadows. Yet that is precisely what obtains in Tibet before the month of June. And then, with startling suddenness, comes the monsoon, with its damp air; for some months the landscape is entirely altered, and also much beautified. The blue haze of the monsoon converts the distant shadows from their crude purple-brown to the most magnificent and sometimes brilliant blue. Once or twice one looked in vain on one's palette for a blue of sufficient brilliance and intensity to reproduce the colour of the shadows 20 or 30 miles away. Then the monsoon brings clouds and rain-storms, all of which tend to give variety to the scene, and to endue the distant peaks with that effect of mystery which renders them so alluring and so beautiful.

As far as the scenery among the higher mountains is concerned, the comparison of photographs of the Everest group of peaks with those of the Alps will give one more idea of the differences between the two districts than can a mere verbal description, save in the matter of scale and colour. In colour, the Alps are more varied and the rock is, as a rule, a darker brown; the snow-shadows are more blue and the outlines less clear; while Alpine foregrounds so often contain trees which are totally absent from the foregrounds of Tibet. There both rocks and stones, scree and valley-bed are of a light reddish-brown, almost uniform in tone from near foreground to extreme distance; Makalu, for example, is a colossal rock-pyramid of quite a light ochre colour; the rocks of Everest are of a light amber brown relieved in the neighbourhood of 27,000 feet by a lighter yellowish band of quartzite. The snow of the range on its northern side resembles that of Alpine peaks, but on the southern face the festoons and grooves of ice, so well known to many from photographs of Himalayan mountains, decorate the much steeper and more uncompromising slopes. Most of the higher peaks are swept by continual gusts of wind which whirl clouds of snow from the topmost ridges into the sky.

CHAPTER XIV

TIBETAN CULTURE

The Tibetans are a very simple folk, though not without a very definite civilisation of their own. Art and music exist in all nations, if the art be merely the fashioning of utensils, and the music be the crudest of rhythms played on a tom-tom. Yet in Tibet the rudimentary music and art associated with so many Eastern races is carried a stage farther, and what is in wilder people merely natural instinct has become in Tibet a definite culture. For I presume that culture is merely organised art, and certainly on that criterion the Tibetan is to some extent cultured.

He is a fine architect, and many of his houses have a simple stateliness which raises them in artistic value high above the average dwelling-house of most other Oriental countries, to say nothing of our own garden suburbs. The Monasteries of Tibet are still more imposing, and some of them are real objects of beauty, for the dignified simplicity of the buildings themselves is combined with an elaborate and often beautiful decoration of windows and cornices. The Tibetans have learned the true principles of decoration—they do not cover the surfaces of their buildings with unnecessary ornament, but reserve the wooden parts alone for elaboration. The cornices are often intricate in workmanship, but throughout the great principle of design is carried to perfection—the principle that all ornament should be founded on utility. Thus economy in the use of scrolls is combined with the multiplication of brackets, supports, and rafter-ends, so that the whole is satisfying to the eye as being beautiful, rather than useless. Considerable Chinese influence is shown in their decorative art, but the Tibetans have a personal, or rather national, touch which distinguishes their work in all branches of art from the Chinese. In painting, too, the influence of China, and very occasionally of India, is felt: though through it all the refined austerity of the better-class Tibetan shines unmistakably. The older pictures, nearly always of sacred subjects, are drawn with consummate skill, coloured with great taste, and in the matter of design rank much higher than the contemporary art of India. But, alas! the story of painting in Tibet is the same as it is everywhere in this commercial world of ours; the modern Tibetan picture is worthless, careless and meretricious. No doubt the demand for "native art" at the bazaars of Darjeeling and other places around has caused this deterioration of what was once a fine and noble art; pictures which used to be the life-work of devoted lamas and conscientious hermits are now "dashed off" to satisfy the capacious maw of the tasteless traveller. Though Tibet is still in measure "The Forbidden Land," yet the tentacles of commercialism cannot but penetrate between its bars, and the same thing is now happening to Tibet as happened to Europe last century and

Religious Banners in Shekar Monastery.

produced oleographs and official artists. It seems almost as if man by nature does bad work only when he is working for reward.

This is a mere flashlight sketch of the art of Tibet, for details of which other books must be consulted; but the music of Tibet will be described more fully, for two reasons—first, that no accurate record of it has to my knowledge been obtained until now, and second, that the writer is himself particularly fond of music, which he believes to be the highest of the arts.

Just as in Europe to-day we have both the traditional folk-song and the highly organised orchestral music, so in Tibet both these forms of the art exist. The two are also more or less interdependent in Tibet, while in Western nations each often goes its own way without the other.

The airs sung by the Tibetan people are usually simple, short, and oft-repeated. They are nearly always in the pentatonic scale, represented best to the general reader by the black notes of the piano. Most isolated races evolve this scale at some time during their history, and the tunes of the Highlands of Scotland, the Forests of Central Africa, the Appallachians of America, and the Tibetans are all in this scale.[1]

[1] Sir Walford Davies has pointed out that, starting (on the black notes) from A flat, and using only the perfect fifth, this scale is very soon developed. From A flat one gets E flat and D flat, each a fifth away; from D flat one obtains G flat, a fifth down, and from E flat a fifth upwards gives us B flat. Thus we get the five notes of the scale by a simple series of fifths, the fifth being the most perfect interval in music, and the one which will appeal most readily to a primitive people.

A typical well-known pentatonic tune is "Over the Sea to Skye." Those who know, for instance, the songs of the Western Highlands, will be able to appreciate the cheerful and non-Oriental character of the tunes of Tibet, which are more akin to those of Russia and Eastern Europe than to the music of China or India. This general spirit of the music which the Tibetans play or sing points to a common origin of the folk-tunes of Tibet and Russia. It seems probable that in Turkestan was the real origin of this music, which very likely spread eastwards into Tibet and westwards into Russia; or if Turkestan is not the country of origin of the music, it may be the musical link between Russia and Tibet. The tunes of Nepal, as sung by our coolies, are many of them of a similar nature to those of Tibet, though more often the whole major or minor scale is used, giving them often a strangely European sound; some of the Nepalese airs have a jolly lilt and swing; others in the minor key have quite a haunting beauty; and they too are quite unlike the music of the plains of India with its rather pointless wailing characteristics.[1]

In Tibet, then, the folk-tunes are simple, short, and emphatically not such "good tunes" as the airs of Nepal. But, in addition to the songs of the peasants and beggars, there is the more highly-organised and orchestrated music of the monasteries. This is usually played with three

[1] A more technical article on the subject of Tibetan Music, with musical quotations, will be found in the *Musical Times* for February 1, 1923.

groups of instruments—first and foremost the percussion; drums of all sizes from those made of a human skull to others 3 and 4 feet in diameter, and cymbals of great resonance and good tone, coming often from China. The cymbals are taken very seriously, and each different way of clashing them has a special name and a special religious significance. The hard-worked percussion department keeps up a continuous rhythm throughout the performance of a devil-dance or other musical festival; and to its strenuous and often sinister efforts are added from time to time the sounds of the two groups of wind instruments. The first of these, playing airs which often possess great charm, are the double-reed oboes, about twice as long as our European oboe, and very often provided with equidistant holes, rendering them incapable of playing save in the scale of whole tones (or a close approximation to it). The second and larger wind instrument is the long straight trumpet, 8 to 12 feet long, of which the fundamental note is almost continuously blown. Most monasteries have two of these, about one tone apart in pitch; but as the longer of the two is blown so as to play its first overtone, while the fundamental note is played on the other, a drone bass of a minor seventh is the resulting sound. This adds to the sinister impressiveness of the music, and provides an effective accompaniment to the quaint tunes of the oboe-like instruments. At a devil-dance performance, the orchestra plays for a whole day, or perhaps two, almost without rest either for itself or for its listeners.

In addition to these instruments, a fairly civilised violin is used in Tibet, especially by wandering beggar minstrels. This is about two-thirds as long as our violin, and has four strings, tuned A,D,A,D, in that order. The bow has two hanks of hair, one of which passes between the first and second strings, while the other goes between the third and fourth. Thus, by pressing the bow in one direction the two A strings are sounded, producing a reinforced note (i.e. two notes in unison); by pressing the bow in the other direction the sound of the D strings is obtained. The strings converge towards the top of the instrument, so that they can all be fingered at once. The Tibetans become very agile with their fingers, and I have heard very skilful performances of rapid, jolly dance-tunes by wandering minstrels; these tunes, like the songs of the peasants, are usually in the pentatonic scale.

One more instrument must be mentioned—the trumpet made from a human thigh-bone. This is not very commonly used in the larger monasteries, but occasionally sounds a note in the ritual of the worship of smaller villages.

NATURAL HISTORY

By

T. G. LONGSTAFF, M.D.

CHAPTER XV

NATURAL HISTORY

Previous experience of the conditions of Tibetan travel had taught me that collection and observation was a task requiring complete immunity from other duties ; but to the doctor of such an Expedition this condition was not attainable. In the collection of specimens we were, however, fortunate in obtaining the assistance of several other members of the Expedition. But it is especially to Major Norton that the thanks of the Everest Committee are due, for in addition to his other duties, he took over the whole of the botanical work and worked equally with myself in all other branches of Zoology. His gift of painting was particularly valuable in leading to the certain identification of birds in districts where collecting was prohibited. At the time of writing he is on duty at Chanak, and the following notes lose half their value through lack of his promised collaboration, which I had anticipated with particular pleasure.

In his absence I must omit all reference to botany, for personally, owing to the wintry conditions during our outward march and to the speed of my journey back with the invalids, I saw nothing that has not been already better described by Wollaston. But Norton, with our Lepcha collector Rumoo, obtained some 350 flowering plants in Kharta, and we also sent back samples of agricultural seeds.

It must be remembered that it was the constant aim of General Bruce to render it easier for any subsequent party to pass through the country. The objection of the Tibetans to the taking of any wild life is almost universal amongst the clerics and is devoutly shared by the lay population in certain localities. These considerations unfortunately applied particularly to the districts of Tengkye, Shelkar Dzong and Rombuk, where the killing of even domestic animals is prohibited.

There are, however, other parts of Tibet where the same restraint is unnecessary, and even where hunting is habitually practised by the semi-nomadic population. This immunity in our case applied especially to the Chumbi Valley and the country round Phari, and in consequence we have been able to bring back some material which it is hoped will add to the value of the larger collections brought back last year by Dr. Wollaston.

That portion of Tibet visited by the Expedition, and indeed it is typical of most of its provinces, is a region of bare uplands and naked mountains. Such physical conditions combine with a violent type of radiation in the thin dry air to evolve a daily strife of winds, ceaselessly seeking to rectify the balance of atmospheric stability; this continual wind is indeed the foundation of the traveller's

Romoo, the Lepcha Collector, who assisted Dr. Longstaff and Major Norton.

Karma Paul, the Expedition's Interpreter.

discomfort and the worst enemy of the mountaineer.

Owing to its aridity, due to the intervention of the rain-catching Himalaya, the country is practically treeless. Distant open views prevail over vast landscapes, lit by strong lights in an atmosphere devoid of fogs or softening mist effects. Usually nothing can move without being visible from a great distance. Hence, though it is not a region particularly rich in life, yet those forms which do prevail are not easily overlooked. Concealment is only to be obtained by burrowing underground, or by immobility combined with protective coloration.

Nowhere is this more obtrusively shown than on the great stony uplands, at an altitude of from 14,000 to 17,000 feet East and South of Khamba Dzong. Here we were in constant sight of bands of wild asses, gazelle, and sheep: from a distance of a couple of miles a prowling wolf was easily discerned. The ground is nowhere here covered by a continuous carpet of grass or herbs, but each plant is several yards from the next. Hence even a small herd of game will cover the ground with innumerable tracks, suggesting to the uninitiated a far greater number of individuals than really exist. To watch a flock of Tibetan sheep or goats grazing seems like watching a migration, for the herd moves at a smart walk, often breaking into a run, each individual racing for the next mouthful a few yards ahead. They move on a wide front, with the shepherd and his wolf-dog well in evidence. On one occasion we came on a wolf devouring a lamb: 50 yards away lay the guardian dog, waiting apparently for any scraps the robber might leave.

It might be supposed that as in the Arctic the birds and animals would turn white in winter. But two sufficient reasons against this necessity have already been indicated. Firstly, the snow line is so high, probably between 19,000 and 20,000 feet, that vegetation does not extend up to it: even the predatory beasts are dependent on vegetation for the pasture of their prey. Secondly, evaporation is so rapid that the country is never snow-clad for long even during the winter season.

But some modification of habit to meet the hostility of winter, under conditions of life already so severe, is to be looked for. Of Marmots we saw nothing during the journey to Everest; probably they were still hibernating. Norton found them later in Kharta and obtained a welcome specimen. Yet Hares were very common at 16,000 to 17,000 feet, several haunting the old moraines of the Rongbuk Glacier even above our Base Camp. Here also, at 17,000 feet, was a small herd of Bharel, or Blue Sheep, which having some familiarity with the hermit monks permitted a fairly close approach.

More interesting are the Mouse-hares, or Pikas, of several varieties, small friendly creatures which live in colonies, mainly (*Ochotona curzoniæ*) on the open plains, where even their small burrows sometimes undermine considerable areas so that one must ride with care. They are quick and lively in their movements, darting from hole to hole with extreme rapidity, and peeping from their burrows at the stranger with obvious amusement. They are often first seen sitting up on their hind-legs. They lay in stores of grass for winter use, though the evidence all goes to prove that they do not regularly hibernate. They frequently utter a nearly inaudible high-pitched whispering call, a sort of subdued whistle, from which no doubt comes the (Shoka) Bhotia name of *shippi*, "The Whisperer," which I obtained in Gnari Khorsum in 1905. Certain birds, as will be subsequently noted, live in association with these small rodents, and add a further note to the charm of their colonies. It appears impossible to trap them, and as their skulls are usually damaged by shooting, a good series of skins, in both summer and winter pelage, of the different species, is still much wanted for study in our museums.

The collection of small mammals is always difficult, and under the circumstances already detailed our collection of skins was necessarily a very small one. Geoffrey Bruce, however, obtained a perfect specimen of the Panda (*Ailurus fulgens*) from the forests on the Chumbi side of the Jelep La. This curiously aberrant animal, sometimes called the Bear-Cat, is about the size of a fox, and has rich thick fur of a chestnut colour on the back, black below, and with a thick bushy ring-marked tail; in appearance it resembles somewhat the badgers, the bears, and the cats. Its relative, the Great Panda of Tibet, is one of the rarest of large mammals, owing to its very circumscribed distribution.

A Hamster and a few Pikas of three varieties were caught

at night in our tents. A Weasel (*M. temon*) shot in Sikkim, with another Weasel and a Marmot from Kharta, complete our list of mammal skins. We are much disappointed at our failure to see or obtain any specimens from 20,000 feet, where Wollaston's Pika was actually handled last year—the greatest known altitude for resident mammals.

As to the birds, we were fortunate in having been able to go over Dr. Wollaston's collection with Mr. Norman B. Kinnear of the Natural History Museum, who provided us in addition with a series of careful notes by which we could identify those likely to be met with in localities where we could not shoot. It is hoped that our material will be found sufficient for Mr. Kinnear to publish a supplement to his recent paper in the *Ibis* on last year's collection.

Dr. Percy R. Lowe, Keeper of Birds of the Natural History Museum, was particularly anxious for us to obtain for him a specimen of the Himalayan or Ibis-billed Curlew (*Ibidorhynchus struthersi*) in the flesh, for purposes of dissection, nothing being known of its anatomy up to the present. Luckily this bird haunts the Chumbi Valley, and Norton and I were able to spend a day in its pursuit. It is of the form of a small curlew, of a general french-grey hue with bold dark markings, and coral red beak and legs. There were several of these birds, not yet (April 3) paired, about Yatung in the Chumbi Valley, but they were very wary. They utter a high-pitched wader-like note not at all resembling our curlew. They always flew directly over the main river, whence we never could have retrieved them. The shores of this river are fringed by beaches of large round grey pebbles, and resting amongst these the birds were invisible. Eventually I lay up under the bank and Norton succeeded in driving a bird on to an island in mid-stream, where I shot it. With an outward display of truly scientific eagerness we divested ourselves of our nether garments and waded waist deep through the torrent. We came near quarrelling as to whether the water or the air was the coldest. But at any rate we retrieved our bird, and what is more brought it, duly preserved in spirits, through all the trials of travel and climate, safely back to Dr. Lowe.

In the Chumbi Valley also we obtained the Great or Solitary Snipe (*Gallinago solitaria*), an addition to last year's list. But my favourite family, the Redstarts, were the most interesting. The beautiful White-capped Redstart (*Chimarhornis leucocephalus*), mostly widely distributed in the Himalaya, was still with us. The Plumbeous Redstart (*Rhyacornis fuliginosus*) and the Blue-fronted Redstart (*Phœnicurus frontalis*) we had already obtained in Sikkim. These also were present at the beginning of April in the Chumbi Valley. We obtained in addition the beautiful Blue-tail or Red-flanked Bush-Robin (*Tarsiger rafiliatus*). I understand that the three latter species have not been previously recorded from this locality. The Blue-tail frequents dense bushes over marshy spots and is very quiet and furtive in its habits, while the Redstarts are the most obtrusive of birds, as to me they are one of the most beautiful of families. At Phari I luckily obtained a specimen of what I thought was the Indian Redstart, but the bird in the hand proved again to be the Blue-fronted sort. At 17,000 feet, above the Base Camp over the snout of the main Rongbuk Glacier, I saw a cock-bird of Güldenstadt's Redstart (*Phœnicurus erythrogaster grandis*), fortunately a very easily recognisable bird, and one I had previously seen in Nubra and the Karakoram country.

Although I had previously become somewhat familiar with bird-life in Tibet, I was not prepared to see the teeming flocks of finches, buntings, and larks which we met with on the bare stony uplands at every old camping ground or village we encountered. A portion of this swarming bird population appears to have been due to the spring migration being at its height. Of this we had evidence before and during our passage of the Jelep La, from Sikkim into the Chumbi Valley. At Phari and at Khamba Dzong especially, the birds appeared not yet to have dispersed in pairs to their breeding territory, but, though actually arrived at their destination, to be still collected in migration flocks. Yet this condition of things may be more apparent than real, for neither Norton nor I ever managed to find any evidence of nesting behaviour in such an extremely common bird as Brandt's Ground Linnet. It is conceivable that the inimical climatic conditions of Tibet are such as to condemn a larger proportion than usual of the bird population to a celibate existence, a condition which is at least by no means rare even in the British Isles. A small piece of evidence is that the only four nests of larks and wagtails which I found contained only three eggs each, as if the altitude had reduced the number of eggs laid. It is to be noted that in each case the eggs were incubated, and so the clutches were presumably complete. But as an exception to this rule, at Chushar, on June 13, I found a nest of the Eastern Desert Wheatear with a normal clutch of five eggs.

In writing of nesting, it may be recorded that we obtained the eggs of the Tibetan Snow Cock (*Tetraogallus tibetanus*) from nearly 17,000 feet on the Pang La. At the Base Camp (16,500 feet), a Brown Accentor (*Prunella f. fulvescens*) commenced building its nest in a crevice between a stack of provision boxes in the middle of the camp on May 16. Laying did not commence till May 25—a long period of delay—and was completed with the third egg on the 27th. The hen commenced to sit at once, and no more eggs were laid. Norton observed Alpine Choughs and Rock Doves nesting in the cliffs above the Base Camp at an altitude of 17,000 feet. Besides the usual Ravens, and the species already named, the Base Camp was visited by Brandt's Ground Linnet (*Leucosticte brandti*), a Sparrow, a Snow Finch, the Ground Chough (*Podoces humilis*), and the Shore Lark (*Otocorys alpestris elwesi*).

Noel, during his vigil on the Changla (23,000 feet), saw a small bird fly above him, borne on the Westerly gale. But Wollaston's Lammergeyer maintains still the first place in altitude with a record of over 24,000 feet.

At Trangso Chumbab, on June 11, I had the opportunity of observing the habits of Blandford's Mountain-Finch (*Chion-*

ospiza blandfordi). This bird seems to live in amity with the Pikas (*Ochotona curzoniæ*) in their burrows. I marked the birds bringing food to a Pika burrow, and wishing to see what the young in down were like, Finch and I commenced to dig out the hole. It proved, however, beyond our powers in the sun-baked ground, so I fell to watching again. We had laid open the burrow for about 2 feet. The hen-bird at once returned with food, but alighting at the spot where the burrow formerly commenced, began immediately to tunnel into the ground, quite oblivious of the true opening in full view only 2 feet away. What would our nature writers say to such a lapse of intellect ? The bird burrowed with its beak, diving its head into the ground and boring with a very rapid jerky twist so that the sand was scattered in a small cloud. This was repeated several times and on several visits. I then filled up the trench, leaving the nesting hole open. On the next visit the bird flew down the hole, which I then stopped with loose earth. In the morning the burrow had been completely cleared and the birds were busily feeding their young again. This seems to point to the conclusion that these birds are naturally ground-dwellers, and are fully capable of making their own tunnels, but that the abundance of Pika burrows has induced lazy habits. Mandelle's Snow-Finch (*Montifringilla mandelli*), not obtained by last year's Expedition, was shot by us at Pika warrens at Phari (April 7), and seen, always associated with Pikas, on the following days.

On June 11, also, we were witnesses to what must be a

common tragedy. A family of small Brahminy ducklings—the Ruddy Sheldrake of Europe—were making their noisy way down from some nesting site on the steppe to the head-waters of the Arun—and safety. The parent birds may have taken fright at our camp, through which the ducklings scuttled fearlessly. The loathsome Ravens, gathered, as always, for carrion or camp refuse, swooped down and attacked the hapless family, bolting a whole duckling at each mouthful. Surely a gun would have done no harm here.

Norton made the interesting discovery that the Meadow Bunting (*Emberiza cia godlewskii*) breeds in the Kama Valley, thus extending its breeding range far to the South. It may, indeed, be expected that several species now believed to breed only in Siberia may in fact be found nesting on the Northern slopes of the Himalaya, and even in other highland regions of Tibet. For here altitude comes to the assistance of latitude to produce an arctic type of climate, flora, and fauna ; though it must be admitted that the aridity of Tibet must produce very different climatic conditions to those obtaining in the far North. In Gnari Khorsum, 400 miles West of Everest, I had obtained specimens, with young in down, of the Large Eastern Sand Plover (*Cirripedesmus mongolicus atrifrons*), which previously was only known as a breeding species from much farther North ; and again, the day we left Tibet, at 17,000 feet, on the Serpo La, I found another pair of these Dotterel, from their behaviour obviously nesting, so to speak, at the very gates of India, for

10 miles further on we had left everything Tibetan behind us—landscape, flowers, birds, beasts, and insects were all different. Nowhere else in the world can there be a sharper natural division than between the Tibetan Highlands and the true Himalayan Zone.

The physical and climatic conditions prevailing in this part of Tibet produces an environment hostile to reptilian and amphibian life. The single Toad obtained last year was quite new to science, and Norton's capture of a second specimen is a great piece of luck. Miss Joan B. Procter, F.Z.S., of the Natural History Museum, has described and named it (*Cophophryne alticola*). It is remarkable by having the toes fully webbed. She also writes that the Toad, together with the Frog (*Nanorana pleskei*) and the Lizard (*Phrynocephalus theobaldi*), are all devoid of external ears, the tympanum itself being absent in the Toad. This unusual modification is attributed to the effect of altitude, but it has also been suggested that the absence of ears is due to inherited atrophy following generations of frost-bite—an interesting subject for the followers of Weissman!

The fish, rejoicing in the name of *Schizopygopsis stoliczkæ*, is stated by Mr. Norman never to have been previously obtained from such an altitude.

With the Molluscs we drew blank, in spite of Norton's energetic dredging of tarns and pools at Kharta. Nor did any member of the Expedition produce a single snail-shell, though all were armed with pill-boxes and on the look out for them.

It is probably only among the various families of insects that any important biological results may be hoped for from this Expedition. Our collection from the Base Camp, greatly due to the assistance received from Morris, of more than 300 beetles of a dozen or more species, may be sufficient to show some evidence of the effect of environment. A number of them are new to science, and, with one or two exceptions, were not obtained last year. There are already described over 100,000 kinds of beetles, and under these circumstances it is obvious that even such a modest collection as ours will take some time to work out. Mr. K. G. Blair, of the Natural History Museum, has it in hand, and, with the assistance of Mr. H. E. Andrewes and Dr. G. A. K. Marshall, will certainly make the most of it. His preliminary note gives 160 specimens of four or perhaps five kinds of Ground Beetles (*Carabidæ*) belonging to genera of Palæarctic distribution. Of the Tenebrionids there are 140 specimens belong to six species, probably all new, but characteristic of the mountainous regions of Central Asia. Of the Weevils there are only seventeen specimens, but they appear to belong to seven new species. Two of these were kindly collected by Norton's Toad.

Mr. B. P. Uvarov is working out the Orthoptera, and writes that our Stick-Insect (Phasmid) is of great interest because the family is essentially a sub-tropical group and has never been recorded from any such high altitude before. We were lucky, also, in getting three more specimens of Wollaston's curious new Grasshopper (*Hypernephia everesti*,

Uvarov). At the same time, my old specimens from Purang have been elevated into the type of a new species of a new genus (*Hyphinomos fasciata*). Future visitors are earnestly requested to collect every grasshopper-like insect they meet here, for the orthopterous fauna of High Asia is wholly unexplored.

It must be remembered that we constantly passed through localities in which it was inadvisable to show even a butterfly-net. When recrossing the Pang La (17,000 feet), I lagged behind and spent a laborious hour collecting disconcertingly quick-flying, woolly-bodied flies; these and others are being worked out by Major E. E. Austen, D.S.O.

There is also a Burrowing Bee (*Ammophia sp.*), the most interesting insect I met. It is of a repellent ant-like aspect, of an evil black and red pattern. It flies astonishingly fast, and can only be netted by careful stalking when it lands to burrow in the sand. It is preparing a tomb for a paralysed grub in which it will lay its own egg; on hatching, the bee grub will feed on the living corpse of its entertainer. I first observed it by noticing, as I rode along the banks of the Phung Chu, tiny jets of sand being shot violently upwards from the ground, the insect itself being quite invisible. My pony, a true Tibetan, loathed the sight of a butterfly-net; I had no companion to hold him, and the pursuit of science was attended by more than the usual trials.

A series of small Moths was obtained at the Base Camp, and Norton collected more in Kharta. These are being worked out by Mr. W. H. T. Tams, but in the case of Moths, identification is a particularly lengthy and laborious business.

The Butterflies are naturally few in such an environment; nor does the constant wind make their breathless capture any easier. Captain N. D. Riley is working them out, and tells me that in general they resemble our English butterflies, with other Alpine families. On a recent visit to the Museum, I was excusing the scantiness of our collection, explaining that, as a rule, I had only been able to collect while crossing high passes. Indicating a series of small dark brown "Ringlets," rather the worse for wear, I said that that was all I saw above 16,000 feet. "Why that," said Riley, "is a new species of a new genus!" So may our successors seize every opportunity that offers of collecting even the least and most inconspicuous-looking insects in the endeavour to assist our research workers in adding some particle to the sum of our knowledge of nature.

INDEX

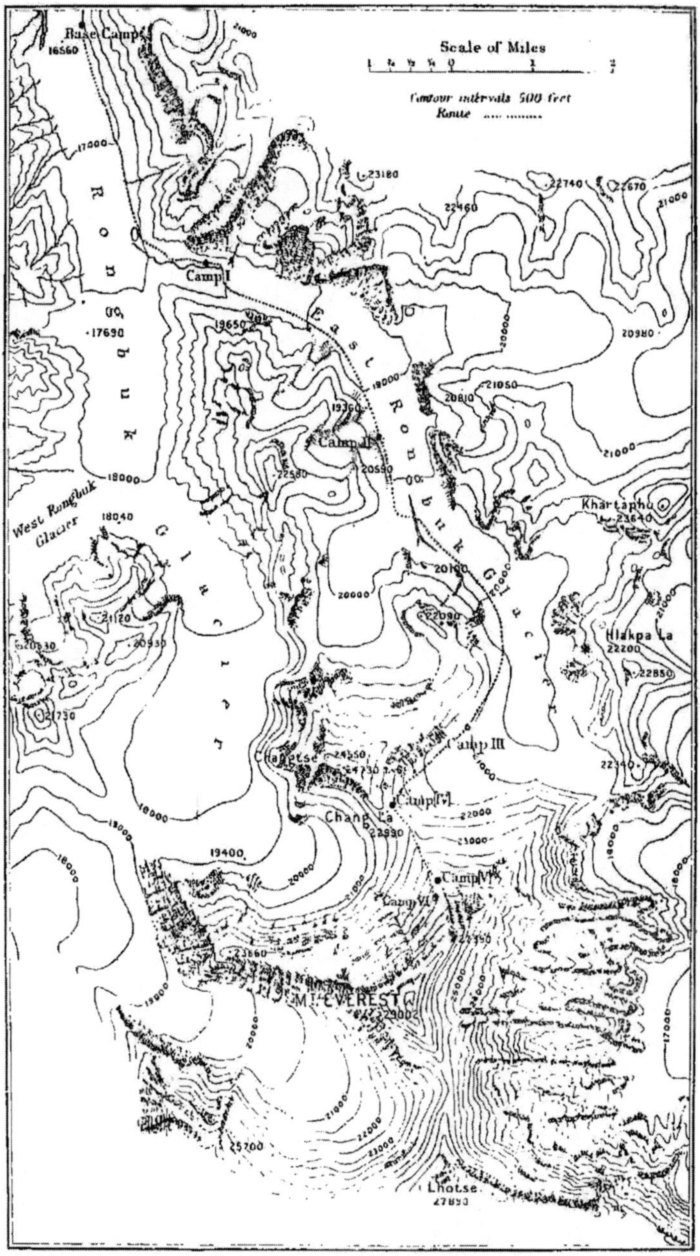

SKETCH-MAP OF MOUNT EVEREST AND THE RONGBUK GLACIERS.

From surveys by Major Wheeler, with Route and Camps of the 1922 Expedition added by Colonel Strutt.

London: Edward Arnold & Co

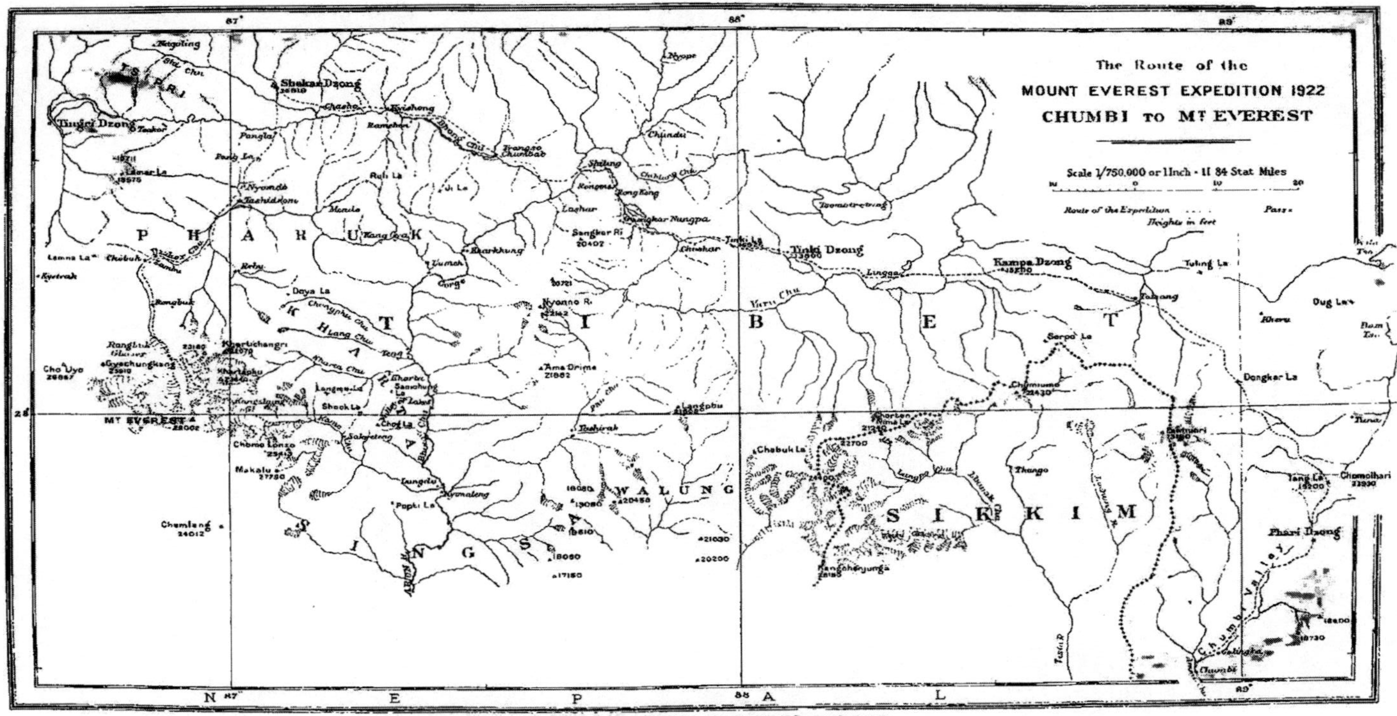

Published by Edward Arnold & Co. for the Mount Everest Committee from maps prepared by the Royal Geographical Society.